French Cinema in the 1990s

French Cinema in the 1990s

Continuity and Difference

ESSAYS EDITED BY

Phil Powrie

OXFORD

UNIVERSITY PRESS

OXFORD

UNIVERSITY PRESS

Great Clarendon Street, Oxford OX2 6DP

Oxford University Press is a department of the University of Oxford.
It furthers the University's objective of excellence in research, scholarship,
and education by publishing worldwide in

Oxford New York

Athens Auckland Bangkok Bogotá Buenos Aires Calcutta
Cape Town Chennai Dar es Salaam Delhi Florence Hong Kong Istanbul
Karachi Kuala Lumpur Madrid Melbourne Mexico City Mumbai
Nairobi Paris São Paulo Singapore Taipei Tokyo Toronto Warsaw

with associated companies in Berlin Ibadan

Published in the United States
by Oxford University Press Inc., New York

First published 1999

British Library Cataloguing in Publication Data

Data available

Library of Congress Cataloging in Publication Data

Data available

ISBN 0-19-815958-7
ISBN 0-19-815957-9 (Pbk.)

1 3 5 7 9 10 8 6 4 2

Typeset in Sabon
by Cambrian Typesetters, Frimley, Surrey
Printed in Great Britain
on acid-free paper by
Biddles Ltd.
Guildford and King's Lynn

Pour Nanou, Nick, Josie, Adeline,
et Manon et notre 'air de famille'

Preface

THIS book was prompted by a conference on French cinema organized by Russell King in the University of Nottingham (UK) in
December 1994. Many of the participants were surprised to see
how many colleagues both in the UK and the USA were teaching
and writing on contemporary French cinema in their institutions of
higher education. The essays in this volume were commissioned
from some of those colleagues and from others to explore the way
in which the 1990s have seen a continuation of practices established in the 1980s, for example the heritage film. The volume also
explores what has been seen as a vibrant new young cinema with
its origins in 1970s realism, but very much of the 1990s in its
preoccupation with a variety of social problems facing French society. The two most obvious problems which surface in the films of
the 1990s are issues of ethnicity arising out of racial tension, and
the marginalization of youth, the two issues colliding in the new
cinéma de banlieue.

I would like to thank the contributors for their patience as I set
up this volume; Sophie Goldsworthy, my editor at Oxford
University Press; Caroline Jeanneau of the CNC, John Saunders,
and the Tyneside Cinema, Newcastle, for their help in providing
statistical information; Jackie Pritchard for her invaluable copy-
editing; and, finally, Keith Reader, once again, for his sympathy
and erudition in all things cinematic.

A version of the introduction to this volume appeared in
Modern and Contemporary France (Nov. 1998). A first version of
the chapter on *Chacun cherche son chat* appeared in
Contemporary French Civilization (Fall 1998). I am grateful to
these periodicals for allowing the material to reappear in this
volume. The other chapters are here published for the first time.

Newcastle upon Tyne   P.P.
Christmas 1998

Contents

List of Plates

(between pp. 144–145)

List of Contributors

RUSSELL COUSINS lectures in French at the University of Birmingham, where he teaches Zola and film studies. He has contributed extensively on French cinema to the *International Dictionary of Films and Filmmakers* (Gale Research, 1996), published on film in *Literature/Film Quarterly*, and written a study of Zola's *Thérèse Raquin* (Grant & Cutler, 1992). He is currently preparing a book on screen adaptations of Zola's novels.

MARTINE DANAN teaches French and film at the University of Memphis. Her publications on the issue of film, language, and identity include articles in the *French Review, Contemporary French Civilization, Film History, Journal of Popular Film and Television*, and A. Higson and R. Maltby (eds.), *'Film Europe' and 'Film America': Cinema, Commerce and Cultural Exchange* (Exeter University Press, forthcoming Sept. 1999).

JULIA DOBSON teaches French at the University of Wolverhampton. Her main areas of research are contemporary French cinema and the work of Hélène Cixous. She is currently co-editing a book on French women directors since 1968.

WENDY EVERETT teaches French and film at the University of Bath. Recent publications in the field of contemporary literature and European film include *European Identity in Cinema* (Intellect, 1996). She is a member of the editorial board of *Literature/Film Quarterly*.

ELIZABETH EZRA teaches French studies at the University of Stirling in Scotland. She has published widely on images of colonialism in inter-war France, and has written a book on the films of Georges Méliès (Manchester University Press/St Martin's, 1999). She is currently working on a study of French cinema of the fantastic.

GRAEME HAYES teaches French, film, and politics at the University of Wolverhampton.

SUSAN HAYWARD lectures on French cinema at the University of Exeter. She is the author of *French National Cinema* (Routledge, 1993), the first in a series for Routledge for which she is the general editor. She is the author of *Key Concepts in Cinema Studies* (Routledge, 1996). She has recently completed a book on Luc Besson for Manchester University Press (1998).

RUSSELL KING teaches film and poetry at the University of Nottingham. He has published extensively on Verlaine and Baudelaire, and on Truffaut and Blier. He has recently edited volumes of essays on modern poetry and French cinema.

MYRTO KONSTANTARAKOS teaches at Middlesex University in London. She is writing a book on *The Centre Elsewhere: Suburbs in Film (Hollywood and Europe)* and editing a volume on *Space in European Cinema*, both to be published by Intellect.

KATHRYN LAUTEN teaches at Kalamazoo College and the University of Michigan. Her works on francophone texts include French cinema as well as North and West African literature and film. Most recently she has published an article entitled 'Discontinuous Continuities in Assia Djebar's *L'Amour, la fantasia*' and has completed a work entitled 'Ex-hum(aniz)e/Re-hum(aniz)e: Disturbing Bodies in "Post-Colonial" Francophone Literature and Film'.

CYNTHIA MARKER teaches French at Old Dominion University, Norfolk, Virginia. She is a contributor to *Columbia History of 20th Century French Thought*, a forthcoming publication of Columbia University Press.

LUCY MAZDON is Senior Research Fellow at the University of Southampton. She completed a Ph.D. thesis on Hollywood remakes of French cinema in 1997 and is currently preparing this work for publication. She is now engaged in research on contemporary French television, working closely with the Institut National de l'Audiovisuel in Paris.

PHIL POWRIE is the director of the Centre for Research into Film at the University of Newcastle upon Tyne. He has published *French Cinema in the 1980s: Nostalgia and the Crisis of Masculinity* (Clarendon Press, 1997), and numerous articles on French cinema. He has also published books on surrealism, and French women's writing. He is currently preparing a book on the films of Jean-Jacques Beineix for Manchester University Press.

KEITH READER teaches French at the University of Newcastle upon Tyne. He has published widely in the fields of contemporary French culture and cinema, and is the joint editor of the Routledge *Encyclopedia of Contemporary French Culture* (1998). He is currently working on a book on Bresson for Manchester University Press and two articles on Renoir.

BRIGITTE ROLLET teaches French cinema and literature at the University of Portsmouth. She has written articles on contemporary French cinema, and a book on Coline Serreau (Manchester University Press, 1998) is forthcoming. She is currently working on a book on contemporary French women directors.

MIREILLE ROSELLO teaches culture and literature of French expression at Northwestern University, Evanston, Illinois. Her recent work includes *Infiltrating Culture* (Manchester University Press, 1996) and *Declining the Stereotype: Ethnicity and Representation in French Cultures* (University Press of New England, 1997).

DINA SHERZER teaches French cinema in the Department of French and Italian at the University of Texas at Austin. She has edited *Cinema Colonialism Postcolonialism: Perspectives from the French and Francophone Worlds* (University of Texas Press, 1996) and is the author of *Representation in Contemporary French Fiction* (University of Nebraska Press, 1986), as well as articles on cinema and postcolonialism, and on works by Duras, Simon, and other twentieth-century writers.

PAUL SUTTON lectures in film studies at the Bolton Institute. He is currently finishing a doctoral thesis on deferred action and spectatorship and has published a number of articles on film and critical theory, including, most recently, an interview with Jean Baudrillard.

CARRIE TARR is Senior Research Fellow at Thames Valley University, London. Her work on gender, sexuality, and ethnicity in classic and contemporary French cinema has been widely published, and her book on the cinema of Diane Kurys for Manchester University Press is forthcoming.

Heritage, History and 'New Realism': French Cinema in the 1990s

PHIL POWRIE

CONTINUITY and difference, the subtitle of this volume, are terms used by Susan Hayward in her introduction to *French National Cinema*. As Hayward points out, however, the issue of a national cinema is a complex one, and not always useful in defining the panorama of French film production at any given time. At best one might be able to distinguish a mainstream cinema, or cinema of the 'centre', as Hayward calls it, following Gauthier, and a vaguely oppositional cinema of the 'periphery' (Hayward 1993: 13). And yet the terms continuity and difference can be profitably used, less in relation to defining any national specificity than in isolating certain key moves in the complex network formed by French film production in the 1990s, which is the focus of this volume. In what follows, I shall outline these key moves, linking them to social and political factors, before returning to the issue of 'national' cinema.

The first of these key moves is the conjuncture of the GATT negotiations (culminating in 1993) and the ascendancy of heritage cinema to mainstream dominance in French production at the expense of popular genres such as comedy and the *polar*.

The second is the attempted return of the auteur through the influential 1994 television series *Tous les garçons et les filles de leur âge* (All the boys and girls of their age). In terms of the simplistic binarism centre/periphery, auteur cinema is complex, since arguably, for historical reasons, it is central to French film production and its sense of cultural worth (a marketing issue), while also being peripheral, since much auteur work defines itself in opposition to mainstream cinema (more of a stylistic or narrative-specific issue).

Finally, overlapping to some extent with the return of the auteur is the arrival of a new generation of film-makers whose political impact in the call for civil disobedience of February 1997 has undoubtedly affected the way in which the French view the films of this younger generation of directors. *Positif* (unlike *Cahiers du cinéma*) ran a number of strongly committed pieces on the issue (see Jeancolas 1997; Garbaz 1997).

GATT 1993 and heritage

Two types (rather than genres) of cinema became dominant (both in terms of audience figures and in terms of media coverage) during the 1980s in French cinema—the *cinéma du look* and heritage cinema—increasingly disestablishing what might until then have been seen as the most sensible way of articulating French film production, namely a generic distinction between comedy and *polar* as the most popular genres, and auteur or art-house cinema. The *cinéma du look* became a spent force by the early 1990s. In a sense, it was less a set of films or directors (Beineix, Besson, Carax) than a critical debate, since the three directors in question had always pursued different agendas. Heritage cinema, on the other hand, retained its quantitative (if not qualitative) hold into the 1990s, arguably becoming the hegemonic French cinema of the 1990s. However, it shifted its focus significantly, becoming considerably less idyllic, and more problematically nostalgic, at the same time as it was exhausting itself into stereotype, to the extent that, at the time of writing (Christmas 1998), heritage cinema appears less hegemonic than it did in the earlier part of the decade.

Heritage cinema was hegemonic despite the immense popularity of some films in the comic genre, such as *Les Visiteurs* (Poiré, 1993), the second best-selling film in the history of French cinema. The success of *Les Visiteurs* is unusual, even if it is paralleled by a similar success in the mid-1980s for *Trois hommes et un couffin* (Serreau, 1985). These two films are isolated, however; French comic films have in general diminished in number and in popularity. In 1994, to take a single year, Frodon notes that a larger number than usual of comedies which would have been expected to be popular either because of their director (Leconte's *Tango*, 1993; Blier's *Un, deux, trois soleil*, 1993; Oury's *La Soif de l'or*, 1993) or their star (Adjani in Esposito's *Toxic Affair*, 1993) were not very successful at the box office (Frodon 1994: 22). And to take a longer timespan, in the period 1984–93, only 20 out of 47 French films with more than 2 million spectators were comedies. Frodon notes that of the 47 films, some 17 are specifically 'historic' in the sense that they reconstitute the past, and that many of them are based on recognizably classic literary texts (Frodon 1995a: 678), both characteristics of the heritage or nostalgia film (see Powrie 1997). Audience figures for French films rose sharply in 1990, the year of the heritage film, with Yves Robert's Pagnol diptych La Gloire de mon père (6.2 million) and Le Château de ma mère (4.2 million), and also Cyrano de Bergerac (Rappeneau; 4.5 million). There was then a sharp decline in 1991, where what might be seen as a Cyrano sequel, Tous les matins du monde (Corneau), again starring Depardieu and Brochet, was the only French film in the first twelve box-office successes. Audience figures for French films have been rising since then from some 35 million to almost 50 million. No doubt Les Visiteurs, with its 14 million spectators, was partly responsible for this rise, but 1993 was also the year of Germinal (Berri; 6.2 million), another heritage film. The extent to which heritage cinema has become dominant can be adduced by two further factors.

The first is connected to the age of spectators in France. A 1997 survey covering films with over 500,000 spectators in the period 1994–7 showed that the average age of spectators had risen to 31.1 (Médiamétrie 1997). The nostrum that the majority of spectators are in the 15–24 age bracket, which served as a partial explanation for the success of the cinéma du look during the 1980s, seems to be no longer as true as it was. It is arguable that the rise in the average age is due in large part to the increasing popularity of the heritage film, with its evident appeal for older spectators, as well as, quite possibly, for a youth audience.

The second factor which might indicate the ascendancy of heritage cinema is that the comic film not infrequently seems dependent on it, in so far as it might be read as a pastiche of heritage, whether it be the costume comedy of Ridicule (Leconte, 1996), or the postmodern and Almodóvarian televisual comedy of Le Bonheur est dans le pré (Chatiliez, 1995) or even, arguably, Les Visiteurs itself, with its play on notions of medieval heritage. It is for this reason that this volume contains studies on the three films just mentioned, but does not have a section on that other popular genre, the polar, or police thriller. Frodon points out that this genre too is on the wane, with only five films in the top forty-seven with over 500,000 spectators (Frodon 1995*a*: 678).

My suggestion that these three comedies might be seen as heritage pastiche is contentious. It clearly gives short shrift to popular comedies such as Poiré's Depardieu/Clavier vehicle *Les Anges gardiens* (1995; 5.5 million spectators), or Blier's controversial black comedy *Merci la vie* (1991; 1 million spectators, marking, as Frodon points out, a steep decline in the popularity of Blier's films (Frodon 1995*a*: 700) and suggesting that Blier was an auteur whose time was the late 1970s through to the late 1980s). It takes no account of the extremely successful *Gazon maudit* (Balasko, 1995), which ran for forty-six weeks (thirty-four more than *Les Anges gardiens*) with almost 4 million spectators. Less contentious is the cartography of heritage that I would like to outline now, around three broad categories: 'official' heritage, 'postcolonial' heritage, and 'Vichy' heritage.

The archetypal 'official' heritage film is undoubtedly *Germinal*, which, as Russell Cousins points out in his essay in this volume, assumed iconic significance at the height of the very difficult GATT negotiations, where the French were arguing for what became known as a 'cultural exception' to the free market in the cinema. Worried by US hegemony in the audiovisual industries, the French argued that these 'industries did not belong in the GATT agreement at all, because, as culturally-driven businesses crucial to the national identity, they were not comparable to other export/import industries' (Finney 1996: 6). *Germinal* represented the uniquely French Other to the Same of Hollywood, and was very visibly supported by the Minister of Culture, Jack Lang: the première of the film was government-sponsored, and Lang had videocassette copies sent to schools free as a form of 'national education' (Austin 1996: 167). As Vincendeau points out, such films' high budgets and production values, prestige producers, directors, 'literary sources and stars all form part of a strategy to fight an industrial battle (against Hollywood) and an aesthetic one (against television)' (Vincendeau 1995: 32). Although a high-budget spectacular, like Spielberg's *Jurassic Park* (1993) with which it was compared at the time, *Germinal* was triply defined as indigenously French: by virtue of the status of the original novel by Zola in the French literary canon; by virtue of its major star, Depardieu; and by virtue of its director, Claude Berri, who had arguably launched the heritage cinema boom in the mid-1980s with his Pagnol adaptations *Jean de Florette* and *Manon des Sources* (1986).

This type of heritage is 'official' because it is normally a combination of a high-profile actor and a cultural icon. The icon can be a novel from the literary canon (*Le Colonel Chabert*, Angelo, 1994; *Le Hussard sur le toit*, Rappeneau, 1995; *La Reine Margot*, Chéreau, 1994), but need not necessarily be. It can also be a play, as in *Cyrano de Bergerac*, or a literary figure (*Beaumarchais, l'insolent*, Molinaro, 1996, a much underrated film with an extraordinary performance by Fabrice Luchini in the title role; he had been a revelation in *Le Colonel Chabert*); or music (*Tous les matins du monde*, with its emphasis on the French baroque musical tradition of Lully and Rameau); or, even, a location, or collocation, such as Provence and Pagnol in the two Yves Robert films of 1990, or Giono and Provence in *Le Hussard sur le toit*.

A feature of many of the 1990s films mentioned is their darkness, 'doubt and suspicion' as Vincendeau says of *Le Colonel Chabert* (Vincendeau 1995: 32), which suggests a difference within the continuity of heritage cinema: class-based dispossession (*Le Colonel Chabert, Germinal*), or the turbulence caused by internecine strife and disease in *Le Hussard sur le toit* and *La Reine Margot*. In the case of the latter, the film is a conscious metaphor, according to its star, Adjani, and its director, Chéreau, for the Bosnian war (Austin 1996: 168), although given its ostensible subject, it could be read just as easily as a commentary on Mitterrand's last years and the troubled atmosphere in his 'court'. Austin makes a similar comment on films dealing with French history in the Mitterrand years: 'Over the decade the focus switched from revolution [Austin is here referring to *Danton* (Wajda, 1982) and *La Nuit de Varennes* (Scola, 1982)] to imperialism (*Fort Saganne*, Corneau, 1984) and ultimately—with Socialist power declining and Mitterrand's presidency clearly doomed—to decolonization and the end of Empire' (Austin 1996: 145). Fundamentally, though, these official heritage films based firmly in French history are struggling to negotiate a new French identity in troubled times:

The contemporary recourse to Balzac's and Dumas's mediations of the past must also be seen in the light of struggles over French national identity, which a conflation of factors are destabilizing: the passing of the last great populist leader (de Gaulle), the end of the *trente glorieuses* years of economic boom, the demise of the colonial empire and the rise of multi-culturalism. (Vincendeau 1995: 30)

It is to the demise of the colonial empire that I shall now turn. As Brigitte Rollet points out in this volume, 1992 was remarkable for producing no less than three films focusing on Indo-China: *L'Amant* (Annaud), *Indochine* (Wargnier), *Diên Biên Phu* (Schoendoerffer), and it is to these three that Austin is referring in the above quotation when he mentions 'decolonization and the end of Empire'. Less speculative than the end-of-reign argument is the fact that these films occur, along with 'post-war' films, at a time when the issue of colonialism had become of major interest to historians and anthropologists (Sherzer 1996: 8). These films, in a process typical of the heritage film, 'memorialize' the colonial past, to use Norindr's term (Norindr 1996: 138), in a veritable work of mourning. What is being mourned is not just the war dead in a film like *Diên Biên Phu*, officially sanctioned by the French government by virtue of Schoendoerffer's presence at Mitterrand's side on the state visit to Vietnam in 1993, but also 'the loss of an era, of a colonial empire, of a utopian world; the loss of France's influence and prestige' (Norindr 1996: 140).

The third and final type of heritage film I would like to isolate is the 'Vichy heritage' film. This, like the postcolonial film, is anchored in a move by historians to review the past which came to haunt the French with highly public trials of Vichy officials in the 1990s and which has been called the Vichy syndrome (Rousso 1991). René Bousquet, for example, was indicted for crimes against humanity in 1991 and assassinated two years later; Maurice Papon's trial saw interventions by academics on the use of history during 1997, amongst them Henri Rousso. The postcolonial heritage films on Indo-China are relatively simplistic nostalgia, even if *Diên Biên Phu*'s theatrical framing to some extent questions colonialist norms (see Austin 1996: 41). Norindr is unconvinced that this minimalistic lip-service to self-consciousness diminishes the film's failure, located in its 'inability to question its structuring vision, its will to contain the heterogeneous and bind the subject' (Norindr 1996: 131). However, some of the Vichy films of the 1990s have tended to be more critical in their approach.

This is not the case, however, with Marbœuf's wooden biopic of *Pétain* (1992). More interesting is Berri's *Uranus* (1990), which does to Marcel Aymé's text what *Jean de Florette* did to Pagnol: grand, melodramatic heritage, with broad historic sweeps and key heritage actors (Depardieu, Jean-Pierre Marielle, also to appear, like Depardieu, in *Tous les matins du monde* two years later). Berri returned to the period in 1997 with *Lucie Aubrac*, the story of a Resistance fighter separated from his wife, which included scenes with the 'butcher of Lyons', Klaus Barbie. As Darke points out, the film is predictably revisionist, and 'sacrifices much-needed suspense in order to generate the oceanic feeling of the French as one big anti-Nazi family' (Darke 1998: 47). *Docteur Petiot* (1990) is in fact so calqued on the horror genre (see Austin 1996: 34–6) that it is not a heritage film in the sense in which I have been using the word, its Caligari-inspired opening sequence suggesting a meditation on Franco-German cinematographic relations.

On the other hand, Miller's *L'Accompagnatrice* (1992), although a disappointingly banal film (see Frodon 1994: 706) in terms of its sentimental and indirect critique of Vichy collaboration, is interesting because the events are viewed through the eyes of the adolescent musician, the accompanist of the title, who merely observes what goes on around her from her privileged position as a musical servant, deresponsibilized, a mere accompanist to the music of history. More interesting still is Audiard's *Un héros très discret* (1996), where, as Kathryn Lauten argues in her essay in this volume, there is a direct link between the narrative and the archival tendencies of current French historiography. The film also forces the 'hero' to confront moral quandaries when his chosen career of modest functionary becomes by force of circumstance inflated beyond his capacities. The film thus forces the spectator into a more critical view of collaboration by its structure, which dwells on the fabrication of identity, and by its narrative, which focuses on individual responsibility. Given the sensitivity of collaboration as an issue in France, it is hardly surprising that the Vichy heritage film should be considerably more interested in the individual and his or her construction in history, and considerably less in any 'memorialization' of this period which many French would prefer to forget.

It is precisely because the Vichy film is more critical that it shades off from heritage *stricto sensu* into areas which are of interest to the two other key moves in the 1990s: autobiography and biography on the one hand, and on the other an irreverent view of the past more in tune with the younger directors (indeed, both Miller, the director of *L'Accompagnatrice*, and Audiard, the director of *Un héros très discret*, were co-signatories of the February 1997 call for civil disobedience). *Un héros très discret* interrogates historical reconstruction in a way which the three postcolonial films cannot, and in so doing shows us how heritage is a postmodern spectacle which uses history to show the impossibility of using history to relocate the individual subject. The latter is either a stereotype caught in 'illustration' as Frodon calls it with regard to *L'Amant* and *Indochine*, or 'memorialization' as Norindr calls it with regard to *Diên Biên Phu*, or, at best in *L'Accompagnatrice* and *Un héros très discret*, an eye disembodied from the flux of events, positioned in ironic contemplation. The autobiographical films which I shall now briefly discuss are in this respect an attempt to 'incorporate' that disembodied eye.

The auteur and autobiography

One of the most successful of French cinema's marketing strategies has been the notion of the auteur, and it remains for many the principal player against the dominance of what Frodon calls the 'Programme' (Frodon 1995a: 692–4), a loose amalgam of Hollywood dominance in the cinema, combined with television, the fetishism of the advertising image, and digital technology. Whilst admitting that cinema's disappearance into this popularizing amalgam with its emphasis on the exotic and the sensational in a sense returns cinema to its popular roots, Frodon is keen to retain the auteur as a guarantee of quality and/or of national integrity against the 'audiovisual continuum' (Frodon 1995a: 692) initiated by the 'Visual' of the 1980s, by which he means the *cinéma du look* of Beineix and, in particular, Besson. Already in the 1980s French cinema had attempted to reinvigorate the notion of the auteur by an emphasis on 'art cinema' in a very literal sense: films which dwelt on painting (e.g. Godard's *Passion*, 1982; Cavalier's *Thérèse*, 1986), coupled with a sustained attempt by the *Cahiers du cinéma* to valorize auteurism through the academic link between cinema and painting (see Darke 1993). A new attempt was made in the early 1990s by the newly established Franco-German television channel Arte, catching the mood of much academic interest in autobiography in the late 1980s, and an increasing interest in biography, interfacing with issues of memory, oral testimony, and archives, as mentioned above in relation to *Un héros très discret*.

As Wendy Everett explains in her chapter for this book, the channel commissioned a series of nine films, *Tous les garçons et les filles de leur âge*. These were to be autobiographical in nature, focusing on the director's adolescence. The films were broadcast over a period of nine weeks in the autumn of 1994, following a historically chronological order: *Le Chêne et le roseau*, André Téchiné (early 1960s); *US go home*, Claire Denis (mid-1960s); *Portrait d'une jeune fille de la fin des années 60*, Chantal Akerman (late 1960s); *La Page blanche*, Olivier Assayas (early 1970s); *Paix et amour*, Laurence Ferreira-Barbosa (mid-1970s); *Travolta et moi*, Patricia Mazuy (late 1970s); *L'Incruste*, Émilie Deleuze (early 1980s); *Bonheur*, Cédric Kahn (mid-1980s); *Frères*, Olivier Dahan (late 1980s). The directors concerned covered the well established (Akerman, Téchiné), as well as directors who had made their name in the late 1980s (Denis, Mazuy), and up-and-coming new directors of the 1990s generation (Assayas, Ferreira-Barbosa, Kahn; these three were co-signatories of the 1997 call for civil disobedience). Three of the films (those by Assayas, Kahn, and Téchiné) were also made as feature films, recalling a similar procedure by Kieslowski who turned two of the films of his *Dekalog Krótki film a milosci* (1988) and *Krótki film o zabijaniu* (1988), into feature-length theatrical releases. A number of films by younger filmmakers subsequent to this series were in this vein, for example, Cédric Klapisch's *Le Péril jeune* (1994).

Quite apart from the fertile if ironic collaboration between television and cinema which Everett mentions, the point to retain from this exercise is its strongly auteurist slant. The films' rationale is as a personal statement located in personal history; the history of the nation is refracted through these distorting lens in a kind of nostalgic memorialization of epoch. A more sophisticated memorializing can be found in Assayas's *Irma Vep* (1996) with its very self-conscious references: Truffaut's *La Nuit américaine* (1973), since the director of the film within the film is Jean-Pierre Léaud; the films of Musidora from the silent period, since the film within the film is a remake of one of these films; and, finally, because the actress who plays Musidora in the film within the film is Maggie Cheung, Hong Kong action films, which, along with other films from the Pacific ring, have became the latest interest for art-house audiences (after the closer-to-home exoticism of New German Cinema in the 1970s). Similar reverential and intertextualizing moves can be found in a film such as *Le Confessional* (Lepage, 1995; strictly speaking Canadian), with its references to Hitchcock's *I Confess* (1953), or *L'Appartement* (Mimouni, 1996), a narratively tortuous thriller with all-too-obvious references to a variety of Hitchcock thrillers, *Vertigo* (1958) being the most evident. Such intertextuality could be seen as an auteurist art-house's response to the more ironic pastiche of postmodern 'Visual' films such as Besson's *Le Cinquième élément* (1997).

There is little to distinguish between some of the auteurs mentioned in this section and many of the newer generation of young film-makers who were associated with the February 1997 call for civil disobedience.

New generations: the return of the 'political' and the return of 'realism'

On 11 February 1997 sixty-six film directors held a press conference protesting against the regressive Debré immigration law which was being debated in the National Assembly, and against one clause of it in particular, requiring individuals to declare *sans-papiers* at their local town hall. The following day a petition (an 'appel', a term I shall use from now on) drawn up by Pascale Ferran and Arnaud Desplechin and signed by fifty-nine of them appeared in *Le Monde* and in *Libération*. The signatories were mostly from a younger generation of directors, such as Assayas, Audiard, Denis, Kassovitz, Klapisch, but also included older directors such as Breillat, Chéreau, Miller, and Tavernier. The 'appel' read as follows:

We, the undersigned French film directors, declare that each of us is guilty of having recently sheltered *sans-papiers*. We did not denounce our foreign friends. And we will continue to shelter, not to denounce, to sympathize with, and to work with our friends and colleagues without checking that their papers are in order.

Following the verdict pronounced on 4 February 1997 against Mme Jacqueline Deltombe, 'guilty' of having sheltered a Zairian friend whose papers were not in order, and following the principle that the law is the same for everyone, we ask that we be investigated and judged as well. Finally, we appeal to our fellow citizens to disobey and not to submit to inhumane laws.

We refuse to see our freedom thus constrained (Manifesto 1997).

A second 'appel' in the run-up to the French elections was published on 14 May with sixty-eight signatories. Together with thirty-five of the original signatories, there were thirty-three new ones, which this time included many more of an older generation of directors (Chabrol, Corneau, Godard, Lanzmann), as well as those who had come to prominence in the 1980s (Charef, Chatiliez, Chibane). The first text was subsequently adopted by many in the arts and liberal professions, with tens of thousands of signatures.

The context for this declaration is the struggle by the *sans-papiers* themselves to move the state. On 18 March 1996, 300 Africans occupied a church in Paris, demanding to be given authorization to stay in France. Ejected by riot police four days later, they occupied a series of buildings, ending up in the Église Saint-Bernard. Ten of them went on hunger strike on 3 July 1996, and they were again evacuated by riot police on 23 August 1996, amidst protestations by a number of personalities. These included the actress Emmanuelle Béart, whose contract with Dior was as a result subsequently not renewed. This was not said Dior, because, they disagreed with her support for humanitarian causes, but because the star 'no longer corresponded to the chic image of the brand' (Kiosque en vue 1997: 31). The *sans-papiers*' tenacity and their innovative use of the media, of which the picture taken of Béart in tears holding a young African child was but one example, seems to have brought about a repoliticization of a generation of intellectuals and artists, spearheaded by the film-makers' 'appel' on 12 February 1997.

The two leading signatories, Pascale Ferran and Arnaud Desplechin, published an open letter to the French *députés* a week later, saying that 'immigrants were being used as scapegoats for a French society in crisis' (Ferran and Desplechin 1997: 13) and pointing to the paradox that the French were being asked to 'renounce their freedom' so as to 'de-integrate' immigrants. Béart, the film-makers, the *sans-papiers*, and the trade unions joined forces for a large demonstration on 22 February. As usual in these circumstances, numbers were disputed, but the demonstrators claimed some 150,000 people participated.

The film-makers, anxious to avoid ossification, not only ensured that public statements were made by as many of their number as possible, effectively 'refusing the label of leader which the media wanted to pin on us' (Klapisch 1997: 25), but also dissolved their group immediately after this demonstration.

Twelve of the signatories published short reflections on what had happened in Le Monde on 19 March. The common thread running between these brief pieces is that nearly all claim to have no party-political experience, and speak of the collapse of traditional left-wing party politics. This is coupled with a renewed sense of 'something having to be done', and that film-makers are as well qualified as anybody else to do this. What this meant in practice was an awareness of non-party-political action, 'the invention, or re-invention of a political practice', according to one (Goupil 1997: 25), community politics (militantisme de proximité), according to the ex-communist Guédiguian (Guédiguian 1997: 25), whose film Marius et Jeannette is a utopian Pagnolesque exercise in working-class community, with touches of Brechtian didacticism (see Guédiguian 1998: 60; the film became one of the more popular in 1998, with over 500,000 spectators in the Paris area by April 1998). In terms of social rather than cinematic practice, this meant supporting individuals, according to Desplechin (Desplechin 1997: 24) and Cahen, as well as carrying on making films, because, in Cahen's words, 'the cinema is made for representing social relationships', and films therefore 'work on the imaginary of social relationships within which can be found the fantasies concerning immigrants' (Cahen 1997: 25).

The dissolution of the group of younger-generation directors did not prevent further action, however. Many pursued the issues in different ways. Jeanne Labrune, for example, organized a meeting between sans-papiers and intellectuals at the Le Trianon cinema in Paris on 24 March; and a three-minute film, Nous, sans-papiers de France, was shown before feature films in selected film theatres during April both in Paris and in the provinces. This film was made by some fifteen film-makers co-ordinated by Nicolas Philibert, including, amongst others, Lucas Belvaux, the co-director of the Belgian film C'est arrivé près de chez vous (1992), and Claire Devers, whose uncompromising study of sadomasochism Noir et blanc (1986; see Powrie 1997: 184–6 and Austin 1996: 92–4) deals with ethnic issues. In addition, some 175 film-makers and others involved in the industry added their names to the film, which is a close-up of one of the *sans-papiers*, Madjiguène Cissé, speaking the following text:

We, the *sans-papiers* of France, decided to come out into the open by signing this appeal. From now on, in spite of the risks we run, it is not just our faces which will be known, but our names too. We proclaim the following:

Like all of the *sans-papiers*, we are just like anybody else. We live amongst you; in most cases, we have done so for years. We came to France because we wanted to work and because we had been told that it was the 'fatherland of the rights of man': we could not endure the suffering and oppression in our own countries, we did not want our children to go hungry, and we dreamed of freedom. In general, we came into France legally. We were arbitrarily thrown into illegality by the hardening of successive laws which meant that town halls were able not to renew our residence permits and by the restrictions imposed on the right to asylum, which was only accorded sparingly. We pay our taxes, our rents, our bills, and our social security contributions when we are allowed to work regularly! When we are not unemployed and living hand to mouth, we work hard in clothing, leather, building, catering, cleaning. We put up with conditions of work which are imposed on us and which you can refuse more easily than we can, because being without papers we are without rights. We know that this is in a lot of people's interests. We produce wealth and we enrich France by our diversity. We are sometimes single which often allows our families to subsist back home; but we also frequently live with our partners and our children born in France or who came to France when they were very young. We have given French Christian names to many of these children; we send them to state schools. We have opened the way for them to obtain French nationality, which many French, sometimes the proudest, themselves hold from parents or grandparents born abroad. We have our families in France, and friends too. We are asking for papers so as to be no longer the victims of the arbitrariness of administrations, of employers, and of landlords. We are asking for papers so as to be no longer the prey of informers and blackmailers. We are asking for papers so as to suffer no longer the humiliation of police checks based on what you look like, detention, being escorted to the border, the break-up of our families, living in perpetual fear. The French Prime Minister had promised that families would not be separated: we demand that this promise be kept at last and that the government's frequent statements concerning humanitarian principles be put into practice. We demand that the European and international conventions to which the French Republic subscribes be respected. We are counting on the support of a large number of French people, whose freedoms could well be under threat if our rights carry on being ignored. As the examples of Italy,

Spain, Portugal, and on several occasions France herself, show that a global regularization is possible, we demand that our papers be regularized. We are not clandestine. We appear here in the full light of day.

There were other ways in which film-makers pursued their initial aims. Several of the signatories participated in a conference on 30 April whose aim was to find ways of bridging the gap between the workerist Left concerned with issues of employment and working conditions, and the 'moral' liberal humanist Left concerned with immigration issues. And a number of documentaries on the *sans-papiers* were announced at the Cannes Film Festival in May, for example *La Ballade des sans-papiers* (Abdallah and Ventura, 1997), *Carnet d'expulsions de Saint-Bernard à Bamako & Kayes* (Girardot and Baque, 1997). Nils and Bertrand Tavernier made a two-part documentary on life in the *banlieues*, *De l'autre côté du périph'*, screened on France 2 on 7 and 14 December 1997.

Film directors were not the only section of society to be protesting against the proposed law. Thirteen immigrants were on hunger strike in Lille at this time, and a variety of civil rights pressure groups, as well as several town mayors, were in noisy public opposition to the proposed law. Nevertheless, the fact that the directors, following Emmanuelle Béart's very public stand, had made a call to civil disobedience was significant. This was because it was the first time that such an 'appel' had originated and been signed only by film directors, who in the past, more typically, joined larger groups incorporating writers and intellectuals. As Frodon, *Le Monde*'s cinema correspondent, points out on the same page as the 'appel', the 'Manifesto of the 159' against the Algerian war had been signed by five film directors, Resnais, Sautet, and Truffaut amongst them (Frodon 1997a: 9). Similarly, many actresses had signed the 1971 'Manifesto of the 343' supporting abortion, but nothing of this kind had occurred since the heavily politicized years following the events of May 1968. Clearly, the protest was more symbolic than real, all the more so because the films of the better-known directors were not 'political' in the way in which films were political in the 1970s, and Frodon, as a historian of the cinema, is at pains to make the link between the political action and the films they had produced: '[They] show a very real relation with the world in which they live, and an attitude to that world. A relation which, although it may not be like the good old days of films with a "message", is also very much in their films' (Frodon 1997*a*: 9).

Frodon seems to be suggesting that the films of these younger directors are somehow more engaged in a contemporary 'reality', a sentiment echoed by one of the twelve directors who had written a short reflection in *Le Monde* in March, Bertrand Tavernier, who said that 'contrary to what has been said, the majority of [the directors signing the 'appel'] make films which are in step with social reality' (Tavernier 1997: 24). It is worth pausing to reflect on the nature of this 'new realism'. Jeancolas, picking up on Guédiguian's 'militantisme de proximité' (which I have rendered as 'community politics'), calls this new realism 'un réel de proximité' (Jeancolas 1997: 57), the 'proximity' being double; it is both the documentary style of the observation, and the objects of the film-maker's observation, 'people of their own age, and who are probably much like them. Intellectuals and the unemployed . . . students, actors and worried-looking bums (*des glandeurs inquiets*) in the metro' (Jeancolas 1997: 58). This leads, Jeancolas suggests, to a third element of 'proximity', a closeness to the sense of social change in a fragmented society.

Naturally, there are differences within the new generation of film-makers. Garbarz, pointing out that the new generation has moved away from the metropolo-centric, suggests three types of realism. The first is the 'films du constat', films which say things as they are (a 'constat' being both the acknowledgement of a state of affairs and a quasi-official report on those affairs); such films bring an austere, often ethnographic gaze to bear on their subjects. The second is the 'films signaux d'alarme', films which sound the alarm, and which are more politically engaged; and, finally, the 'films de la solidarité' (films of solidarity), best exemplified by those of Guédiguian (Garbaz 1997: 74–5). Not all film-makers in this generation show evidence of the 'réel de proximité', even if they may display the same signs of social disarray in their films. Herpe, reviewing the only book to have been written on this generation at the time of writing, points out, somewhat disapprovingly, how the films of Desplechin and Ferran fetishize form by their postmodern attachment to intertextuality, to Truffaut in Desplechin's case, and to Demy and Resnais in Ferran's case, both signatories to the 'appel' (Herpe 1998: 53–4; the book is Trémois 1997, which is more a descriptive compendium than an analytical history). Nevertheless, the defining characteristic of the new realism, which Herpe likens to British film-makers (presumably Loach and Leigh, both Cannes winners in the 1990s), is an evident engagement with social realities, inhabiting an uneasy middle ground between the ethnographically dispassionate and the dramatically compassionate. A thoughtful piece by another signatory of the 'appel', Tonie Marshall, points out that the political cinema of the 1970s was part of a specific political context, and that because cinema has now spread more widely socially and geographically, the nature of the political engagement was different: 'Those who are making films at the moment come from everywhere, which was not the case necessarily ten, twenty or thirty years ago. But that brings society into the cinema and it is no longer cinema which goes in search of society' (Marshall 1997: 47). The *Cahiers du cinéma*, who supported the call to civil disobedience somewhat lamely, merely reproducing the original call in their March 1997 issue with a statement of support, made much the same point, coining the phrase 'retour du politique' in the title of Toubiana's survey of the young cinema. For him, this new cinema showed a 'preoccupation with social and political affairs', and was characterized by 'the *banlieue* [the term is difficult to translate, as Myrto Konstantarakos points out in her chapter on *La Haine*, 1995, in this volume], the crisis in urban lifestyles, the cultural and musical mix (*métissage*), the taking account of an elsewhere (*la prise en compte de l'ailleurs*), a real feel for otherness, the refusal of consensual morality' (Toubiana 1997: 28).

This might be thought to be best exemplified by Kassovitz's *La Haine*, a film of which Kassovitz notoriously said that it was 'against the police', playing to the disaffected youth audience which ten years earlier flocked to see a considerably less politicized, but equally anomically oriented *37°, 2 le matin* (Beineix, 1986). *La Haine* is undoubtedly one of the major films of the 1990s by its focus on contemporary issues of youth alienation, and accordingly much attention was lavished on it, extending to government ministers watching it so as to understand what might be ailing the disaffected youth of the *banlieues*. To put this attention in the perspective of other successful 1995 films, however, *La Haine* garnered merely 2 million spectators to the 5.5 million of *Les Anges gardiens*, or the 4 million of another comedy, *Gazon maudit*, or even the 2.5 million of *Le Hussard sur le toit*. It also has to be said that *La Haine* is not particularly representative of the 'return to the real' (Frodon 1995*b*: 32) in the vein of early films by Maurice Pialat, which many of the younger generation's films exhibit, such as Karim Dridi's *Bye Bye* (1995), or Richet's *État des lieux* (1995), which quotes Marx and the situationists, making it a return to May 1968 as well. As Dridi points out in a striking metaphor, 'our political, social and humanist thinking must be seen in our films. That is the struggle which I have chosen, without necessarily being militant, making films with a message. I try to make films like antibodies, to fight against the virus' (Dridi 1997: 24).

Sandrine Veysset's *Y aura-t-il de la neige à Noël?* (1996) is reasonably typical of this 'return to the real' reminiscent of Pialat's early work, and is used by Garbarz as an example of his category of 'films du constat': a mother of seven struggles to survive as a tenant on the farm belonging to the father of her children (there are echoes of the Taviani brothers' *Padre padrone*, 1977, here). The whole family almost literally slaves on the farm, with few moments of relief. The title refers to the snow the children long for at Christmas. On Christmas Eve the mother puts the children to bed in one room with her and switches on the gas, but is awoken by the snow as it falls; this small act of Nature is enough to make her, at least for the moment, forget her attempted suicide. Coming in the final sequence of the film, this attempted suicide, by its sudden drama, resembles Akerman's *Jeanne Dielman, 23 quai du Commerce, 1080 Bruxelles* (1975), collocating and repositioning 1970s realism and 1970s feminism. It might seem like an unpromisingly stark subject, but, surprisingly perhaps for an independent film unsupported by funds from TV channels, it was relatively successful with some 600,000 spectators in the three months after its release on 25 December 1996 (see Balsan 1997: 4–5).

The attention lavished on *La Haine* with its focus on youth difference was very much to the detriment of at least two other major issues which surfaced in the 1990s. Kassovitz's first film, *Métisse* (1993), focused less on youth alienation than on another aspect of difference, that of ethnicity. Ethnicity in the form of *beur* films is clearly a defining feature of 1990s cinema, just as it had been in the 1980s. The difference between the 1980s and 1990s as far as *beur* cinema is concerned is that the appellation itself causes problems (Rosello 1996*b*). For obvious reasons of ghettoization amongst others, Bosséno has called *beur* cinema transitional (Bosséno 1992), which should not lead us to underestimate its importance in a France wracked by ethnic tension. *La Haine* is again a key film in this respect, because its preoccupations might well seem only incidentally linked to problems of ethnicity, as Konstantarakos points out in her chapter in this volume, and much more an example of social tensions. And yet, the chapter by Carrie Tarr which follows it attempts to show how problematic *La Haine*, amongst other 'return-to-the-real' films, is in relation to problems of ethnicity, suggesting that the attention given to it has obscured the issue of ethnicity.

The second issue, no less pressing in some respects than the marginalization of ethnic minorities, is AIDS. Unlike the USA, however, where AIDS films increased in number during the 1990s, and became a feature of the mainstream cinema, AIDS films in France are few and far between. This is all the more surprising in the light of the scandal of the contaminated blood supplies of 1995 which at one point threatened to seep up to ministerial level (see Riedmatten 1996 and Sanitas 1995). There are only a handful of films which deal with AIDS, of which the most obvious to date are Blier's allusive *Merci la vie*, a less allusive but poor film starring Nathalie Baye, *Mensonge* (Margolin, 1992), whose main protagonist is bisexual, just as is the main protagonist of *Les Nuits fauves* (Collard, 1992), a film whose neo-romantic self-indulgence was for a brief period obscured by its flamboyant style.

Although in this Introduction I have tried to articulate French cinema in the 1990s around three major focuses, the sections of the volume cannot be neatly mapped onto them. The first section, 'History, Heritage, and Pastiche', shows varieties of heritage (official, postcolonial, and Vichy), which demonstrate continuity in the form and purpose of the heritage film by an older generation of directors (Berri and Wargnier), while also demonstrating different approaches by other directors, whether Wendy Everett's combination of the personal and the historical in *Les Roseaux sauvages*, or the questioning of historical discourses by Kathryn Lauten in Audiard's *Un héros très discret*, or what I have claimed is heritage pastiche in a number of comedies: *Ridicule*, which, Mireille Rosello suggests, redefines the heritage genre by using 'a historical setting to ask very specific questions about our contemporary ways of relating to history, to words, to images and, in the end, to the film itself'; *Les Visiteurs*, examined as a discourse on the 'national' by Martine Danan; and *Le Bonheur est dans le pré*, which Keith Reader associates with right-wing anarchism.

The second section, 'Inscribing Differences', explores a variety of films from the perspective of difference. Carrie Tarr takes a critical look at the iconic AIDS film *Les Nuits fauves*, while Brigitte Rollet examines the position of Josiane Balasko with particular reference to the 'first lesbian comedy' *Gazon maudit*. Issues of ethnicity are broached in a number of chapters focusing on gender relations. Cynthia Marker examines Denis's very noir *J'ai pas sommeil*, and Dina Sherzer looks at the imbrication between gender, ethnicity, and comedy in two comedies, one by Coline Serreau, *Romuald et Juliette*, an updated *Romeo and Juliet* which followed the more popular *Trois hommes et un couffin*, and Kassovitz's *Métisse*. The two following chapters by Myrto Konstantarakos and Carrie Tarr set up a debate on the extent to which ethnicity should be seen as central in the newly emerging *cinéma de banlieue*. Finally, a chapter by Russell King explores Blier's *Merci la vie* from the perspective not of AIDS or history, as has often been the case for this film, but as an example of a new viewing practice more attuned to youth culture and zapping.

The final section, 'Defining the "national" ', is an attempt to bring together studies on several films. By their collocation these films, although they are very different from each other, throw light on the difficulty of defining a 'national' cinema in a televisual global market. Graeme Hayes's chapter on *Les Amants du Pont-Neuf* (Carax, 1991) shows how the film is the site of multiple crises in masculinity, representation, and national identity. The film, I would contend, is not only an elegy for the 1980s and for Mitterrandism, but also for the possibility of a national cinema based in consensus. The collapse of that consensus is here figured by a number of events or items within the film, which are undermined. First there is the historical anchor of the bicentennial, ironically seen from a distance, and serving as a backdrop to a very personal love affair. Second, the geographical anchor of the bridge, eventually reconstructed in Montpellier, and illustrating, by the return to the studio, the impossibility of the 'real' at the beginning of the 1990s. Third, there is the typically Caraxian nostalgic return to pre-1940 cinema with the reference to Vigo's *L'Atalante* (1934).

Chacun cherche son chat (1996), by one of the younger generation of film-makers, Cédric Klapisch, is also located in Paris, and also gestures to the films of the past, but is a more successful articulation of contemporary anxieties about fragmentation. Elizabeth Ezra examines the film as a meditation on what it means to be part of a community, and the film is affecting as an echo of the social-observation films of the 1930s, similar in many respects to Salvadori's *Les Apprentis* (1995) in its whimsy, and its oddball characters, as Darke points out (Darke 1996: 62), but with a more careful address to problems of gender and ethnicity. The internationalization of the French cinema is made clear in a variety of ways by the other four films. Lucy Mazdon's chapter on *Mon Père ce héros* shows how the phenomenon of the remake recycles cultural attitudes (and icons like Depardieu), whereas Besson's *Le Cinquième élément* can be seen as the most startling combination of French postmodern style and Hollywood action movie. Its camp Gaultier costumes and references to other French films, combined with the trappings and the stars of the Hollywood action movie in a kind of hyper-postmodern transnational commodity fetish, require a different analytical approach, as Susan Hayward shows in the final chapter of this volume. It is curiously paralleled by *Alien Resurrection* (1998), directed by Jeunet, the co-director of *Delicatessen* (1990) and *Cité des enfants perdus* (1995), and starring, amongst others, one of the main actors in those two films, Dominique Pinon, suggesting that transatlantic crossover is a developing mode of film-making. Ranged against such films, there is auteur cinema, although here too, Ang Lee's *The Ice Storm* (1998), as well as the work of some independent US film-makers such as Hal Hartley, suggests that auteurist art-house cinema is no longer confined to Europe. It is paradoxical that the director whom many might consider to be the quintessential French/European auteur, Kieslowski, was a Pole working in French, over whom opinions, as Julia Dobson's chapter points out, are considerably divided, and divide over issues of the 'national'.

I began this Introduction by alluding to the problem of the 'national' in French national cinema, and suggesting that heritage cinema is the hegemonic cinema in France today, precisely because its anchoring in French history makes it the most easily identifiable 'national' cinema. Arguably, the new realism of some of the younger generation of directors could also suggest a claim to a national authenticity, perhaps less problematic than the melodramatic heritage film which is too much in thrall to its Hollywood cousins. But it is as well to remember that French cinema in the 1990s is more variable than the categories I have been arguing for. Quite apart from the internationalism and transnationalism of several of the films studied in the final section of this volume, quite apart too from the increasing interest in francophone cinema, whether Belgian (see Reader 1999), French-Canadian (see Donahoe 1991; Pallister 1995), or African (see Diawara 1992; Nwachukwu 1994; Downing 1996; Brahimi 1997), it is worth mentioning two less well-known films, both released in the UK: *Total Eclipse* (1995), a turgid biopic of the relationship between two eminently French *poètes maudits*, Verlaine and Rimbaud, starring the British David Thewlis, the lead in Mike Leigh's *Naked*, and Romane Bohringer as Mr and Mrs Verlaine, directed by Agnieska Holland, a French/UK/Belgian co-production. Details of the second film demonstrate even better the difficulty of defining national production. It is *Décroche les étoiles* (1996), directed by John Cassavetes's son Nick, starring his mother Gena Rowlands, set entirely in the USA, but a French production starring and produced by that icon of French heritage, Depardieu. These two films, it could be argued, are examples of exceptions which prove more general rules, just as it is arguable that Besson's *Cinquième élément* is also an unusual exception, which merely compounds most other directors' (and critics') difficulties in defining French cinema and/or 'fighting against' Hollywood (as Finney points out, this is a misguided approach; Finney 1996: 8). However, most of the films studied in the final section of this volume, and indeed some of those in the preceding sections, such as *Irma Vep*, prove only that in the (post?)postmodern world of super-productions and co-productions, France's new young directors will find it hard to maintain the new realism anchored in the diffuse, marginalized 'national' of French national cinema.

Part I

HISTORY, HERITAGE, AND PASTICHE

2

The Heritage Film and Cultural Politics: *Germinal* (Berri, 1993)

RUSSELL COUSINS

ZOLA'S *Germinal* (1885), an epic novel about a mining community driven by starvation wages to strike action and destructive violence, was inspired by the 1884 pit strike at Anzin which was brought to a brutal and murderous end by troops. The author's uncompromising fictionalized version of these events shocked and shamed contemporary readers who, perhaps for the first time, came to realize the human price of coal.

Berri's 1993 film version appeared against a rather less dramatic background, but one nevertheless of rising unemployment, social unrest, and industrial decline, with a now nearly defunct mining industry retaining only a tenuous link with its proud history. Growing disillusionment with the political centre-left under Mitterrand's presidency had brought, in May of that year, the return of a centre-right government led by Édouard Balladur. The moment was propitious for a resonant restatement of Zola's original challenging account of the economic and moral issues facing a troubled nation uncertain about its place in the economic and social structures of the new Europe.

Berri's painstaking reworking of Zola's text, emphasizing spectacle rather than political critique, was, apart from its sheer cost, an unremarkable example of the dutiful heritage film genre which in part defined French cinema in the 1980s. If Berri's film is in itself unexceptional as a heritage product, it none the less merits further consideration not only for its anodyne ideological inflection but also for its unexpected transformation into a national cultural icon during the acrimonious GATT negotiations of 1992–4 which set France against the USA. Berri's ideologically bland reading of Zola's narrative and the film's embroilment in the GATT negotiations reflect aspects of the cultural-political climate in France of the early 1990s.

The immediate origins of the GATT dispute between the two countries over free trade in audiovisual products may be traced to policies introduced in the 1980s by Jack Lang when he was Minister of Culture in the newly elected socialist government. During the 1970s, with its small indigenous market, the French film industry had declined sharply in the face of stiff competition from television and Hollywood's increasing penetration of the domestic market (Prédal 1991: 388). To remedy this situation, Lang increased film production subsidies, found additional funds for prestige block-busters, and offered new tax incentives to encourage film finance companies or SOFICAs to be more adventurous (Finney 1996: 131–2). American negotiators argued that such subsidies, along with protective quotas, contravened GATT protocols on free competition.

Contrary to free-marketeers' expectations, the return of a centre-right government in France did not change the French position on state support for the film industry. Traditionalists opposed to the all-pervading influence of American values in French society, exemplified for many by such transatlantic implantations as Eurodisney and McDonald's, stiffened political resolve. This defensive nationalism, in the face of perceived American cultural imperialism, found specific expression in Jacques Toubon's protective legislation for the French language which sought to outlaw Anglo-Saxon loanwords (*La Loi Toubon* 1994).

As for the French film industry, a reasoned justification for state intervention was articulated by Jack Lang: the cinema was not simply a commercial enterprise, but an art form expressing a nation's history and values and, as such, should be deemed to constitute a cultural exception to the general trade regulations (Lang 1993: 63). Whereas Hollywood could easily reach a vast anglophone market and be self-sufficient, the economics of the French film industry, with its more limited language base, were entirely different and, for the French voice to be heard, production subsidies and protective quotas were essential. Almost inevitably, the high-budget, government-subsidized *Germinal*, produced as part of a rolling programme of films to challenge the Hollywood blockbuster, became entangled in the GATT negotiations. Berri was forthright in his defence of the French support system to counter American cultural hegemony: 'I'm not about to be buggered by the US industry. We shouldn't allow them to deal with us the way they dealt with the Redskins' (Finney 1996: 5).

After the success of his previous heritage super-productions, *Manon des Sources* and *Jean de Florette* (1986), Berri seemed well placed to challenge the Hollywood blockbuster with a quality version of *Germinal*. Zola's best-known canonical text, the enduring mainstay of literature syllabuses, was safe territory for the heritage treatment. A cast of established French actors and personalities provided domestic box-office guarantees: Gérard Depardieu, the international embodiment of the French male, as the respected Maheu; Miou-Miou, more readily found in comic roles, extending her range as the tragic wife La Maheude; the popular singer and working-class icon Renaud making his film debut as Zola's proletarian hero Étienne Lantier. The major financial backing came from the banking community (BNP, Crédit Lyonnais, Société Générale) and television companies (Canal Plus and Antenne 2), while additional support was provided by government agencies: the Ministry of Education; the Regional Film Board; the Regional Development Agency (Assouline 1993: 157). With its broad spectrum of institutional support, both governmental and financial, *Germinal* was readily perceived as a quasi-national undertaking. With French opinion convinced that Depardieu had been cheated out of an Oscar for his role in *Green Card* (Weir, 1990) by an American magazine slur imputing involvement in a teenage gang rape, his presence in the film became a further reason for resisting American pressures.

Previous adaptations of *Germinal*, notably Capellani's silent transposition of 1913 and Allégret's condensed rendering of 1963, had disappointed largely because of technical limitations and budgetary constraints. Berri's prestige version costing over 170 million francs sought to avoid such pitfalls with some 42 million francs spent on set construction, costumes, and special effects. Some 8,000 extras (ironically mostly unemployed miners) provided Zola's northern France pit community: the cheaper East European locations imposed upon Allégret were deemed incompatible with a heritage cinema movement concerned with historical authenticity, but above all Frenchness.

After weeks of carefully orchestrated publicity, *Germinal* was launched with a gala performance in Lille on 27 September 1993. Against the background of the contentious GATT negotiations and the imminent release of Spielberg's much-trailed *Jurassic Park*, the event assumed unusual political and national significance. A special

TGV, symbolizing French engineering achievement, brought President Mitterrand, Jack Lang, Jacques Delors, and other high-profile politicians to Lille to head the invited audience of regional deputies, French businessmen, representatives of the various funding bodies, and local mining families. The glittering populist occasion embodied Mitterrand's carefully fostered all-embracing designer socialism, with *Germinal*, the nation's most expensive film, acquiring a totemistic significance for the embattled French film industry.

Journalists readily fuelled the GATT dispute by taking *Germinal* and its future box-office rival *Jurassic Park* as symptomatic of competing and contrastive cultural values. Whereas the Hollywood spectacular dealt in puerile escapism, the French film was a reflective cultural product, confronting socio-political issues and marking an important stage in the nation's coming to terms with its past. In the prevailing atmosphere, attending a performance of *Germinal* was deemed by ironical newspaper columnists to be a civic duty (Lefort 1993), while the only important consideration was not the quality of the film but whether it constituted a 'victory for French culture over Yankee imperialism' (Evin 1993: 35). Released on 29 September throughout France, *Germinal* attracted an audience of 867,000 in the first week alone, and within seven weeks passed the break-even figure of 5 million spectators. However, this French triumph was relatively short-lived, for ultimately, Hollywood's version of escapist fantasies was more in tune with the French mood than the darker tones of, albeit synthetic, heritage social realism and, by the end of the year, the much-feared and derided *Jurassic Park* had outdistanced *Germinal* with 6.3 million spectators. The reasons for the relative failure of *Germinal* to see off the Hollywood super-production may lie in the undemanding narrative conventions of the heritage genre with its attendant self-serving ideology.

Berri's screen version of Zola's narrative fits squarely within the heritage film mould and as such is overly reverential in its treatment: '*Germinal* . . . is a prime example of literalist cinema that deadens the imagination' (Romney 1994: 33). Although Berri claimed his adaptation to be a personal reading, and not a slavish illustration of Zola's text (Berri 1993: 19), the heritage genre requires all but total submission to the literary source material, privileging author over film-maker, especially where the writer enjoys canonical status. Audiences, and reviewers on their behalf, are primed to expect a version corresponding as closely as possible to a faithful, uncontroversial visualization of the well-known story, rather than a creative reshaping or politically committed treatment. Berri's film assiduously follows Zola's general narrative development, though in the omission of particular episodes or characters, and the reworking of material, shifts of emphasis may be observed.

In Berri's reworking, a more positive, less critical image of the mining community emerges. The miners are more abstemious, less promiscuous, and more morally conscious citizens than Zola allows. Problem families, dirty households are not represented, nor are the sexual couplings which Étienne found so difficult to accept. Negative aspects of individual characters are eradicated: La Levaque, the miner's wife, is no longer coarse and unfaithful; Jeanlin, Maheu's injured son, does not commit the vicious murder of a soldier; the good-hearted La Mouquette is not allowed to seduce the hero Étienne. The cumulative effect of omissions and reworkings is to provide a more attractive image of the mining community. Here are reasonable, hard-working French people let down by the system they loyally serve. In the more forgiving tone of the film, their bourgeois masters, often stereotyped to the point of caricature and as such more figures of fun than of evil disposition, are spared the cutting edge of Zola's presentation. Greater emphasis is given to their common humanity, their marital difficulties (Hennebeau), their financial problems (Deneulin), the painful loss of Cécile strangled by the demented Bonnemort. Only the despicable grocer Maigrat, trading food against sexual favours, is treated with the same degree of violence that Zola envisaged. The film's representation of the nation's immediate history to itself seeks an accommodation with past mistakes rather than confrontation. Errors are made as society constructs itself and, in line with Mitterrand's comfortably anodyne version of the nation's development, a better future (now the present) is guaranteed in the reconciliatory tone Berri provides, especially for Zola's already irrationally upbeat ending.

In the film version, the broad canvas presented by Zola is more tightly concentrated in the destiny of the Maheu family, and through the sympathetic Depardieu/Miou-Miou couple, a sanitized reading of Zola's narrative is constructed. Miou-Miou, after her successful television portrayal of another mature and resolute Zola female character (Mme Caroline of *L'Argent*), interprets La Maheude as the eternal mother figure, an indestructible Marianne, determined to fight on when the men around her are ready to compromise, somehow surviving a succession of tragic losses and still providing for her family at the end. Gérard Depardieu, the iconic modern French male, endows the role of Maheu with his characteristic gentle strength and considerateness. He is the family man, the hard-working, dependable, and moral representative of the miners, driven to violence only under extreme provocation. His centrality to the action (emphasized when he takes over part of the outsider Étienne's political role from the novel) brings a measured dignity to the miners' cause, preferring compromise to conflict.

Berri's insistence on action and spectacle rather than debate and reflection reduces discussion of politics and economics. The emphasis is shifted from analysis to dramatization with a focus on individuals and personalities. This displacement, which obfuscates any objective critique of the free-market system, may not be unconnected to Berri's entrepreneurial reflexes and the involvement of the large financial institutions in the film's funding arrangements. With the mood of political pragmatism abroad in the 1990s, crystallized in Mitterrand's accommodation with the centre-right and his concessions on privatization (Hewitt 1998: 67), the reduction of political content in the film was perhaps not unexpected and this particular reworking was favourably viewed by sections of the establishment press (Siclier 1993).

Zola's account of political issues and Berri's inflection merits more detailed analysis. The author's understanding of ideologies was rudimentary and Étienne's fumbling engagement with political concepts may be seen to reflect Zola's own limited grasp of his ill-digested research. His distillation of his narrative as the struggle between labour and capital (Becker 1986: 43) was shaped less by political concerns than by his creative sense of the dramatic: here was a clear antithetical structure to illustrate opposing ideologies. Political positions are distributed to members of his cast who exemplify, as though in a morality play, an identifiable stance.

Étienne is given a strong sense of justice which leads to outrage as he discovers the conditions forced upon the miners. His limited grasp of politics and power structures is gradually refined by more politically aware characters: Souvarine, an anarchist; Rasseneur, a moderate socialist; Pluchart, a trade unionist. Zola charts his protagonist's heteroclitic political education through a series of formative discussions and his ensuing, frequently muddled, reflections. Étienne's confusion and self-doubt are conveyed through interior monologue (Zola 1964: 1274), with Zola's editorializing alerting the reader to his character's deficiencies (Zola 1964: 1281) and effectively undermining his protagonist's actions by implying naivety and arrogance (Zola 1964: 1328). The author's attitude to the ideological stance of other characters is similarly signposted by his presentation: Souvarine, who provides the most lucid analysis of the politico-economic situation, is marginalized as a cold intellectual; Pluchart is condemned as a careerist; Rasseneur, the sympathetic former miner advocating moderation and accommodation with the employers, emerges clearly as Zola's surrogate voice. Of the employers, Deneulin, the private mine owner representing paternalistic capitalism, is treated with greater understanding than the Grégoires or the Hennebeaus, who are cast as unquestioning devotees of the free-market system which has served them so well.

Berri in part reflects this emblematic distribution, faithfully borrowing both dialogue (thus emphasizing his literary source material) and situation to illustrate Zola's thesis. His film, however, is more concerned with providing dramatic action than with exploring political concepts. The lengthy political discussions at Rasseneur's, in which Souvarine provides a clear analysis of the situation, are curtailed, as are the revealing dinner party exchanges at the Hennebeau household. The scaling-down of Souvarine's contributions and the virtual elimination of Pluchart diminish the film's political content, while even the moderate Rasseneur is condemned to a reduced role. The red-coated Étienne never for a moment seems to doubt his purpose or to struggle with political concepts: he becomes a man of action, not analysis and reflection. Entirely committed to the cause, he is the untainted hero not given to self-importance, happily rejecting La Mouquette's advances while remaining true to his devotion for Catherine. The tragic turn of events confirms his naivety and, in the miners' eyes, he is seen as a false prophet.

For both author and film-maker the meeting of the striking miners in the forest is a dramatic set piece which illustrates how the political material is handled. Zola's preparatory notes reveal a careful stage-managing of effects as he conjures up the forest clearing atmospherically lit by the full moon. The political positions of the main participants are indicated with the substance of Étienne's arguments located in Zola's reading of the socialist theoretician Laveleye (Becker 1986: 163). An atmosphere of religious exaltation is suggested as the moonlit events reach their climax. The stage is set for Étienne to stir the miners into action, propounding the ideas he has uncritically absorbed from conversations with Souvarine. Rasseneur, counselling restraint, is shouted down; the respected Bonnemort is moved to speak in support of strike action; Chaval, when challenged, agrees to demonstrate solidarity by stopping work at the Jean-Bart pit which has remained open.

Berri's version differs considerably in both content and enunciation, though the essential theatricality of the sequence is retained. Portentous music floods the screen as the camera moves with the gathering crowds to the darkened forest where a crucifix stands out amongst the trees, thus giving concrete illustration to Zola's indication of religious exaltation. The action is considerably shorter with fewer individual contributions. Neither Rasseneur nor Bonnemort participates in the meeting, while in contrast to his silence in the novel, Maheu takes over from Étienne as the principal speaker. In dispensing with Rasseneur, Berri silences Zola's voice of caution, a loss which is balanced by the elimination of Bonnemort's enthusiastic support for action. By removing these contributors and curtailing Étienne's speech the sequence effectively becomes a vehicle for Depardieu at the expense of the less commanding Renaud. The shift of focus from Renaud, with his limited acting range, to Depardieu, with his greater screen presence, may be explained in part by matters relating to the star persona but, with the strike message now identified with his Maheu, the action acquires a more solid sense of moral justification.

For the heritage film-maker committed to spectacle, Zola's text offers several opportunities to experiment with cinematic equivalences. However, Berri's enunciation is frequently inadequate and his misguidedly literalist approach frequently betrays a misapprehension of the function and purpose of documentary and descriptive elements in Zola's discourse. The author's aim was not simply mimetic, but didactic. Detailed accounts of the environment were deemed essential to an understanding of the physical and moral conditions shaping consciousness, and Zola conveys this conditioning through various narrative techniques including authorial observation and characterial perspectives. The initial presentation of the pit in novel and film illustrates the differences between Zola's multilayered account and Berri's impressive, but less resonant, presentation.

After evoking a marrow-chilling, pitch-black night by repetition and accumulation of a lexis denoting cold and dark, Zola introduces his starving newcomer to the mysterious pithead. The unknowing stranger is important to Zola's relation, for it is through Étienne's untutored subjectivity that he registers the terrifyingly inhuman conditions of capitalist exploitation. Through internal focalization Zola transmits the thoughts and impressions of his protagonist: the icy wind appears to Étienne as the metaphorical cry of the starving unemployed (Zola 1964: 1140) while the pit in his incomprehension appears like a monstrous ogre swallowing up miners (Zola 1964: 1135). But in these subjective reactions lies an objective reality: unemployed workers *are* starving and miners *do* sacrifice their lives to the mining industry. Zola's framing of Bonnemort's attitude towards his anonymous masters reinforces this view: 'His voice had taken on a sort of religious awe as though he was speaking of some inaccessible tabernacle' (Zola 1964: 1141). The author's editorializing and evocation of the pit as a devouring monster moves beyond simple description to reveal an ideological position: an implicit criticism of unregulated market forces as dehumanizing and destructive.

Berri's opening sequence imitates the structure of Zola's narrative, but lacks the criticism implicit in the novelist's account. After close ups of feet pounding a dark track and images of a distant industrial landscape with braziers flaming in the wind of the bleak night, the camera invites identification with a newcomer staring blankly ahead. These establishing images are overlaid by Rouques's majestically sombre music, occasionally interrupted by discordant groans and clanking from the barely discernible pit machinery. The characterial point of view is maintained as the camera foregrounds Étienne observing the pit constructions with subsequent eye-match shots of the various buildings, but no access to his thoughts or impressions is offered: the pit remains an observed pit and does not become an imagined monster. As Étienne explores the pithead or watches Bonnemort going about his work, the viewer discovers further aspects of the mining process, but in this visualization there is no authorial voice to explain the significance of what is perceived. Neither is there the editorializing presence of an omniscient narrator revealing the awe in which Bonnemort holds his employers. In Berri's presentation, the pit may be an impressive sight, but there is not the same sense of it being a monstrous threat to human life.

Whereas Zola shocked readers by his raw reworking of contemporary events and damning exposure of mining conditions, Berri's visualization, without informative commentary, characterial perspectives, or Zola's richly evocative discourse, loses the critical edge. A nostalgic, unchallenging visual essay on a defunct industry safely belonging to a bygone age results. Angelo's camera provides the viewer with a series of naturalizing guided tours: now visiting the mine's underground workings, now dropping in on the miners' fair, now showing the comfortable lives of the bourgeoisie in picture-book mansions. This commitment to illustration provides an umproblematic version of Zola's narrative, where the past is lovingly recreated as living tableaux, but drained of historical significance and emotional involvement. Rarely does the camera participate in the creation of mood or meaning for the viewer, preferring to show rather than involve. Notable exceptions are during the vertiginous pit descent, where disconcerting angles do suggest the shaft's depth and Étienne's discomfort, or during the pit explosion where, like the trapped miners, the audience is faced with a hurtling fireball.

The highly visual miners' fair in Zola's novel constitutes a ready-made heritage film set piece, with its potential for spectacle and historical recreation. The author's explicit intentions in this episode were to advance the plot in terms of Zacharie's marriage to the pregnant Philomène, to establish the creation of the miners' hardship fund, and to portray the miners enjoying themselves (Becker 1986: 113–15). This diegetic pattern is carefully replicated by Berri.

To establish an authentic setting, Zola researched common fairground attractions in mining communities. These elements form the basis of his description and, to give them narrative immediacy, he deploys characters as witness-participants: Chaval and Catherine will serve to relay the fair as they tour the sideshows (Becker 1986: 112). Zola evokes the good-humoured, milling crowd, the heaving pubs, the pedlars with their wares, the sweetmeats, a cock fight, an archery stall, and a game of boules in a composite picture of collective festivity. Allusions to heat, noise, and food smells complete this atmospheric verbal canvas (Zola 1964: 1265–6).

Berri's street fair lasts no more than 100 seconds but manages to embrace a wealth of detail. The sequence opens dramatically with a character descending a greasy pole, a detail not found in Zola's text, though interestingly reproducing the opening of Allégret's 1963 version of the street fair. Berri does not deploy the presence of observer-participant characters, as does Zola, to legitimize the scene, but observes events in documentary style from a series of vantage points. After the establishing shot of the greasy pole, the camera pans slowly across the village square to reveal characters engaged in myriad activities: testing their strength (Berri's invention), watching a cock fight (cut from the English video version), eating food, or simply strolling. Music from the on-screen organ grinder accompanies the action. The omniscient camera does not privilege any particular individual, nor is any image of the fair relayed through an individual consciousness. By his all-embracing overview, including cameos of established characters, Berri conveys a sense of the community at large enjoying itself. The dynamic immediacy of the Bruegelesque sequence, with its many activities simultaneously in view, achieves the desired sense of joyful specta-cle as the community, or perhaps even Mitterrand's France, is at one with itself.

As an example of heritage film-making, *Germinal* embodies many of the genre's defining characteristics: a French literary clas-sic as source material; a conscientious, though unchallenging, rendering of the narrative; a carefully researched authentic period recreation; high production values with an emphasis on spectacle; an inherent sense of Frenchness conveyed though national stars and French locations; an anodyne account of French social history with an emphasis on aesthetic values rather than political content.

Berri's ambitious and expensive venture into Zola's world confirms many differences in novelistic discourse and film practice, but, more significantly, his film serves an ideology validating consensus rather than conflict. Released during the contentious GATT negotiations, Berri's *Germinal* inadvertently acquired a political presence as the champion of the struggling French film industry: here was a quality film about the nation's recent past to set against the facile escapist fantasy of *Jurassic Park*. In reality both films shared similar goals as crowd-pleasing entertainment: only the degree of misrepresentation of the past with its accommodation with the present was in question.

The protracted confrontations between Hollywood media magnates and representatives of the threatened French film industry assumed, in a curious twist, a *mise en abyme* re-enactment of the power struggle at the heart of *Germinal*: individuals caught up in an unregulated free-market system seeking to defend their work and to voice their opinions against the pressures of the international market.

Berri's film, a characteristic, but stylistically unexceptional, end-product of Lang's cultural renewal policies of the 1980s, had unintentionally crossed the boundaries of conformist domestic heritage cinema to enter the unmapped and dangerous domain of international cultural politics. In so doing, *Germinal* became a political statement in itself and a rallying point for the embattled French film industry, thereby enjoying a critical attention which it scarcely merited either in terms of film-making or of the vacuity of its sanitized political content.

3

Identity and Alterity in *Indochine*
(Wargnier, 1992)

BRIGITTE ROLLET

FRANCE has always been reluctant to confront its own past; 'amnesia' is a word frequently used when referring to colonization and decolonization, even in recent historical work such as *Les Lieux de mémoire* edited by Pierre Nora. As far as the wars which led to decolonization are concerned, the silence is even greater. Since both the Indo-Chinese and Algerian wars were 'lost' by France, the painful memories of such 'events' (as the Algerian war has long been called) are more often than not suppressed in the national memory. Indirect or direct recollection of this aspect of recent French history has often led to controversy and to vivid reactions whichever side one stands on.[1]

Indo-China and Algeria have been described as 'non-lieux de mémoire' and this partly explains the fact that there are few films which refer to these conflicts. This is particularly the case for Indo-China, dubbed 'the pearl of the Empire', but which inspired directors less than the North African colony Algeria. Around 150 films (including co-productions) were shot in the Maghreb between 1911 and 1961 (Boulanger 1975), whereas only a few documentaries and fiction films were made in the 1920s–1930s in the eastern colonies. Film representations were even rarer during the Indo-Chinese war, when, as Baldizzone points out, film footage was limited to government propaganda: 'between 1945 and 1956 cinematographic representations of Indochina and its inhabitants were limited for the audience to the weekly "news" [which] always expressed . . . the views of the governing political party' (Baldizzone 1992: 40–6). A few fiction films addressed the issue after the war; recent filmographies suggest either thirteen or fourteen (Delemeuille 1992: 63–72; Gauthier 1992: 52). Other fictions such as Becker's *Goupi mains rouges* (1942) or Tavernier's *Le Juge et l'assassin* (1976) addressed the issue obliquely by including former expats from Indo-China. Despite Benjamin Stora's recent attempts to prove differently (1997), French cinema has not addressed its colonial past the way the USA has in relation to Vietnam. Censorship alone cannot explain the persistent silence of French cinema on the subject.

It is all the more surprising then that three big-budget films dealing with the Indo-Chinese conflict were released in 1992: *Diên Biên Phu* by Pierre Schoendoerffer (with the biggest budget in French cinema until Besson's *Le Cinquième élément* (1997)), *L'Amant* by Jean-Jacques Annaud, and *Indochine* by Régis Wargnier). This sudden interest in the Far East could be explained by a number of factors: the recent political turmoil in North Africa; a desire for exoticism; a conscious or unconscious nostalgia for the lost empire; and/or the late acceptance of decolonization. Superficially, it is difficult not to agree that it was the desire for exoticism which prevailed, since not only did travel agencies use extracts from the films to sell package holidays to Vietnam, but most critics in their reviews emphasized the iconography of the film, especially the stunning landscapes, rather than focusing on France's troubled relationship with its former colony and the ambiguities of its 'mission civilisatrice'.

Before the release of these three films, French cinema had not reconstructed France's past the way British heritage films typically do, that is by attempting 'to forge a national consensus based on the celebration of a nationhood deeply rooted in a colonial empire' (Jäckel and Duverger 1993: 23). Wargnier declared that he wanted 'to show colonization as people did not know it' and to make a 'tough' film where 'nothing was invented' (Wargnier 1992: 37). I shall argue on the contrary that the film offers a consensual vision of colonialism through a reconstruction of the past based on stereotypes. Far from being as radical as its director would like us to believe, his critique of colonialism is often ambiguous. This chapter will also analyse the issues of national, sexual, and racial identity/alterity raised in the film.

Wargnier's choice of co-scriptwriters might have led one to assume a serious perspective on colonial matters. Erik Orsenna won the Goncourt prize in 1988 for his book *L'Exposition coloniale*, and Louis Gardel wrote about the North African 'Empire' in his book

Fort Saganne which the director Alain Corneau adapted for the cinema in 1984, starring Gérard Depardieu and Catherine Deneuve. Wargnier had often expressed his great admiration for David Lean and his 'passion for *Lawrence of Arabia*', which he described as his 'favourite film of all time' (Wargnier 1992: 37). Initially, the intention had been to rewrite *Madam Butterfly* in the context of the French colonization of Indo-China. By changing the content of the film (even if the element of the young Asian woman falling in love with a French army officer remains), Wargnier also changed the perspective. The main character of *Indochine* is not a young native any longer, but a Frenchwoman, Éliane Devries. The love affair becomes a triangle as both Éliane and her Indo-Chinese adoptive daughter Camille are in love with Jean-Baptiste, a young French army officer. The story takes place during the last twenty years of the French presence in Indo-China, and is constructed as an epic drama. Some historical events (such as the massacre of Yam Bay and its consequences both in Indo-China and in France, and the general amnesty decided by Blum's Popular Front government which led to the release of all the political prisoners in the Poulo Condor prison) are interwoven with the individual lives of the fictional characters to add a historical touch to the film.

Besides the traditional ingredients of melodrama (the competing demands of love, family, and duty), the film offers features typical of the colonial film as described by Boulanger in its extensive use of natural settings and local colour. The film's opening sequences evoke a traditional funeral in images reminiscent of the early twentieth-century documentaries on 'native customs'. Instead of the Ankor Palace, a typical location in these films, Wargnier dwells on Along Bay with aerial views characteristic of the documentary series *Découverte du monde*.

More important is the predominance of the white and western gaze. Secondary Indo-Chinese characters or extras are foils whose presence is always justified by the presence and indeed the gaze of a western protagonist. There is always a western character in all the scenes with a crowd of natives, be they the opening funerals of Camille's parents, the release of the prisoners of Poulo Condor, or the 'fête de la tranquillité'. Even the scenes where Camille discovers with other Indo-Chinese what appalling conditions of life colonialism brings in the countryside are narrated by Éliane, who comments in voice-over what Camille thinks. The overall presentation of the colony is stereotypical. In other words, the film gives colonized and colonizers alike the 'roles' defined by Albert Memmi in his famous essay *The Colonizer and the Colonized*, despite a few variations to which I shall return. Where the colonized are concerned, the emphasis is on the exotic setting and the daily life of the natives is often depicted only as a backdrop for spectacular travelling shots.

The first minutes of the film give in the space of a few shots a variety of relationships between colonizers and colonized, from the rarest to the more traditional. Camille, a young Indo-Chinese woman belonging to the local aristocracy and adopted by a western woman (Éliane), appears first, driven in a luxury car by an Indian before dancing the tango with her adoptive mother. In a simultaneous scene, a young Indo-Chinese woman is shown with an older man who strokes her hair in the stereotyped situation of the 'encongaillement' (the word is formed from the Annamite 'congai', which means Annamite woman). In the following sequence, Éliane talks patronizingly to her Indo-Chinese cook. In three segments therefore we see the different situations of the colonized: they are either economically and culturally 'equal' with the western population (local bourgeoisies), or in a 'privileged' situation (the young native lover of a western middle-aged man), or at the bottom of the social scale where they are employed as domestics.

In the first 'category', none of the characters presented seems to suffer from the western presence except a young man called Tanh. The son of local middle-class Indo-Chinese, he realizes while studying in France the situation his country is in and, after being expelled from France, he joins the clandestine struggle of the illegal Indo-Chinese Communist Party. Although Tanh's role is rather limited within the narrative, he portrays the intellectual elite disillusioned with the 'mission civilisatrice' realizing the gap between the theory of the declaration of human rights and the reality of life in the colonies. By choosing the struggle against France, he rejects both his biological family who accept France's rules and his adoptive cultural one.

More disturbing than the stereotypical representation of both colonizers and colonized are the negative depictions of natives used to soften the negative aspects of westerners. Thus, when political prisoners are tortured in the police station (controlled by French officers), the 'torturer' is an Indo-Chinese policeman. Later in the film, during the 'slave market' supervised by the French army, the most shocking behaviour with the 'slaves' comes from an Indo-Chinese merchant who is shown examining the eyes and teeth of his compatriots. We do not see the French officer killing a child a few minutes before. Similarly, Éliane is not seen beating her workers (although we can hear her doing so), while in another scene an Indo-Chinese worker does so. This suggests that the distinction suggested by Memmi between the 'colonial subject' or 'colonialist self' and the 'colonized other' is not clear as far as the protagonists are concerned.

Although Camille is both Indo-Chinese and one of the main characters, she is never clearly identified as different from the Europeans. She looks like them, speaks like them, and is dressed like them (whereas her 'mother' often wears Indo-Chinese clothes). She says 'them' when referring to her compatriots, which illustrates both her position as a 'colonialist self/subject' and her dissociation from the 'colonized other'. She also embodies Memmi's view that 'another sign of the colonized's depersonalization is what one might call the mark of the plural. The colonized is never characterized in an individual manner; he is entitled only to drown in an anonymous collectivity' (Memmi 1965: 85). From a religious and cultural point of view, she is also on the westerners' side, even if, in the second half of the film, she joins her compatriots, talks their/her language, wear similar outfits, and suffers comparable pain and discomfort. Despite her break-up with her adoptive family, she does not seem to be politically aware early in the film, and her conflict with her mother seems more linked to a sexual jealousy than an ideological conflict. She never questions what her mother stands for, even if she tells her at the end of the film that '[her] Indo-China is dead'. When she discovers the 'bad' side of colonialism she justifies her becoming a communist (the red princess) by saying that 'it was the only way to survive'. Camille seems to escape categorization by being both of Bhabha's self and other (1993), and by becoming a sort of 'colonized self or subject'. Her mother indicates this process when she says that 'Camille is with her people', and that 'now she has Indo-China inside herself'. The fact that from the moment she becomes the Other either through her clothes, her language, or her way of life, she becomes linked with Jean-Baptiste, last representative of the white world, further blurs the easy distinction between self and other.

This lack of differentiation, or to say the least the extreme ambiguity between 'Self' and 'Other', can also be found to a lesser degree in the character of Jean-Baptiste and more especially with Éliane. Jean-Baptiste could be described as what Memmi calls 'the colonizer who refuses' (Memmi 1965: 19), or in other words and for the colonizers who accept, 'a colonizer [who] is nothing but a traitor' (Memmi 1965: 21). Because he is an army officer, the army's role in colonization being essential, there is an extra ambivalence to the character. Initially presented as a young and disciplined officer who obeys and respects orders whatever they are, Jean-Baptiste differs from the other colonizers by his apparent disrespect for the non-written rules of colonialism. He tells Éliane that she is a 'bird of prey. You treat men as you treat your trees. You buy them and then make them bleed.' His reaction does not mean that he wants to fight on the colonized side; on the contrary, his struggle is highly individualistic. He is outraged that a woman can influence his fate, and only identifies himself with the colonized at this precise moment because, like them, he has no power whatsoever. He illustrates Memmi's comment that 'such an indignation is not always accompanied by a desire for a policy of action. It is rather a position of principle' (Memmi 1965: 20). His rejecting his 'side' does not necessarily mean that he wants to join the other. He does not choose to become a deserter, and therefore deviates from Memmi's assertion that 'to refuse means either withdrawing physically from the conditions or remaining to fight them' (Memmi 1965: 19). His desertion/treason are not motivated by a political awareness, but by personal reasons. None of his actions is political and despite the help he receives from the illegal Indo-Chinese Communist Party (led by Tanh), he never expresses any interest in their struggle. His 'neutrality' is exemplified by the character he has to perform with the drama band he is hiding with. Unlike the other actors, his stage persona does not represent anything or anyone. He accepts the slave market by remaining silent. He deserts because of Camille's murderous act and not because his superior kills a child a few minutes before. Despite all the ambiguities of such a character, he is presented as a 'moral' hero, for the audience of the film as well as for the fictitious Indo-Chinese audience of the drama performed in the film. He embodies the stereotype of the principled soldier associated with the army, at the other end of the moral spectrum to the amoral if not immoral police chief Guy.

All the roles are symbolic in the film, although it would be superficial only to read the film as a metaphor on Camille (i.e. Indo-China) split between her adoptive mother (i.e. France) and a French 'rebel' (as the officer deserts to save the young woman, as other soldiers did during the war). The most obvious element in this regard is the choice of Catherine Deneuve as the star who embodies Éliane. Although the film was, according to the director, 'written for her and thinking about her' (Wargnier 1992: 37), Wargnier's choice goes beyond his desire to direct the 'top female French star of all time' (Vincendeau 1993a: 20). Deneuve is also 'a semi-official ambassador for French fashion on and off screen' (Vincendeau 1993a: 22). It is even more tempting to say that she embodies France, as her image has been used since 1985 in French town halls (after Brigitte Bardot) as a model for Marianne, the symbol of the French Republic. The link between the actress and her role is therefore extremely significant. Despite its title, the film does not tell the story of Indo-China as such but of Indo-China seen through the gaze of the key character Éliane Devries. The choice of the flashback through the use of voice-over in the film (which recalls the opening sequence of *Out of Africa* (Pollack, 1985) with Karen Blixen's 'I had a farm in Africa') clearly expresses the subjectivity of the narrative mode. As Maurin Turim suggests, 'flashbacks in film merge the two levels of remembering the past, giving large-scale social and political history the subjective mode of a single, fictional individual's remembered experience . . . One of the ideological implications of this narration of history through a subjective focalization is to create history as an essential and emotional experience' (Turim 1989: 2, 17). The story told is hers and the fact that her fictitious character was inspired by a 'real' woman is not important. What is interesting is on the one hand the extreme symbolism of her role, and on the other the apparent and varied contradictions it comprises.

Éliane Devries is presented as a rich and beautiful single landowner, born in Indo-China where she lives with her father. She owns one of the biggest rubber plantations in Indo-China which she refers to as her 'domain', a domain she inherited after the death of Camille's parents, a couple of rich local aristocrats. She is very close to the upper-class natives, speaks their language, and knows the country and its inhabitants very well. She also has very good connections on the European side, and more especially with the

Security Chief who is in love with her. Although everything seems to identify her as the colonizer par excellence, she, even more than the other Europeans in the film, is presented in ways which problematize that status. First and foremost, she is the main character, a woman, the narrator, and a star, leading to unequivocal audience identification. Second, she represents the acceptable side of colonialism, a humanitarian and patronizing colonialism, typical of Meryl Streep's character in *Out of Africa*. She has a similar relationship with the expatriate community, as both Devries and Blixen are 'outsiders' from a social and sexual point of view. She is presented as a 'good' colonizer, although she never rejects her role. During a boat race at the beginning of the film, for example, where 'her' team, made up of the Indo-Chinese workers of her plantation, competes with the French soldiers, she only differs from the other Europeans making racist comments by her silence; she does not speak in their defence. More important is the fact that her character, like Blixen in *Out of Africa*, does not change in the course of the film, despite the massive upheavals the country is facing. All the other colonizers act in ways which demonstrate their belonging to Memmi's category of the 'colonizers who accept'. Éliane is neither in this group nor in the other of the 'colonizers who refuse'. This reinforces the ambiguity of her character, who represents a hybrid form of colonialism generated by both her sexual and national identity.

According to Shohat, 'the intersection of colonial and gender discourses involves a shifting, contradictory subject positioning, whereby Western woman can simultaneously constitute "center" and "periphery", identity and alterity' (Shohat 1991–2: 63), to which one could add 'Self' and 'Other'. Éliane offers an interesting combination of identity and alterity. Unlike Yvette, another European woman, she is single, she has a job, indeed a 'male job' as Jean-Baptiste tells her, and she is Camille's adoptive mother. Although she is French, she sees herself as what she calls an 'Asiate', is often dressed in Indo-Chinese clothes, likens herself to a mango (which she opposes to the European apple), and calls Tanh's mother 'aunt'.

More interesting is the way her character combines colonialism and gender through the notion of motherhood. Indeed, she is perhaps less 'paternalist' than 'maternalist', as what Éliane encapsulates is the recurrent idea of motherhood on the one hand and the opposition between the links of blood and property on the other. Éliane's relationships with the other characters are almost always related to the idea of motherhood, despite the fact that she is not a biological mother. Éliane has an affair with Jean-Baptiste, who is much younger than herself, something which is not new in the actress's career; she has already illustrated 'the familiar screen conflict between a woman's sexuality and motherhood' (Vincendeau 1993*a*: 22). She behaves with her father as a tolerant mother who would accept her child's bad conduct. She finally confesses the reason why she never slept with the Security Chief Guy by telling him that she never wanted to have him in her womb. She is the adoptive mother of Camille and indirectly of Camille's son Étienne, who tells her at the end of the film: 'you are my mother'. She sees herself as the mother of her coolies, far removed from any notions of sexuality. When Jean-Baptiste asks her: 'Don't you mind the way they look at you . . . they are all male,' she answers: 'they are just my coolies.' She tells one of them after physically punishing him: 'do you think a mother likes to beat her child?' His answer in broken French is: 'you are both my father and my mother.' She illustrates perfectly Fanon's comment on the familial relationship fundamental to colonialism:

On the unconscious plane, colonialism   did not seek to be considered by the native as a gentle loving mother who protects her child from a hostile environment, but rather as a mother who unceasingly restrains her fundamentally perverse offspring from . . . giving free rein to his evil instincts. The colonial mother protects her child from itself, from its ego, and from its physiology, its biology and its own unhappiness which is its very own essence. (Fanon 1971: 169–70)

By choosing a female character to embody the stereotyped and unfashionable cinematographic role of the colonizer, by slightly modifying the idea of 'fatherland' and making it a 'motherland', with all the clichés it suggests, Wargnier has succeeded in renewing the established genre of the colonial film, although the message remains the same. He has also managed to create a female role model which combines toughness and glamour, a model French audiences are not familiar with, and which suggests a shift away from an unproblematically eroticized to-be-looked-at-ness: 'the discourse of gender within a colonial context . . . suggests that Western woman can occupy a relatively powerful position on the surface of the text, as the vehicle less for a sexual gaze than a colonial gaze' (Shohat 1991–2: 43).

Notes

* The author acknowledges the support of the British Academy for the writing of this chapter.
1. Thus, after *Indochine*, a television programme in three parts, made by Henri de Turennes and broadcast in France in 1984. See Tignères 1992 for the reaction triggered by the film.

4

Film at the Crossroads:
Les Roseaux sauvages (Téchiné, 1994)

WENDY EVERETT

DEALING with themes of memory, identity, and personal choice, offering perspectives which are simultaneously retrospective and prospective, and structured by a dialectic in which the spectator is directly and actively implicated, *Les Roseaux sauvages* emerges as a key film for the turn of the century. Directed by André Téchiné in 1994, the film provides a vivid and convincing autobiographical account of adolescence in France in the early 1960s. Set in and around the small town of Villeneuve-sur-Lot, in south-west France, its narrative traces the complex and shifting relationships between four teenagers: three boys (François, Téchiné's serious and intellectual alter ego; Serge, the son of an illiterate peasant family; and Henri, a *pied-noir*, that is to say, a French colonial, born in Algeria), and one girl (Maïté, the daughter of one of the teachers at the local lycée), following them through their final year at school leading up to their baccalaureate examination. The narrative ends as they set off together to find out the results which will shape their futures.

The film fits comfortably into the concerns of contemporary French (and, indeed, European) cinema, through its status as autobiography, its essentially subjective exploration of the nature of memory and personal identity, articulated through its reconstruction or visualization of the director's own past (Everett 1996: 103–11). But the various personal issues it raises are intricately entwined with the social and political problems facing France in the early years of the Fifth Republic, at the height of the Algerian war; and the doubts and conflicts which mark the protagonists' transition from childhood to adulthood are mirrored by those of France itself, uncomfortably poised on the brink of postcolonialism, and deeply riven with guilt, uncertainty, and fear. Whilst this aspect gives *Les Roseaux sauvages* a breadth of vision which is perhaps unusual in autobiographical accounts, so often criticized for their extreme narcissism and self-absorption ('nombrilisme') (Prédal 1996: 644), in fact it is precisely because of the intensely personal nature of its discourse, with its shifting tenses and viewpoints, that the film is able to achieve its striking relevance and modernity.[1] This often paradoxical coincidence between public and private, present and past, history and fiction will provide the critical parameters of this chapter, in which I shall use the crossroads analogy, with its rich symbolism of choice and indecision, trace and *errance* (after all, suicides were buried at crossroads, and gallows were erected there), to examine the points of intersection which mark both the status and the narrative impetus of *Les Roseaux sauvages*. My aim will be to discover how Téchiné uses the polyphonic discourse of autobiography to create an essentially dynamic account of history which, as in the model proposed by James Young (Young 1993: 730–43), posits memory as a continuously evolving reading of events, a dynamic relationship between present and past.

French cinema has, of course, long been concerned with memory, and with the notion of history as personal viewpoint, and *Les Roseaux sauvages* openly acknowledges its position within this tradition. Indeed, it actively explores its own filmic identity, with the repeated and self-conscious references to, and quotations from, earlier films which constitute one of the characteristics of autobiographical form. However, it also takes the less common step of acknowledging the role played by television in mediating memory (in a lengthy shot of television news coverage of the Algerian war), and this apparent 'truce' between traditionally antagonistic media may well refer not only to French cinema's marked failure to deal with the Algerian issue, but also to the production methods and context of *Les Roseaux sauvages*, as one of a series of autobiographical films commissioned in 1993 by the television producer Chantal Poupaud for the French national arts channel La Sept/Arte. For this series, *Tous les garçons et les filles de leur âge*, nine directors of different ages were each invited to make a film dealing with his/her own adolescence; thus with no pretensions to documentary objectivity, the series would nevertheless effectively provide a broad historical and social panorama covering the lives of young people in France (and, in the case of Chantal Akerman, Belgium), over a period stretching from the 1960s to the 1980s.

The films were required to be autobiographical, to concentrate on the directors' teenage years, and to include a party scene and popular songs from the relevant period. Further shared constraints were a limited budget (5.4 million francs per film), shooting period (18–23 days), and duration (one hour of prime time television). The series thus instigated an entirely new type of collaboration in France between television and cinema, with La Sept/Arte and the film company, IMA Production, working in close partnership throughout. Potential clashes of interest were minimized by the fact that the producers of the series, Chantal Poupaud and Pierre Chevalier, had both worked in cinema before moving to television, while the earlier career of the director of IMA Production, Georges Benayoun, had been in television. The significance of this unprecedented cooperation was widely recognized, and the series was thought to offer a new direction to the French film industry, and a new and positive role for television within that industry (Austin 1996: 171).

However, even within this innovative 'crossroads' collaboration between film and television, the position and status of Téchiné's film was particularly complex for, from the first, Arte had commissioned two versions from him: *Le Chêne et le roseau*, lasting an hour, to open the series, and a second, feature-length version, *Les Roseaux sauvages*, to be given a general cinema release before the televised series. Given the increasing frequency with which French cinema has had to turn to television, 'the very medium which threatens its survival', for financial support (Hayward 1993: 295), Frodon understandably relishes the nice irony of the fact that, in this instance, television needed the prestige of a cinema release to guarantee its own audience ratings (Frodon 1995a: 807). In fact, with the support of IMA Production, two other films in the series appeared in cinemas before their television release, although this had never been Arte's intention. Both Assayas and Kahn also made feature-length versions of their films, and these, like *Les Roseaux sauvages*, were selected for screening at the 1994 Cannes Film Festival, despite their official status as television films.[2]

Clearly, therefore, *Les Roseaux sauvages* stands at the crossroads between old and new, tradition and innovation, which is to say that it is a truly modern film, grounded in the present. However, it is important to reject any simplistic binary oppositions this image may suggest, for if the present (like the future) both shapes and is shaped by the past in a continuous process of reassessment, a crossroads, the moment of intersection or choice, functions as locus of encounter not opposition. And this concept is foregrounded and reinforced in the film's diegetic narration. Thus, for example, the complex issues facing its adolescent protagonists are, initially, perceived by them as discrete (horizontal) alternatives: political (left/right; French Algeria/independent Algeria; combat/pacifism); moral (honesty/cheating; idealism/pragmatism; intellectual/physical); sexual (homosexuality/heterosexuality; fidelity/promiscuity). Within the temporal journey the narrative traces, François and his friends seek resolutions, and equate the reaching of decisions with the transition to the unknown state of adulthood. It is therefore obvious that the film must concern their discovery that there are no final solutions. But more importantly, the shifting tensions which characterize the children's relationships with each other ultimately make them aware that the apparently discrete choices, the binary oppositions and dichotomies they encounter, are in fact complex, ambiguous, and tightly interrelated; that there are, in other words, not even any clear-cut questions.

Take, for example, Algeria, which constitutes an important intersection of personal and public memory for the film's director, and is one of the key issues explored by the film. The conflict can be perceived simplistically in terms of a stark binary choice: whether Algeria should be given its independence or kept under French rule. Thus formulated, the question presents opposing absolutes, and these are articulated by two of the film's characters: Mme Alvarez, Maïté's mother, who, in addition to teaching French at the lycée, is secretary of the local Communist Party, and Henri, the *pied-noir* member of the group. For the former, colonial rule is unjustifiable exploitation, and all colonials are fascist pigs who deserve no understanding. For the latter, France's role in Algeria has been paternalistic, not exploitative, Arabs fighting for independence are murderers, and de Gaulle and his followers are traitors. Mme Alvarez's position is based on political and moral certainty which permits no compromise; Henri's reflects his upbringing and the terrifying experience of his father's violent death in Algeria. Both are inflexible. The question which the young Téchiné seems to face is 'who is right?', and given the importance of the issue, and the hindsight with which the film is formulated, it might at first seem surprising that it is Mme Alvarez who cracks, and Henri who, in the end, may be saved. But this of course is part of the rejection of a simplistic approach to opposition and choice which we have already noted.

Thus the intricate relationship established between the various textual surfaces of the film, its intertextual dialogism, inevitably generates and foregrounds complexity and ambiguity. For example, both Mme Alvarez and we, the spectators, are implicated in the Algerian question right from the opening scene, but it is here posed in very different terms. The scene in question portrays the wedding of one of Mme Alvarez's former pupils, Pierre (Serge's older brother), which she attends, accompanied by Maïté and a reluctant François. As part of his compulsory National Service, Pierre has been drafted to fight in Algeria. He has no political or ethical involvement in the war; he has not elected to fight, and he supports neither cause. For him the battle is one of personal survival: of life or death. His wedding is a ploy to enable him to return to France, and he has invited his former teacher because he knows that, as part of the Resistance movement in the Second World War, the communists helped soldiers in danger to 'disappear', to hide in safety, and he hopes that she will do the same for him. Pierre makes no distinction between the two situations; his view is based on expediency and survival. She, on the other hand, cannot understand this pragmatic viewpoint: since Algeria is in any case going to be given its independence, in other words, since good will triumph, there can be no possible reason for helping him.

When, therefore, she hears that Pierre has indeed been killed, she is overcome with remorse, and has a nervous breakdown. Prescribed a sleep cure, she enters a twilight zone of dreams and whispers, in which contact with the outside world is limited to classical music played on the radio while she is fed her daily meal of puréed vegetables and fruit. Ironically, for Henri, too, the radio provides almost the only link with the world outside school. We see him repeatedly, his radio pressed tightly to his ear, deaf to all else as he listens to news bulletins. In both cases, therefore, rigidity brings isolation and unhappiness. However, whereas Mme Alvarez remains inflexible even after her breakdown, unable to feel concern for Henri's plight because she refuses to look beyond his political beliefs, the possibility of greater tolerance and change is granted to Henri through his relationship with Maïté. In one scene, armed with a can of petrol, he decides to avenge France's betrayal of its own citizens in Algeria, and the communists' role in this, by setting fire to the local Communist Party office where, looking in through the window, he sees Maïté for the first time. In theory, Henri was ready to kill all communists, and Maïté's attitude to fascists was equally extreme, yet they fall in love. Of course, this situation, which in the end is left entirely open-ended, is not proposed as a solution; nor does it suggest that colonialism was justified, or that we should avoid taking sides in moral or political struggles, but it does make us consider the nature and complexity of choice. And the different ways in which the other characters are touched by the war, and the varying viewpoints they contribute to our readings, endlessly extend this process of reflection.

In formal terms too, the film reveals the children's gradual recognition of the complexity of choosing, and their increasingly flexible viewpoints. One of the earliest conflicts between the three boys occurs in the school cloakroom during a class test. Serge has left the classroom armed with the answers to the maths questions which he has offered to François, in a pragmatic attempt to exploit their differences; he will help François with his maths, and François can help him with his French. François follows, indecisively, having already announced somewhat pompously to Serge that he will not cheat; he is already equipped with apparently unassailable moral criteria. In the meantime, Henri too has left the classroom, primarily to listen to his radio, but also to check up on Serge and François. Throughout the scene, the characters are framed on screen within a thick, dark window frame, and the changing positions they occupy in the conflict are visually represented within this frame. Thus Henri, listening to his radio and asking to be left alone, is positioned on the left of the empty window, at one side of the cross formed between its four panes; as Serge starts to argue with him, he appears on the right of the window, at the other extreme of its horizontal bar, while the vertical bar separates them completely. François's hesitant intervention positions him at the base of the frame, directly under its central strut. Thus the triangular conflict which will shape much of their relationship is set out before us. The device is maintained throughout the scene; as different alliances are formed, as one or other of the boys assumes a dominant role, so this is shown in the patterning. But always they are held within the oppositional framework of the window. Later on, when François, attempting to come to terms with his homosexuality, and in search of unequivocal advice, goes to see the manager of a local shoe shop (himself gay, but within a long-term and apparently happy relationship), he is framed through the shop window, held impotently within the vertical and horizontal struts of its frame. (On this occasion, he panics and runs away; on a later occasion, he does ask his questions, but the adult is unable to help, claiming to have forgotten the agonies of his youth.)

As the narrative progresses, and the children become aware of the complex relationships and ambiguities that underlie choice, so too the framings become less restrictive, less polarized. Discussions take place against freer, more mobile backgrounds: a busy classroom or games field, and the final sequence, which brings all four together for the first time, is set in the countryside, beside a river. Here there is no possible stasis, only flux; the children have reached a new awareness and tolerance (whereas Mme Alvarez remains forever imprisoned in the rigid framings which reflect her intolerance). The film's closing shot (with more than a passing reference to the end of Truffaut's *Les 400 coups* (1959), one of the key points of reference in all autobiographical film), is a long tracking shot which follows the children as they walk along a twisting lane, through open fields, and across a bridge, simultaneously walking back to their past (school) and forward to their unknown futures.

The camera's changing viewpoint reflects, of course, the remembering eye of the director, and reminds us of the extent to which Téchiné's success in achieving this open-ended narrative is a feature of the film's autobiographical form. For the Algerian question, like all the others which the film raises, is formulated with the hindsight of the remembering adult; thus superimposed upon the various horizontal divisions which (initially) structure the children's world is a temporal axis which constantly modifies both the initial choices and their repercussions, contributing distance and breadth to the narrative, and making possible an overview to which none of the individual characters within the narrative has access. In this context, we can assess the importance of La Fontaine's 'Le Chêne et le roseau' ('The oak tree and the reed'; drawn from book 1 of his *Fables*), which provides both the title and the central metaphor of the film. That it expresses Téchiné's viewpoint is emphasized by the fact that it is read aloud by François, his younger self. It thus assumes the privileged status of authorial voice-over, establishing a complicity between director and spectator, and indicating that this tale of the pompous, self-satisfied oak tree which pities the wild reed for its vulnerability to the slightest breeze, should provide a key to our reading of the film. For whilst the thin and fragile reed is able to survive a violent storm precisely because of its flexibility, the giant oak is destroyed. It is significant that the fable has been written on the blackboard by Morelli (the replacement for Mme Alvarez), and that, immediately after the class, François overhears him warning Henri that unless he becomes more flexible he too is in danger of being destroyed. However, it is of course the film's autobiographical framework which, imposing a different temporal perspective, enables Téchiné (and us) to assess the broader implications of the fable: to see in it, for example, the contrast between Mme Alvarez's inability to see beyond her rigid opinions, and Morelli, whose fairness and open-mindedness are condemned by both Henri and Mme Alvarez. It further serves to highlight their differing approaches to their pupils: she encourages them to express their personal reactions to Rimbaud, but gives Henri zero because she disagrees with his political stance; he tells them to concentrate on the structure of their arguments, which suggests a more objective, detached, approach, yet—as the narrative will show—remains unfailingly humanitarian and caring.

The autobiographical framework thus creates different temporal viewpoints, involving the spectators in the immediate dilemmas facing the characters, while simultaneously providing distance; we view their present through the perspective of our own. This aspect is clearly important with regard to the film's treatment of Algeria, where Téchiné does not aim to provide a historical account, fixed in the past, but to make us aware that those distant events are part of our present, and indeed our future; that our gaze both shapes and is shaped by them. Thus, within the film's simultaneously retrospective and prospective regard it is the spectator who now occupies the crossroads position; the intersection or conjunction of past and present, history and fiction.

The viewpoint of the characters, however, is narrower; François, for example, is only marginally aware of the Algerian war, scarcely noticing the faint reports emanating from Henri's radio, and involved only very indirectly through its impact on his friends. Awareness of the war's significance and long-term implications is reserved for the remembering adult. Indeed, François is so totally absorbed in his developing identity and sexuality that even the emotions felt by other characters merely constitute an 'otherness' against which he seeks to define himself (a point which Maïté at least recognizes). Central to his search for identity is, of course, his growing awareness that he is gay; all other conflicts are secondary to this one, although he is unconscious of this at the time. For example, his refusal to accept examination answers from Serge, because this would compromise his moral integrity, is overcome not by rational argument but by his increasing attraction to Serge. The adult Téchiné recognizes this, and makes us aware of it (through the shot of François frenziedly undoing Serge's shirt to reach the answers concealed under his trouser waistband), although François has no such understanding of his actions. Similarly, François's outright condemnation of Henri's political position is overcome by his physical attraction, revealed to us by the way that their stark confrontational positioning within a tight inner framing is replaced by shots of them sitting side by side on the rugby pitch, sharing the goodies which François's parents have sent.

The moment at which François confronts and accepts his homosexuality, possibly the key moment in the film, occurs in a brief scene in which, in a direct reference both to the self-absorption of Narcissus and to Lacan's famous mirror phase ('stade du miroir'), he confronts his image in the mirror in search of his real identity (Lacan 1977). We first see François and his reflection as separate, unreconciled: 'the child is divided from the moment it forms a self-conception' (Lapsley and Westlake 1988: 69). However, a series of jumpcuts, as he desperately repeats, 'I am a faggot. I am a faggot,' moves us closer and closer to his reflected image, until it is the only one we too see.[3]

This moment could be represented as a triangle, in which the mirror forms the base (*a–b*), and the child the apex (*c*). The child gazes at his own reflection which he endows with the plenitude he desires; a subjective memory portrayed as the film's present. However, if we recognize the autobiographical context of this scene, we understand that the director himself, the adult Téchiné, is himself using the screen as a mirror in his search for some new understanding of his present identity. In other words, (*a–b*) is acknowledged as both mirror and screen-as-mirror, with the child (*c*) a point on the screen both identical to and different from the adult director, who could constitute a new apex, the presence of which is manifest only through his (invisible) controlling eye.

It is therefore clear that the 'I' of an autobiographical account is multiple; that the subject/object distinction is unclear and unstable. An inevitable further consequence of the form is that temporal perspectives too are forever shifting, for if, in the first 'triangle', the child's reflected image (which is both self and other, first- and third-person) is adopted as his present and future identity, nevertheless we are aware that the looking I/eye is simultaneously that of the adult director, and that his gaze is retrospective. Thus the autobiographical gaze crosses time; both the child's present and his hypothesized future belong, in reality, to the director's past. At the same time, it is in the nature of the filmic image to be in the continuous present tense, actualizing or re-presenting the past. In other words, the autobiographical framing of the filmic narrative inhibits temporal closure; its gaze is self-reflexive and open-ended.

Given that it is yet another in a long line of autobiographical memory narrations, it would be easy to dismiss *Les Roseaux sauvages* as just one more nostalgic and sentimental search for a lost childhood. Similarly, both the film and the series of which it was a part could be blamed for their backward-looking references to the French New Wave, and the auteur tradition, long since out of fashion among critical theorists. To do so, however, would be misguided, as my description of it as a crossroads film is an attempt to indicate, for *Les Roseaux sauvages* is a film of its time; it is, as Téchiné himself explains, an exploration not of the past but of the present, since the past is always a construction of the present (Perrin 1994). As such, it is essential to recognize the extent to which its innovative qualities are a function of its traditional autobiographical form. Indeed, it is the essentially mobile, polyphonic, and open-ended nature of autobiographical discourse that enable Téchiné to instigate a dynamic dialogue not only between different times and viewpoints but also, essentially, between text and spectator. Because, of course, as that self-conscious discourse constantly reminds us, throughout all the levels of looking, all the various I/eye dualities the film explores, the ultimate one, the one whose gaze alone can impart meanings to the film, is that of the spectator.

Notes

1. For a more detailed development of the nature of autobiographical film about which, despite its increasing popularity, there is still considerable confusion, see Everett (1995: 3–10).

2. One indication of their cinematic success is the prizes these films were awarded. *Les Roseaux sauvages* received the Prix Louis Delluc (1994), and a César (1995), with Téchiné winning the Best Director award (1995); while *Trop de bonheur* (1994), the full-length version of Kahn's film, was given the Prix Jean Vigo (1994).

3. It is interesting to see this as an example of the intertextuality which underlies the film's polyphony; this scene is closely related to an earlier one in which François admits his homosexuality for the first time. He and Maïté have just been to see Bergman's *Through a Glass Darkly* (1961) the French title of which is *A travers le miroir*, literally *Through the mirror*, and Maïté questions the significance of the title, thus drawing our attention to its significance. When we watch François confronting himself in the mirror, our reading is therefore mediated through that earlier reference, and we understand that Téchiné's identity is inseparable from its filmic articulation.

5

'Dusting off' Dehousse:
Un héros très discret (Audiard, 1996)

KATHRYN M. LAUTEN

THE director of *Un héros très discret* (1996), Jacques Audiard, is
quoted in the press releases for this film as saying, 'I remember very
clearly the first time I read the book by Jean-François Deniau, as it
reminded me of why the 1944–45 period had always fascinated
me. It was then that the biggest lie of our generation was created—
the idea of France resisting, the idea of France at the victor's table.
The lie of France as a war resister . . . a country that after five years
of zealous collaboration tries to reconstruct its identity and its
virtue around a great lie.' Certainly when the novel was published
in 1989 the idea that France had woven a post-war tale of non-
collaboration was not new, and certainly the examination of this
phenomenon in the 1996 film is not ground-breaking. The collab-
orationist Vichy government had already been revisited; the early
1970s ushered in a new era of films and works on the Second
World War in the aftermath of May 1968. Robert Paxton's *Vichy
France* had been published in 1972 in the United States, and its
French translation appeared the following year. The film *Le
Chagrin et la pitié* dates back to 1970 even though it was banned
from television until 1981 and initially was not widely released.
The debates over Louis Malle's ambiguous political tensions in
Lacombe Lucien surfaced in 1975, and many other films on the
Second World War era were produced in France through the 1980s
including *Au revoir les enfants* (1987) and *Hôtel Terminus* (1988).
It is precisely the film's repetitive visit to the period that I find
fascinating—the notion that still today French cinema is examining
the role of France in the war. I intend to analyse this near obsession
in two related steps. First, I will consider the post-war era and its
importance today as portrayed in this film. Second, I will analyse
the documentary-style form that this fiction film takes as it builds

a 'history' of 1944–5 France that simultaneously dictates ramifications being felt in France today.

History and memory—two words irreparably separated in the twentieth century yet inevitably examined together. Henry Rousso writes in *The Vichy Syndrome* of how 'the disintegration of rural society and of the ancestral traditions it embodied, the proliferation of sources of information . . . the depth of internal divisions including those born of Vichy—all have caused history and memory to evolve in different directions. . . . Thus a new field of study has been opened up for historians: the history of memory' (Rousso 1991: 3). The echoes of Pierre Nora's *Lieux de mémoire* pervade Rousso's project of trying to understand the '*immediacy* of the period' through the 'history of the *memory* of Vichy' in contrast to and alongside the 'history of Vichy' (Rousso 1991: 1). As Naomi Greene aptly synthesizes Nora and by extension this move in Rousso's work, 'Hence, not only is modern memory lived as a "duty" [or "obligation"] and embodied in the "archive" but— paradoxically—it is "distanced" from the very past it strains to embrace [and has thus become] archival (*mémoire-archive*), obligatory (*mémoire-devoir*), and distanced (*mémoire-distance*)' (Greene 1996: 118).

This distinction between history and memory is critical to the era discussed here, as evidenced in the concept that drew Audiard to make this film, the 'lie of France as a war resister'. At the liberation of Paris, de Gaulle, having returned from London, was determined to unite France through pride and honour (to the extent that he attributed the liberation of France to the French while neglecting to share the glory with the Allied troops). One result of this was that people were put into two categories as either being on the 'right' side as a member of the resistance or on the 'wrong' side as a collaborator/traitor. For the most part, an instinct of self-preservation drove people to deny the collaboration on a national and personal scale and thus to deny any memories that might contradict de Gaulle's rhetoric. To varying extents, people thus *produced* memories of participation in the Resistance, as a nation and as individuals. In *Un héros très discret*, Albert Dehousse, neither resister nor collaborator, since he had quite literally ignored the war and remained out of its grasp for the duration, decides to join in the celebration and become a member of the Resistance—after the fact. As I will show, Dehousse works to his advantage both the tripartite structure of Nora's *Lieux de mémoire*—archive, obligation, and distance—and the attempts of many people to solidify their potentially ambiguous position of having fought in the Resistance. For it was almost fashionable to change politics during this war, as evidenced in *Au revoir les enfants* when Mme Quentin exclaims in shock, 'But no one is Pétainist anymore!' in the same tone as one might use to scoff at another's out-of-date clothing. The passion to document the war provides fertile terrain for Dehousse's scheme. Since the national policy was not just to 'recreate' the past, but to 'create' it, the resulting 'distancing' between present and past allowed this scheme to be all the more fruitful.

Dehousse is first shown as a boy living with his mother, who has falsely told him that his father, a soldier, died a hero in combat. Albert has no reason not to believe her until another boy tells him the truth: that his father, a drunk, died in a bar. Albert gives this boy his satchel in exchange for this information and later lets his mother believe it had been stolen when she asks what has happened to it. This one sequence outlines the larger issue at hand of a country trying to sustain the image of hero. It also shows Dehousse's tactic of letting others believe what they want or need to believe without Dehousse himself directly telling a lie.

Although Dehousse is very observant of his immediate setting and very influenced by it, he is ignorant of the war and related events happening around him. Since his mother is a widow and he is her only child, he is exempt from any service. Thus at the end of the war, Dehousse finds himself lamentably neither a resistant fighter nor a collaborator. Finally, an eye-opening event puts him in motion. One day, his mother is nearly taken down the streets with a group of others to be shaven and shamed publicly for being a collaborator, but Yvette, Albert's wife, is able to save her. Yvette reveals that their house is a 'house of the Resistance', a place where American, English, and Canadian soldiers are hidden. Dehousse, previously oblivious to this and struck by the notion that his wife acted without confiding in him, decides not to return home that night after work.

Audiard uses present-day talking head narration by Jean-Louis Trintignant as an aged Dehousse whose words are interspersed with Mathieu Kassovitz's portrayal of Albert Dehousse in the mid-1940s. At this crucial point in Dehousse's development, the present-day narration by Trintignant interjects to explain how 'you', the viewer, could not have returned to that life either after such a sequence of events for 'you would have been destroyed (*anéanti*)'. Thus Audiard draws the viewer into a complicitous role in the events that follow, and he quite clearly begins a connection between Dehousse's life and with the post-war national rhetoric that France was an *active* country of resistance.

Rousso explains in *The Vichy Syndrome* an effort that is evident in this film. He describes the post-war campaign to rebuild the French nation in the wake of the war trauma as threefold: (1) 'to minimize the importance of the Vichy regime'; (2) 'to construct an object of memory, the "Resistance" ' and (3) to create the 'identification of this "Resistance" with the nation as a whole which is a characteristic feature of the Gaullist version of the myth' (Rousso 1991: 10). Instead of going home that night, Dehousse hops on a train to Paris, disappears from his hometown, and is encouraged, once in Paris, to start a new life. He soon sees the opportunity of creating himself as a hero in the midst of this post-war activity with the help of a man named Le Capitaine. Dehousse takes on the task of committing the war and the actions of those in the Resistance to memory, an easy feat at the time for the media was full of photographs, tales, and 'memories' in the push to 'construct the "Resistance" ' through archives, as Nora has explained is part of the 'duty' of modern memory.

Because the country wanted heroes of the Resistance, Dehousse is able to become one by taking calculated advantage of this 'archival obligation'. He trains as an actor would for the part. He mimics different people he finds in newspaper and magazine articles as well as in newsreel footage. He also manages, through 'a strategy of infiltration' as the narration states, to get himself filmed and photographed in post-war trials and various events appropriate to the hero he is creating. And he craftily works his way into a reunion party of Resistance fighters. He establishes himself as a permanent member of that group by becoming a part of their memories. 'Of course you remember me,' he tells people as he supplies necessarily believable information from his research and training. And, of course, they have to remember him. Perhaps their own role is debatable and not remembering him would break apart their personal story. Perhaps everyone wants so much to believe that they just do, similar to Dehousse as a child with respect to his own father's status.

This film shows that memory and forgetting work together. To create de Gaulle's myth, the French enacted this duality. They forgot, or at least repressed, thoughts and actions incompatible with the bombardment of 'memories' of the Resistance that sprouted up everywhere. The past thus became necessarily 'distanced', working to Dehousse's advantage. Recent work on trauma and forgetting, especially in conjunction with the Second World War and the Holocaust, suggests that traumatic events can readily be forgotten on the conscious level. While much of this work has been done strictly with the Holocaust, parts can be extended to general trauma. For France, the Second World War was traumatic on many fronts. Certainly the death and destruction touched everyone, but behind that was the tension of reconciling a 'Franco-French war' (Rousso 1991) and its specifics in the 'denied' actions of the Vichy government and the persecution of Jews. In her work on witnessing and trauma related to the Holocaust, Shoshana Felman writes of the film *Shoah* (Lanzmann, 1985):

The newness of the film's vision, on the other hand consists precisely in the surprising insight it conveys into the radical ignorance in which we are unknowingly all plunged with respect to the actual historical occurrence. This ignorance is not simply dispelled by history—on the contrary, it *encompasses* history as such. The film shows how history is used for the purpose of a historical (ongoing) *process of forgetting* which, ironically enough, *includes* the gestures of historiography. Historiography is as much the product of the passion of forgetting as it is the product of the passion of remembering. (Felman and Laub 1992: 214)

Works already cited on the Occupation as well as others have shown, and tried to reverse, this 'process of forgetting' just as Holocaust museums are created so that we do not forget—which in many cases means that we *learn* what actually happened. What is interesting in *Un héros très discret* is that the success of Dehousse relies on people forgetting that they never knew what they now believe they know. This twist on memory work emphasizes not what people remember or do not remember of what happened, but rather that they remember something that never happened. People with whom Dehousse comes into contact 'remember' Dehousse doing things he never did, just as France was made to remember something that never happened to the extent that the Gaullist myth claimed. Certainly there was a basis of action and conviction both within occupied France and among the exiled community of the

Resistance, but the myth encompasses a denial of Vichy and non-resistance actions that has since been for the most part dispelled. The rationalization was that without this rhetoric France would have been 'anéanti' or destroyed just like Dehousse had he gone back home to Yvette on that pivotal day in 1944. The historical annals thus became very much a *process of forgetting*; not only of forgetting what happened but also of forgetting that what was remembered did not quite happen.

Still today this friction plagues the nation. On the official world wide web page for France's Prime Minister found at www.premier-ministre.gouv.fr, the links to the official history pages send you to de Gaulle's speeches as well as a set of pages on the Resistance. Only a slight mention is made in a chronological table of the Vichy government despite Jacques Chirac's monumental speech that created a divisive split with his predecessors on 16 July 1995, at the 53rd anniversary of the police action of Vel'd'Hiv':

Yes, the criminal madness of the occupier had been, everyone knows, seconded by the French, seconded by the French State. ... I want to *remember* that this summer of 1942 reveals the true face of the 'collaboration', of which the racist character, after the anti-Jewish laws of 1940, no longer allows any doubt; this summer will be, for a lot of our citizens . . . the point of departure for a vast movement of resistance. (my emphasis)

More than fifty years later, Chirac thus makes an official appeal to stop the 'process of forgetting' and to 'remember'—an act that certainly requires remembering that one had been told to forget. De Gaulle, Pompidou, Mitterrand used the very term 'forget' as a command to the French people such as: Let us forget the past and move forward. The resultant ghosts, however, still haunt the country. Rousso suggests in *The Vichy Syndrome* that the 'obsession with the war is not yet a thing of the past: from the Barbie trial to the Touvier affair by way of argument over the Resistance, many events still have the potential to erupt into major controversies' (Rousso 1991: 305). September 1997 brought such an eruption with the trial of Maurice Papon, who was convicted in March 1998 of complicity in crimes against humanity for having sent 1,500 Jews to death camps during the German Occupation. It took sixteen years to bring this case to trial because of the refusal, in this case, of President Mitterrand to 'open old wounds' which would have countered the official edict to 'forget the past'.

Although the Barbie trial induced a national revision of the postwar period, Papon's trial aims directly at the heart of France; for Barbie was a German, the Gestapo chief of Lyons, but Papon was the French secretary-general of the Gironde region of France. He claims innocence, for he was obeying orders as mandated by the Vichy government in its armistice with Germany, and maintains that he sacrificed a few to save many. At issue are certainly his specific actions but also his claim after the war to have been working for the Resistance—a claim that helped him earn promotions for the rest of his career. Gérard Boulanger, the prosecuting attorney, has, however, written that 'the resistance of Maurice Papon is only a fiction' (Boulanger 1997: 55). But regardless of his actual actions, he was able to 'infiltrate' the system, as did Dehousse, and profit from others wanting and needing, at least outwardly, to believe his words at the time. Dehousse too is promoted (a paradoxical term in his case since he does not have a military past or position to be promoted from) to a high-ranking position in French-occupied Germany as a colonel, where he continues with wit and cunning to 'pass' in his new identity. He is able to keep up his charade, marry another woman, and live in comfort until a critical 'event' disturbs his own psyche. Frenchmen who had donned German uniforms and fought in and for Germany during the war wander near Dehousse's military station. He, after much apparent grief and internal conflict, orders them shot for treason, which was the mandated punishment. Due to a series of events, this is more than he can take, and he writes a letter that reveals the truth about his being an impostor. In this act, Dehousse, as the translation of his name suggests, 'dusts off' what has been covered up. Given the climate in France, however, he is not tried for being an impostor in the army so as not to disrupt national unity and discredit the army and the Resistance; instead he is imprisoned for a short time for bigamy while the government hopes that everything else will be 'forgotten'.

Similarly, in France it has taken obtrusive 'events' such as the Barbie trial, the Touvier affair, and more recently the Papon trial to bring debate of the Occupation period to the national level. Henry Rousso wrote in an analysis of a BVA-*L'Express* survey done in connection with coverage of the Papon trial on 5–6 September 1997 that 'the more one talks about it, the more it is necessary to talk about it, the more forgotten moments are erased, the greater the requirement of memory becomes' (Rousso 1997: 15). It is tempting to suggest that if *Un héros très discret* had come out in the autumn of 1997 it would have had a bigger box-office success. For in addition to its pertinence to the Papon trial through events portrayed, its cinematic structure helps one see how the Papon trial is working on the psyche of the French, as I would now like to consider.

Pierre Nora, Robert Paxton, Henry Rousso, and other historians have commented publicly on the Papon trail and/or have been called to testify, which has also put the authority of historians on trial. Jean-Marc Varaut, Papon's principal defence lawyer, followed Paxton's testimony by questioning, not for the first time, the role of historians in this trial on the grounds that Paxton 'did not witness either the facts or the morality of the accused which is in contradiction to the penal procedure code' (Canellas 1997). The trial system places the weight of verdicts on eye-witness accounts, showing its acceptance of their validity. Eye-witness testimony has also had a great influence on the realm of documentary films. As Nichols says, 're-enactment' and 'spoken testimony' are mainstays in documentary films:

More recently, filmmakers resurrected [re-enactments but they] present the threat of disembodiment; the camera records those we see on screen with indexical fidelity, but these figures are also ghosts or simulacra of others who have already acted out their parts. Spoken testimony came to be seen as an antidote for the 'body too many' problem of reenactment. . . . With historical footage from around the time recounted appended to it, indexicality may guarantee an apparent congruity between what happened then and what is said now. (Nichols 1994: 4)

While Nichols is assuming here a documentary that is trying to prove something through 'an apparent congruity', this same postulate can be reversed to service documentaries that seek to make a point or prove something using the same types of elements but ones that are, when assembled, *incongruous*. Films such as *La Hora de los hornas* (Getino & Solanas, 1968) and *Afrique, je te plumerai* (Téno, 1992) use a juxtaposition of testimony, archival footage, and re-enactment to discredit the one giving the testimony or a dominant ideology. Because viewers have been conditioned to expect the 'truth' from a testimonial account, film-makers have used the tactic of discrediting witnesses to make their point even more poignant as viewers learn through the course of the film that they are actually being asked to rethink what the witnesses say. In a similar thread, the 'blurred boundaries' between fiction and documentary have come under much scrutiny as 'recently, documentary has come to suggest incompleteness and uncertainty, recollection and impression, images of personal worlds and their subjective construction' (Nichols 1994: 1). And Nichols continues, 'historical reality is under siege' (Nichols 1994: 2) in this age, as what had been accepted as 'historical truth' has been thrown into question while the possibility of representing 'truth' has been all but thrown out.

While *Un héros très discret* does not fit into even a broad view of documentary, its play on the genre is part of its aim. As I have mentioned, Trintignant propels the narration of the story played by Kassovitz. Also interspersed between those sequences are present-day interviews with people who not only claim they remember Albert Dehousse, but who go on to describe specific actions he carried through as part of Resistance activities, specific places he was in during the war, and specific names of battalions he aided.

Thus, *Un héros très discret* uses the very means of creating this long-standing French National History to expose the process of such a construction. That means is documenting and labelling everything to add an illusion of 'authenticity' and 'truth' to the contents. As Pierre Nora writes, 'to produce archives is the imperative of our epoch . . . Archive, archive, something of it will always remain!' (Nora 1984: p. xxviii). Dehousse inserts himself into the documentation of the time period as 'proof' of his position. And through the present-day interviews that become part of the narrative of the film, Audiard documents others as having known Dehousse during the war. As David MacDougall writes, 'As for most recent historical events, we remember not the events themselves . . . but the films and photographs we have seen of them' (MacDougall 1994: 261). In a circular action, then, people in 1944–5 who met Dehousse would have his purported actions reinforced by the photos or newsreels they saw of him *after having met him* as a war hero. And the claim that what is portrayed in the film's narrative actually happened and that Dehousse did convince others he was a war hero is reinforced in the film for the viewer by the present-day interviews interspersed into the main narrative moments in which we watch Dehousse accomplish his goals. The crowning act, of course, is that Dehousse himself is on film to help narrate his life—the ultimate witness to an event is surely the one who performed it. As Michel de Certeau claims, the 'realistic illusion' is easily created through quoting those presented as authorities and that in turn helps reinforce the perception of the quoted one as an authority. He also writes that 'quoted language . . . introduces a necessary outer text within a text. And reciprocally, quotation is the means of attaching the text to its outer surface, of letting it appear to play a role in culture, and of thus giving it the stamp of referential credibility' (Certeau 1988: 94).

More interviews, or 'quotations' of 'officials' from various occupations who claim to have known Dehousse at different times, end the film. Thus the viewer is left with an image of a man who has occupied many roles, ranging from a promoter of independence for African nations to a French governmental minister. His life blurs together in this final collage of interviews such that few clear images stand out. This onslaught of images serves more than the purpose of showing that Dehousse was capable of carrying on further 'deceptions' as he espoused numerous global roles. As de Certeau establishes above, quotations perform a linkage with outside texts, and in this case, the extension of the image of the 'Second World War hero' serves as an extension of the denial of events during the Second World War to other repressions in France.

I have used the term 'denial' rather loosely, yet purposely, in reference to the French and the Second World War. Its psychoanalytic roots call back to Rousso's comments on French society's repression of Vichy (Rousso 1991: 21). And in her work on censorship Cynthia Marker deftly analyses the appropriateness of considering the Algerian war within a similar framework. She considers veiled attacks and political commentaries on the French presence in Algeria in numerous films and written texts. Interesting to this study here is her analysis of the relationship in the French psyche between the Second World War and the Algerian war. One of Marker's emphases, however, is on rereadings of texts that had previously been seen as commentaries on the Second World War to show them as actually addressing issues of the Algerian war. As Marker shows, analogies can be drawn when one considers the 'Franco-French war' aspects of the Algerian war and the Second World War, that North African Jews migrating to France brought about a re-examination of attitudes towards Jews before and during the Second World War in France (see also Gérard Noiriel's *The French Melting Pot* on this issue), and that atrocities of torture in Algeria (and France) brought back images of Nazi but also Vichy-sanctioned torture during the Second World War. It is not coincidental that Papon, on trial for actions in the Second World War, cannot escape the analysis in his trial of his actions concerning North Africans.

I contend that *Un héros très discret* is addressed to present-day hauntings of the French, coincidentally as the trial of the century asks them once again to evaluate their own complicity not just during the Second World War, but, by a voiced extension at the trial, during the Algerian war. *Un héros très discret*, as a fictional representation of a documentary, is made to look like a documentary that combines re-enactment, archival footage, and eye-witness accounts to keep the French public in check as it considers 'reality' versus 'fiction'. In this age of French cinema where youth in crisis is portrayed as the great problem of society, *Un héros très discret* suggests that the ghostly ancestors of those young people have not stopped haunting the present. As Nichols tries to answer his question in *Blurred Boundaries* of how the past can be represented if 'historical reality is under siege', he postulates that 'this particular search will be for forms that intensify the need for retrospection, that require recall in order to grasp the pattern they propose, that heighten the tension between a representation and its historical referent, that invoke both past and present in the dialectic of constructing a future' (Nichols 1994: 119). *Un héros très discret* was created in such a form, as are the conversations resulting from the Papon trial. According to the justice system, Papon was tried for events that happened more than fifty years ago, but the very quotation of those events in outside conversations has created referential texts that cannot help but affect the past and present, and surely form the future as France examines its role during the war(s).

6

Remaking the Remake:
Irma Vep (Assayas, 1996)

PAUL SUTTON

OLIVIER ASSAYAS'S sixth film, *Irma Vep*, charts the difficulties that beset a film crew remaking Louis Feuillade's *feuilleton Les Vampires* (1915–16) for television. Reviewers have generally referred to *Irma Vep* as a film about film-making and as such it has been compared with Truffaut's *La Nuit américaine*, which also featured Jean-Pierre Léaud. This comparison is pushed even further when Assayas and Truffaut are linked by their respective writings for *Cahiers du cinéma*. However, *Irma Vep* is not concerned simply with film-making, but is in fact a film about remaking. Ironically, the comparisons made by reviewers appear to position Assayas's film as a kind of remake of Truffaut's. This chapter is primarily concerned with the remake as a cinematic and cultural phenome-non and will argue that spectatorship itself may be regarded, as *Irma Vep* demonstrates, as a form of remaking. It will be asserted that the spectator 'remakes' the film viewed, afterwards, in and through memory. This process is a function, it will be suggested, of Freud's concept of *Nachträglichkeit* (*après coup* or deferred action). The idea of the photographic *punctum* proposed by Barthes will serve as a temporary point of origin for the develop-ment of this concept of spectatorial remaking. The chapter will be divided into two broad sections. The first will contextualize, briefly and somewhat schematically, Assayas's film and the phenomenon of the remake. The second will extrapolate from *Irma Vep*, with reference to a specific sequence—the intradiegetic remake—a 'theory' of spectatorial remaking, a critically productive mode of spectatorship.

The cinematic remake is as old as the cinema itself, in part an inbuilt effect of the cinema's technological status, its mechanical reproducibility (Benjamin 1969). However, the cinema has also always 'adapted, copied, plagiarized, and been inspired by other works' (Mazdon 1996: 47). Remaking in the cinema might refer to any number of technological and cultural activities, ranging from, for example, the transfer of Cinemascope films to video formats (the spectatorial remaking that this would imply is foregrounded by Mireille (Bulle Ogier) in *Irma Vep* when she refers to watching Feuillade on video: 'Thank God I could fast forward'), to instances of generic self-reflexivity or the remaking by Hollywood of other national cinemas.[1] In France anxiety over the remake largely concerns the latter category, where attitudes have tended to be negative. As Ginette Vincendeau has pointed out, 'Reviewers usually note that these films . . . are based on European (most often French) titles, and then content themselves with pointing out that they are inferior to the originals' (Vincendeau 1993*b*: 23). (For a brief account of the 'real "scandal" of remakes: not the aesthetic copy-cat . . . but terroristic marketing practices', see Vincendeau 1993*b*: 24).

Remakes are discussed in terms suggestive of a kind of criminality. They are 'described as an act of violence against the films from which they develop and it is claimed that only very rarely is a remake not worse than its "original". The "original" is by definition given a status which renders it unassailable' (Mazdon 1996: 48). Assayas's film can be seen as an intervention in this debate on the remake, which in Europe, and in France in particular, is also fuelled by concerns over the future of cinema (and perhaps also of Europe itself). Assayas's film is about remaking specifically for television and one reviewer has gone so far as to describe Irma Vep herself as 'the exterminating angel of an expiring culture' (Herpe 1996: 36). Other films, such as Rivette's *La Belle Noiseuse* (1991), for example, have questioned the continued possibility of cinema itself (Elsaesser 1992: 20). Godard's *Histoire(s) du cinéma* (1988–97) is also significant in this context and its serial structure has been explicitly compared with Feuillade's *Les Vampires* (Temple 1998: 22).[2]

'Le remake' in French cinema can be seen, then, to occupy a site of extreme tension. It contains (and gives expression to) a number of fundamental anxieties: questions of national, racial, and sexual identity, economic imperialism, authenticity, and the status of cinema as the 'seventh art'. The recent celebration of cinema's centenary, and the increasing focus upon the end of the twentieth century, have further heightened this sense of unease. As Showalter says, 'the crises of the fin de siècle . . . are more intensely experienced, more emotionally fraught, more weighted with symbolic and historical meaning, because we invest them with the metaphors of death and rebirth that we project onto the final decades and years of a century' (Showalter 1991: 2).

Thus, as cinema reaches 100, thoughts of its death, and rebirth in new technology, occupy the minds of both its supporters and detractors. As a period of self-reflection, the *fin de siècle* recalls Europe's colonial legacy and occasions a re-examination of Europe's cinematic and cultural identity, or what might more properly be called 'identities in Europe' (Petrie 1992: 3). Past, present, and future converge at the *fin de siècle* in a process of re-evaluation that has found expression in the works of contemporary European film-makers. (For a detailed discussion of these issues, see Everett 1996: 7–28 and Petrie 1992: 1–8.)

This sense of anxiety is captured powerfully in Assayas's obviously self-conscious and self-reflexive film, not only in terms of questions of remaking but also through the conflictual and complex cultural and personal relationships represented within it. Thus a whole series of binary oppositions operate at a number of different levels. The tension between the weight of French cinematic history and the desire to produce original films is represented in the remake project itself and in the different approaches adopted by René Vidal (Jean-Pierre Léaud) and his replacement José Murano (Lou Castel). The former is paralysed by the legacy of Feuillade and by his desire to recapture a lost moment of cinematic origin, the latter mired in material concerns (Herpe 1996: 35). Somewhat ironically it is the apparently classic auteur, the caricatural Vidal (Morice 1996: 34), who produces a radical reinterpretation of *Les Vampires* for a contemporary audience. As this chapter will demonstrate, his avant-garde 'scratch' film, reminiscent of the Lettrist films of Isidore Isou, productively remakes Feuillade's 'original' as a film that is arguably about spectatorship and the structure of the look in film.[3] As one French critic has suggested, Assayas avoids producing a remake as 'pale copy' but instead 'revives (*réanime*) the spectator's imagination (*imaginaire*)' through an amalgamation of early and contemporary cinema (Morice 1996: 35).

Whilst partly a satire on the figure of the auteur, *Irma Vep* might also be seen as a commentary on the 1980s phenomenon of the so-called 'nostalgia film', a genre that sought to affirm European cultural identity in the face of 'disillusion and failure' (Powrie 1997: 13–27). With reference to this type of film Erickson has argued as follows of *Irma Vep*:

If it's a lament for what the cinema has become, it's a lament without the melancholy nostalgia that characterizes much contemporary discussion of cinephilia. As fast-paced and hip as a Hong Kong action film, *Irma Vep* couldn't be further from the neo-Tradition of Quality period pieces that often seem to be the only new French films American distributors care about. (Erickson 1997: 6)

This rather complex imbrication of genre and national cinema that Erickson references here finds its fullest expression in the figure of Maggie Cheung, who plays herself in *Irma Vep*. Cheung is an actress who has become popularly associated with a particular genre, the Hong Kong action movie. Her Chinese origins and English schooling place her on a kind of racial borderline; her various film roles also place her on a number of generic borderlines. It is this interstitial status that Assayas exploits in his film, just as it is partly this 'borderline status' that appeals to René Vidal. It is Maggie's Otherness that makes her, in his eyes, the only actress for the role of Irma Vep. As he explains to her (in his heavily accented English):

When the TV came to me and asked me to make a remake *Les Vampires*, I think they are out of their mind. Why ask me to do *Les Vampires* when Feuillade did it in 1915. Very simple, magic. Why touch it? They insist. Then I think, not French actress can be Irma Vep. After Musidora, it's impossible, it's blasphemy.

Irma Vep has become a kind of fantasy figure for Vidal, a fantasy that is mirrored by her mythic status in French cinema. He eulogizes Maggie (who tries to puncture his fantasy by pointing out to him that 'her' grace is actually that of stuntwomen): 'You are mysterious like Irma Vep, you are beautiful like Irma Vep and also you are magic like her and also you are very strong. And it's very important that you are modern, I want a modern Irma Vep.'

The nostalgia film mentioned above has been associated with fetishism, in that it functions as a defence against anxiety (Herpe 1996: 35–6). It is not inappropriate therefore, to refer to fetishism in the context of *Irma Vep*, given the clearly fetishistic updating of Musidora's 'original' Irma Vep costume. Musidora, who has been described as 'the original French screen femme fatale' (Abel 1984: 74), wore a silk bodysuit that was 'more suited to erotic adventures' (Callahan 1996: 45) than criminal escapades.[4] However, despite this eroticization, the rubber catsuit that Maggie Cheung wears introduces a more explicitly fetishistic or sadomasochistic dimension to the representation of Irma Vep. It also reintroduces France's cinematic Other—Hollywood—through an intertextual reference to *Batman Returns* (Burton, 1992), a film which is both a remake and part of an expanding serial. Zoë (Nathalie Richard) shows Maggie a still of Catwoman, remarking: 'This is the idea of Irma Vep. I say it's like hooker, but if he wants hooker I say it's okay.' A cruel parody of Feuillade's heroine, 'Irma Vep is (re)produced as a high priestess of sadomasochism' (Herpe 1996: 36). As a caricature of 'the poetry of Musidora (*la poésie musidoresque*)' (Herpe 1996: 36), Maggie Cheung's Irma Vep might be regarded, at a cultural and national level, as a kind of theft of the 'original' Irma Vep. Just as characters in the film attempt to manipulate others (Herpe 1996: 35), so an imperialistic or colonial imperative might be seen to operate here.

It is the very process of remaking arguably that distances *Irma Vep* from any kind of sentimental nostalgia. *Irma Vep* achieves this distance partly as a result of its metacinematic status, but also precisely because it allows itself to be permeated by, and is celebratory of, the denigrated Other (here both the remake and the Hong Kong action movie). Assayas offers the spectator of *Irma Vep* a paradigm for productive spectatorship based upon the idea of the remake and the process of remaking. He illustrates how film-making is (always already) remaking and how spectatorship itself may be considered a powerful and creative process of remaking (or at least may render remaking productive). This assertion will be demonstrated by focusing on the remake (episode 6 of *Les Vampires*) within Assayas's film—Vidal's *Les Yeux qui fascinent*. As the title indicates, this sequence is concerned with cinematic fascination, seduction, and spectatorship as transformation. Transformation, as will become clear, is a significant term for both Musidora's and Cheung's interpretation of Irma Vep. However, before these questions of transformation and remaking are addressed in more detail, further contextual and stylistic analysis of *Irma Vep* is necessary.

Assayas's film has no structuring narrative but consists of a series of episodes and excerpts ranging from *Les Vampires, 3: Le Cryptogramme rouge* (1915) and *Les Vampires, 6: Les Yeux qui fascinent* (1916), to SLON's *Classe de lutte* (1969) and Johnny To's *Dongfang San Xia/The Heroic Trio* (1992). *Irma Vep* depicts a series of transitory encounters between hastily sketched figures, reflected at both a thematic and stylistic level. These intersections, collisions, and partings represent cinema's intertextual character and are mimicked by the mobile camera that shifts speedily and without warning from scene to scene. Interestingly, it has been asserted that the film almost (re)invents itself in its very screening (Morice 1996: 35).

Certain stylistic traits identifiable here are in fact common to all of Assayas's films but are particularly effective in *Irma Vep*. The use of a hand-held kinetic camera and prolonged takes, combined with 'prowling camera-work' (Jones 1997: 37), suffuses *Irma Vep* with a sense of Feuillade's serial and adds to the general atmosphere of criminality. Assayas, much like Feuillade (impecunious in war-torn France), made this film on a small budget and within the constraints of a four-week shooting schedule (Pithon 1987: 50). Describing the making of *Irma Vep*, Assayas commented on the ad hoc, and perhaps vampiric, nature of the experience: 'I was trying to make the film feed itself, something I had never done before' (Jones 1997: 76).

Ostensibly a satirical film about the remaking process, then, a demystification of 'cinema magic', *Irma Vep* is ultimately a film about cinematic spectatorship. As one US reviewer of the film has remarked, 'It's a languorous ballad, and a daring one, about the way moving pictures move, the way they hold the light, the way they steal from us when we're not looking' (Zacharek 1997: 1). The connection made here between theft and spectatorship is entirely appropriate, in the context of both Feuillade's serial and Assayas's fictional account of its remaking. It is in the celebrated scene when Maggie Cheung, playing herself, becomes Irma Vep and burgles a neighbouring hotel room that René Vidal, and of course Assayas himself, comes closest to capturing something of Feuillade's *Les Vampires*.

Irma Vep proffers a critical commentary upon the remake, whilst at the same time enacting, knowingly, the very tensions identified within it. The defining tension of the remake, that between original and copy, which is also central to any notion of transformation, is represented through the figure of the vampire and the associated notion of crime. Feuillade's labelling of the criminal gang 'les vampires' foregrounds the figure of the 'actual' vampire, an interstitial, borderline figure, connotative of transformation itself (White and Sutton 1997: 33). The vampire and the remake share a preoccupation with transformation. Virginia Woolf famously described the fate of the novel in vampiric terms: 'The cinema fell upon its prey with immense rapacity, and to the moment largely subsists upon the body of its unfortunate victim' (quoted in White and Sutton 1997: 31). Irma Vep, as a 'vampire'/criminal, is situated, in the context of Assayas's film, as a signifier for the remake as a crime against the original. She also, in Feuillade's serial, demonstrates the permeability of social boundaries, moving between 'la zone' and central Paris (Callahan 1996: 42). Showalter has noted how this policing of borders is a feature of the *fin de siècle*. It is precisely when these borderlines are experienced as most insecure and mobile that definitions of gender, race, class, and nationality are most frequently contested (Showalter 1991: 4). Similar racial anxieties are clearly discernible in a number of contemporary French films, most notably *La Haine*. The Irma Vep of *Les Vampires* is also renowned for her cross-dressing or 'gender trouble'. It could be argued that Assayas's film induces anxiety at a formal level through the blurring of boundaries: the hand-held camerawork disorients the spectator and the lack of any real narrative adds to this sense of confusion and unease.

Having situated *Irma Vep* and the remake in the context of the *fin de siècle* and its attendant anxieties, this chapter will now turn to the question of spectatorial remaking. This concept has emerged from an incremental exploration of a number of strategically aligned theories, which for the purposes of this chapter will be considered in brief. This synthesis of ideas represents a point of 'origin' that requires, of necessity, further 'remaking' (beyond the 'confines' of this chapter).

To begin, then, with the concept of *Nachträglichkeit* or *après coup*, which might be briefly described as the reprinting of memory in the light of later experience. It was first developed by Freud in relation to trauma and dates from his work with Breuer on hysteria and from the earlier influence of Charcot (Phillips 1994: 33). Trauma, from the Greek for physical wound, describes what Laplanche calls 'an effraction or breach of external origin' (Laplanche 1976: 41). Freud is concerned, however, with psychical rather than physical trauma. This 'internal' trauma results from the interaction of two scenes or phases, neither of which in themselves can be called traumatic. The first scene occurs in childhood and because of a lack of understanding on the part of the child is not registered consciously; it is only when a second event occurs, again not in itself traumatic, that the memory of the first event is reawakened, at which point this second scene is read through the first, thus becoming traumatic: 'It always takes two traumas to make a trauma' (Laplanche 1989: 88). It is the memory, then, and not the event itself which is traumatic. As Laplanche remarks:

If the first event is not traumatic, the second is, if possible, even less so .. . And yet it is that second scene which releases the excitation by awakening the memory of the first one: that memory acts from then on like a veritable 'internal alien entity', henceforth attacking the subject from within. (Laplanche 1976: 42)

Contrary, then, to a deterministic causality, *après coup* asserts that 'it is the later which is important, and alone allows us to understand and to interpret the prior' (Laplanche 1976: 25). The remake in its provocation of anxiety might be regarded as inherently traumatic, for it is, in part at least, its uncanny relationship with its 'original' that renders it so threatening. (For an account of anxiety and its relation to the uncanny and the causality of deferred action, see Copjec 1995: 117–39). The remake, because of the temporality of deferred action, is regarded as a threat to the 'original'. It is that which in its return contaminates the original, remakes the original before itself, so to speak, an example perhaps of Benjamin's assertion that 'To an ever greater degree the work of art reproduced becomes the work of art designed for reproducibility' (Benjamin 1969: 224). As Zizek argues of what he calls, variously, the cause, trauma, or real (or here the 'original' film), 'it is through its "repetition", through its echoes within the signifying structure, that the cause retroactively becomes what it always already was' (Zizek 1994: 32).

This account of the *effet d'après coup*, as that which explains the temporality of the trauma, is taken up by Barthes in his discussion of the photographic *punctum*. Barthes's comments are particularly resonant when one recalls the 'lines of sight' scratched onto Irma Vep's eyes in Vidal's *Les Yeux qui fascinent*. Describing the *punctum*, Barthes speaks of 'this element which rises from the scene, shoots out of it like an arrow, and pierces me. A photograph's *punctum* is that accident which pricks me (but also bruises me, is poignant to me)' (Barthes 1988: 26). The eyes that fascinate are precisely those from which an 'element' shoots which in its piercing traumatizes the spectator. In the novelization of *Les Yeux qui fascinent* attributed to Feuillade and Meirs (1916), it is Irma Vep's eyes (dressed as a man, she has been captured on newsreel) that reveal her identity to Guérande, the journalist/detective, and his companion/assistant Mazamette. In front of 'the most immense screen' (Feuillade and Meirs 1916: 25) at the Gaumont-Palace, an 'astounded Guérande seized Mazamette's arm: "His eyes!... do you see his eyes?... Those are her eyes; it's him, it's her!... It's Irma Vep" ' (Feuillade and Meirs 1916: 24–5). In this scene Mazamette plays the role of cinema's early (in)credulous spectator. He raises a fist at the screen and threatens to clamber over the seats as if 'the beings on the screen might have been real, as if he might find them, in the flesh, behind the projection' (Feuillade and Meirs 1916: 25).

Maggie Cheung as Irma Vep, in Vidal's remake, with her 'gorgeous, captivating, alluring, and . . . savage eyes' (Feuillade and Meirs 1916: 24–5) returns the viewer to a kind of spectatorship that comes close to the kinds of experience that the earliest of spectators supposedly experienced, whilst also representing precisely the kind of 'trauma' that Barthes speaks of in relation to photography. In language that echoes Barthes's, Susan Sontag speaks of being 'kidnapped' or 'overwhelmed by the physical presence of the image' (Sontag 1996: 27). Now, the *punctum* in Barthes's analysis is only revealed 'after the fact, when the photograph is no longer in front of me and I think back on it', in other words, only *après coup*, only once the photograph is remembered (Barthes 1988: 53). Barthes depicts the notion of love at first sight in similar terms, a love that the cinephile would surely recognize, by suggesting that one falls in love with a scene, with an image by which one is fascinated/hypnotized (the French is 'fasciner') and ravished or kidnapped (Barthes 1990: 189).

Celia Lury stresses what she sees as Barthes's insistence upon the metonymic power of the *punctum*, its almost *scriptible* or writerly quality (Lury 1998: 90). What is most interesting in Lury's analysis, however, is her insistence on a relation between the *punctum* and mimesis (Lury 1998: 90). The *punctum*, in its physicality, is understood in terms of 'animation', the expression of a proximity between subject and object that is 'both a copying or imitation and a palpable, sensuous connection between the very body of the perceiver and the perceived, copy and contact, coincidence and metamorphosis' (Lury 1998: 91).

This reference to imitation and metamorphosis gestures towards the kind of productive remaking that is envisaged here, particularly in relation to a notion of spectatorial remaking, where what one might refer to as the cinematic *punctum* of Irma Vep's 'yeux qui fascinent' functions both as 'copy and contact'. Maggie Cheung's Irma Vep copies Musidora's 'original', demonstrating contact with this original' but also engendering a 'sensuous connection between the very body of the perceiver and the perceived'. The cinematic experience, especially that of Vidal's *Les Yeux qui fascinent*, is one that involves an almost corporeal or visceral dimension. This recalls one of cinema's powerful mythic and 'originary' moments: the terrified reactions of audiences at the Lumière brothers' screenings of *L'Arrivée d'un train en gare de La Ciotat* (1895).[5] A recent, somatically grounded account of cinematic spectatorship has asserted that:

Cinema invites me, or forces me, to stay within the orbit of the senses. I am confronted and assaulted by a flux of sensations that I can neither attach to physical presences, nor translate into systematized abstractions. I am violently, viscerally affected by this image and this sound, without being able to have any recourse to any frame of reference, any form of transcendental reflection, or any Symbolic order. No longer does a signifying structure anticipate every possible perception; instead, the continual metamorphoses of sensation preempt, slip and slide beneath, and threaten to dislodge all the comforts and stabilities of meaning. (Shaviro 1993: 32–3)

It is through such a sensual relation that the *punctum*, and it could be argued its cinematic incarnation, functions; not only as simple imitation, but also as metamorphosis. Such a process of transformation pertains in Vidal's avant-garde film, a film that transforms *Les Vampires*, dislodging the weight of historical meaning and interpretation that has attached itself to it. This transformation is also, as previously noted, a function of Irma Vep's characterization as a 'vampire'. This transformation or metamorphosis might also be linked productively to deferred action and memory.

Burgin has described spectatorship as a kind of 'recurrent experience', whereby 'having seen a film, all that remains of it in [my] memory is an image or a short sequence of images' (Burgin 1986: 86). He might well have been speaking of the cinematic *punctum* (as that which claims remembrance) and the kind of spectatorship envisaged here in relation to the remake. The fascinated spectator pricked by the cinematic *punctum*, which is only revealed *après coup*, remakes the film for him- or herself in and through memory, afterwards. Returning to mimesis and the *punctum*, Lury develops the concept of 'seeing photographically'. Mimesis, as that which 'has the potential to enable a dissociation of the senses that disturbs the coherence of the individual' (Lury 1998: 5), enables a process of transformation, or 'self-extension' (Lury 1998: 3). It is the 'prosthesis'—'seeing photographically'—that makes such 'self-extension' possible. There is in this idea what appears to be an element of performativity:

In adopting/adapting a prosthesis, the person creates (or is created by) a self-identity that is no longer defined by the edict 'I think, therefore I am'; rather he or she is constituted in the relation 'I can, therefore I am'. In the mediated extension of capability that ensues, the relations between consciousness, memory and the body that had defined the possessive individual as a legal personality are experimentally dis- and re-assembled. (Lury 1998: 3)

The notion of the *punctum* as a traumatic event that subsequently enables a retranscription, *après coup*, is expressed in Lury's concept of 'seeing photographically'. The prosthetic memory activated by the effects of the *punctum* enables the spectator to perform him- or herself, a performance that, it could be argued, is both represented in Vidal's film and required by the viewing of it.

Perhaps ultimately Assayas, through Vidal, is proposing a paradigm for cinematic spectatorship that might allow the anxious French spectator to escape his or her anxiety, to offer up a space in which he or she might perform spectatorship as a process of productive remaking.

Notes

1. Maggie (Cheung) in *Irma Vep* has no French, therefore much of the dialogue occurs in English with French subtitles. For the purposes of this chapter, dialogue cited from the film is based upon either the

English subtitles or the spoken English. This bilingualism emphasizes the theme of cultural diversity in the film. Unless otherwise indicated all other translations from the French are my own.

2. For the history of this project and details of its structure, see Temple 1998. For further comments, an interview with Philippe Sollers, and a dialogue between Serge Daney and Jean-Luc Godard see Baecque 1997.

3. The Lettrist group, led by Isou, were renowned for 'tactics of "détournement" or subversion' (Nowell-Smith 1997: 540). They 'cut commercial found footage literally to pieces, scratching and painting the film surface and frame, adding texts and sound-tracks to dislocate its original meaning further' (Nowell-Smith 1997: 540).

4. For discussions of the femme fatale in film, see Creed 1994, Doane 1991, and Kaplan 1994.

5. For an account that cautions against the myth of the 'enthralled' spectator, see Gunning 1989. Doane explores similar territory, but introduces a gender dimension to the analysis (Doane 1993).

7

Dissident Voices before the Revolution:
Ridicule (Leconte, 1996)

MIREILLE ROSELLO

IN France, Patrice Leconte is probably best known for his popular comedies such as *Les Bronzés* (1978) and its sequel *Les Bronzés font du ski* (1979). Abroad, and especially in the United States, his name was perhaps not as familiar until the end of the 1980s when he directed *Monsieur Hire* (1988) and *Le Mari de la coiffeuse* (1990), the two films most often mentioned by Anglo-Saxon critics. *Ridicule* is one of his most recent films and it is his first incursion into the genre of the period film. It is set at the end of the eighteenth century, six years before the French Revolution, and its plot is linear and straightforward: distressed to see his peasants die of fever because his estate is infested with pestilent swamps, Grégoire Ponceludon de Malavoy decides to go to Versailles to ask Louis XVI for money to drain the swamps, and build locks and canals. He soon discovers, though, that this logic will not get him anywhere at Court where one hegemonic language makes everyone deaf to any other channel of communication. Wit, Ponceludon finds out, is the only acceptable language. Compassion or technical knowledge impress no one, only memorable and typically cruel formulas open doors.

This summary, however, hardly gives credit to one of the most intriguing features of *Ridicule*: its ability to be a convincing heritage film while commenting on cultural and political issues of immediate relevance to a contemporary French audience; that is, its ability to invent a particular past to construct a particular present. If the plot is safely circumscribed between Malavoy's estate, Les Dombes, and Versailles, the hero's dilemma (must he play dirty to achieve his lofty goal?) is narrativized in ways that are almost uncomfortably too close to current cultural debates: after all, Ponceludon's goal is to eradicate a deadly disease, and the tactics that he is implicitly asked to adopt are all tainted with extreme forms of deceit and corruption, malice and self-centredness. The story of a fund-raiser whose noble goal is threatened by corruption and contamination may well remind French spectators of a whole series of recent scandals, including cases that led the public to question the integrity of the medical milieu and of charitable organizations linked to medical research: in 1995, damaging revelations about the maladministration at the powerful ARC (Association of Research on Cancer) led to serious accusations against the director of the Association and the scandal dragged a world-renowned researcher through the mud (Nau 1996: 7). This sordid tale of misused charity funds occurred soon after the so-called 'affaire du sang contaminé', when untested and non-heat-treated blood supplies were used to treat haemophiliacs who were later to discover that they had been infected with the HIV virus (Riedmatten 1996; Sanitas 1995). Even if the film does not bring to mind a specific scandal, references to the commonly accepted notion that associations must raise money to help bring about the eradication of a disease that kills indiscriminately but which threatens certain groups more directly can hardly be more relevant in the age of AIDS, especially if we consider that the film was presented at Cannes only a few weeks before the 1996 Sidaction.[1]

Because the film echoes such pressing contemporary preoccupations, I was not surprised at first to hear Leconte insist that he was determined to leave the heritage film aspect in the background. Yet, the director's claim is puzzling as it is impossible to downplay the period piece dimension. This film is not an allegory, it does not step out of the frame it has chosen for itself, and it would be difficult to ignore the film's attempts at presenting us with a specific vision of a specific eighteenth century. The question then becomes: which eighteenth century does the film construct?

In an interview granted to Pascal Mérigeau at the Cannes Festival, Leconte claimed that he had been afraid of being 'paralysed by the notion of heritage film, of costume film, which "kept resurfacing" ' (Mérigeau 1996: 3).[2] At Cannes, and later at the Toronto Film Festival, Leconte denied making a film about the eighteenth century. Despite most critics noticing and praising the attention to detail (they practically all refer admiringly to the scene where servants blow clouds of powder over the naked Mme de Blayac, the King's beautiful and clever mistress), the director explained to his interviewer, who commented that 'details do not detract from the film's essence, which . . . has little to do with the 18th century' (Cuthbert 1997): 'The modernity of it comes through treating the story as something universal, and why not—something of today' (Leconte in Cuthbert 1997).

But how exactly does Leconte both use and redeploy the concept of the heritage film? What is criticized both in the past and in the present and what solutions are offered? And at what price is the precarious balance maintained?

I suspect, for example, that historians might discover a significant number of factual inaccuracies. Not knowing enough about the period, but aware that most representations of 'academics' in films strike me as hopelessly naive and stereotypical, I can easily imagine that *Ridicule* might, at times, annoy specialists of the pre-Revolutionary French period. Perhaps it is very difficult for some historians to enjoy a fiction set in such a recognizable context if it is marred by what would appear to them as obvious historical flaws. It is quite clear, however, that *Ridicule* is not trying to convince a scholarly public. Not that it lacks ideological or ethical ambitions, quite the contrary, but some questions may be less relevant than others. For example, what would I achieve if I were to point out that Ponceludon's interview with Louis XVI's minister Maurepas, portrayed as a stern old financier who thinks that draining swamps is tantamount to 'draining the kingdom's finances', is most improbable if the film takes place in 1783, because, at that time, the minister in question had been dead for two years? Having revealed a factual 'error' I could, I suppose, grin a self-satisfied grin. But would it mean much? It would certainly not prove that the conversation between Ponceludon and the minister about 'the price of human life' and 'France's destiny' is meaningless within the context of the film or otherwise. It would certainly not be a sign of my superior knowledge of the period in question. Quite the opposite, in fact, since I only discovered that the interview could not be 'realistic' when my total ignorance of Maurepas's historical role embarrassed me to the extent that I felt compelled to reach for the first encyclopedia at hand. In a sense, my knowledge of the hard fact reveals my total lack of knowledge about the most meaningful political aspects of the character. Yet, it gives me a certain power over the film. I know that this detail, at least, is incorrect. I now know that Maurepas died in 1781, but that knowledge is only useful inasmuch as it makes me aware that the film serves a precious educational and critical purpose: it not only tempted me to look elsewhere, to seek more knowledge, more details, but it also forced me to admit that I simply cannot count on being presented with historical 'truths'. As a member of the general public, I discover that the film is both too close to historical truth to be dismissed as unverifiable fiction, as 'universal' truths (as the director would have it), and inaccurate enough to invite critical distance and to require further enquiry. It invites me to formulate my own version of this piece of 'cultural patrimony' which is both mine and the product of others' textual inventions. Far from losing its interest as 'heritage film', *Ridicule* thus complicates the notion of heritage by urging us to ask not only 'what happened?' but 'what are the possible uses of claiming that such and such happened?' In other words, the film invites us to interpret it, to experiment with knowledge, including historical knowledge.

Experimenting with concepts and boundaries, with unacceptable forms of communication, is presented as a valuable if minoritized option: it is the direction chosen by one of the most favourably depicted heroines, Mathilde Bellegarde, who will fall in love with Ponceludon and eventually leave the court to help him in his enterprise. In *Ridicule*, Mathilde is portrayed as an outsider whose ambitions are never nurtured by her environment, not even by Ponceludon, who does not support her research experiments because he finds them too dangerous. A gifted researcher, Mathilde builds a diving suit and wants to break immersion records. She has read Pascal, she knows how to swim, and enjoys discovering underwater universes. Ponceludon, on the other hand, is her metaphorical counter-image: his idea of scientific progress involves separating water from land, and drying out humid terrains. He is afraid of water and refuses to have any contact with it (finding swimming 'unnatural', for example). He wants to drain swamps, he puts his faith in boats, bridges, and locks, he wants to control nature. He only experiences the presence of a liquid element as disease and death; his fever-stricken peasants feeding, as he bitterly puts it to one of the courtesans, both mosquitoes and aristocrats. Mathilde, on the other hand, embraces water as an unknown element to be explored and discovered. As far as the natural world is concerned, she does not hesitate to take risks in making contact with it. Far from idealistic, however, she is fully aware that her research is expensive and she coldly considers marrying old Montalieri, who is willing to trade a generous endowment against the promise that his future wife will stay away from the court and grant him access to her bed twice a month.

Mathilde is obviously presented as a positive model and it is part of the film's happy ending that Ponceludon should give up his doomed and self-destructive attempts to raise money from a profoundly corrupt Versailles to go back to the Dombes with her. But as with Maurepas, this character raises the question of which eighteenth century is represented, and of what the film achieves by this representation: when Ponceludon tries to convince Mathilde's father, the Marquis de Bellegarde, to help him dissuade her from going down into the well, the enlightened Marquis, his host, explains that he has never set any limits to her freedom: 'She was born the year Mr Rousseau published his *Émile*.' Just as Voltaire is regularly hailed as the finest representative of courtly wit, Rousseau is here praised as an author whose writings could influence fathers into allowing their daughters to lead a free and enterprising life. This statement, I argue, is slightly disconcerting. My quibble, this time, is not with dates and verisimilitude: if Mathilde was born in 1762, she is twenty-something when the film begins. At this point, what I am resisting is the idea that Rousseau should be credited with Mathilde's freedom. In fact, those of us who are not exactly great fans of Jean-Jacques Rousseau might well be tempted to snicker: for if the Marquis de Bellegarde was indeed looking for advice on raising a female child in *Émile*, he would certainly not have raised a proud 'Learned Lady'. Surely, the Rousseau referred to here is a vague idea, a stereotypical allusion to a certain canonical eighteenth century: to view Rousseau as one of the most revolutionary philosophers, we somehow need to invent his radicalness according to today's criteria. Otherwise, Mathilde's gender would have had to come into play instead of being conveniently erased by the (admittedly optimistic and generous) notion that freedom was non-gender specific when Rousseau wrote about it. After all, if we reread the ludicrous fifth book of Rousseau's *Émile*, it becomes obvious that 'Sophie or The Woman' (Rousseau 1979: 357), and precisely not the little boy Émile, was meant as the model for women's education. If Bellegarde had indeed followed Rousseau's advice, Mathilde would presumably have learned quite different lessons.[3] She would have internalized the notion that 'woman is made especially to please man' (Rousseau 1979: 358) and, paradoxically, she would probably have become a woman quite similar to the scheming Mme de Blayac, whose success at the court could easily have been prepared by Rousseau's lessons.

Blayac, for example, is quite aware that sexual politics are politics pure and simple. Unlike Mathilde, who very nearly accepts marrying Montalieri to ensure that her research will be properly funded, Blayac acknowledges that her life is governed by intrigue and that her power is indistinguishable from her sexual attraction. She knows full well the extent of both her power and her powerlessness and her devious tactics of seduction are the very logical consequence of the fact that she works within the system: *she* may well invoke the fifth book of *Émile*:

Here then, is a third conclusion drawn from the constitution of the two sexes—that the stronger appears to be master but actually depends on the weaker. This is due not to a frivolous practice of gallantry or to the proud generosity of a protector, but to an invariable law of nature which gives the woman more facility to excite the desires than man to satisfy them. This causes the latter, whether he likes it or not, to depend on the former's wish and constrains him to seek to please her in turn, so that she will consent to let him be the stronger. (Rousseau 1979: 359–60)

What then is the film doing when it allows Bellegarde to equate Rousseauism and freedom for women? Spectators who ask themselves the question without having the opportunity to verify authorial intention will of course be limited to speculation: can it be said, for example, that the film is cynically reappropriating Rousseau's canonical authority by making *Émile* a more liberating and modern text than it really is? Is *Ridicule* then sacrificing a real eighteenth-century Rousseau in the hope that Mathilde's character will benefit from the philosopher's image, even if that image is technically inaccurate? In 'Custody Battles', Garber writes that 'It was only in the eighteenth century that the myth of "Shakespeare" and the reified Shakespeare text, began to be invented. Shakespeare in this sense is an eighteenth-century author' (Garber 1996: 30). Similarly, the Rousseau of *Ridicule* is a 1990s invention. But I would argue that the implications of that particular fabrication are crucial to the overall meaning of the film: first, it divides the audience into two constituencies. If the spectator is aware of the existence of Sophie, one possibility is to imagine that the rewriting of *Émile* and the invention of a non gender-specific enlightened freedom places today's women in a position to claim, as their 'heritage', the model that Mathilde represents: historically, she displaces, or competes with, Sophie. Whether or not the film adopts this strategy consciously, the net result is a sort of feminism at the expense of historical truth, a dangerous proposition which of course mirrors Ponceludon's dilemma: his truth leads him nowhere if he addresses the wrong audience and, in the end, his roundabout and tainted ways fail as well.

On the other hand, if the spectator has never heard of Rousseau's Sophie, if he or she has been taught the same (national) myths as the ones that produced *Ridicule* as a historical fiction, Rousseau's reputation as a revolutionary thinker may be interpreted as the reason for Mathilde's unorthodox positions. Then, the film praises dissidence, a universal definition of dissidence that happens to be embodied by a woman. Mathilde's point of view is promoted as the ethical choice, as if her gender were irrelevant. In other words, the film does to Rousseau what sexist thinking does to women when it pretends that it is one and the same thing to include them in a neutral reference to 'men': Rousseau and dissidence are praised as one and the same thing. Too bad if Rousseau's contribution meant at the same time more, but also less, than our twentieth-century notion of dissidence.

I have chosen the word 'dissidence' to characterize Mathilde because if we translate her position as a twentieth-century concept, she is the only voice that speaks out against the tyranny, not so much of privileges and inequality, but of what the French call 'la pensée unique' (i.e. a worship of economic growth and of the forces of the global market at the expense of any other system). And like contemporary thinkers who worry that western culture is turning into sound-bites, like for example Pierre Bourdieu and Régis Debray who suggest that events only become events once the media credit them with entertainment value (Bourdieu 1996; Debray 1993), Mathilde is convinced that Ponceludon can neither translate his compassion into the dominant language nor transfer back to his peasants the power that such limited acceptance gives him. Admittedly, this is a pessimistic and perhaps unrealistic attitude and we may disagree with her. Her absolute certainty that 'A rotten tree cannot bear beautiful fruit' and that Ponceludon's attempt to have his courtly cake and eat it too is doomed does not provide any solution to his financial quandary. Short of a Revolution (which the end of the film graciously provides), Mathilde's radical refusal does not solve the problem.[4]

Besides, even if the film seems to side with her, one of the most ambiguous scenes suggests that there is some future in cross-pollination and hybridity: when Ponceludon and Mathilde take a walk along the so-called 'lovers' lane' in the gardens of the palace, they are, in fact, conducting a scientific experiment, Mathilde allowing her dress to brush against the flowers to collect the pollen. When she goes back to her own garden and allows Ponceludon to delicately pollinate her own flowers, the dialogue makes it clear that no boundary can be drawn between science and their mutual attraction: he talks about the new species, she wants to know if he blames her for marrying Montalieri. And while her words deny that Ponceludon's caresses are anything but a form of chemistry, the camera lingers on her clenched fist both resisting and expressing her desire. Similarly, her idea to create a new hybrid flower belies her own metaphors: something coming from Versailles might bear fruit.

On the other hand, the film does not fully condone Ponceludon's tactics either. The film insists that no accumulation of knowledge or of power is possible in an environment where the latest *bon mot* is immediately displaced by a new one, where courtesans rise and fall with no predictable pattern.

The redefinition of the heritage film, however, is not the only possible way to oppose the tyranny of a dominant rhetoric. *Ridicule*, a visual work of art, is capable of criticizing the court, or rather, of criticizing a principle that allows wit to become the only acceptable form of language. The film thus makes a very Foucauldian point that power and influence, at the court of Louis XVI or in our own western context, are indistinguishable from the mastery of one type of hegemonic language, wit, or perhaps sound-bites as one of the reviewers suggests (Schwartzbaum 1996; Foucault 1971). If one does not speak that language (and this time Spivak's work comes to mind), then one is literally not heard (Spivak 1996): as the Marquis de Bellegarde puts it to his protégé Ponceludon de Malavoy, 'being invited is easy, my good Sir, but being heard is not'.

Yet in spite of the script's emphasis on the value of unique combinations of words, of what is remembered and repeated, the images reveal another dimension: the film as a whole is fascinated by the *physical* effects of words. As Leah Rozen puts it, *Ridicule* is about the 'treacherously slippery arts of social climbing and political intrigue' (Rozen 1996), but the originality of the film is to take the 'slipperiness' literally and to represent the rise and fall of characters as a physical event. The attention to language is never theoretical: wit is, quite seriously, a matter of life and death. 'Action' in the traditional sense is not *replaced* by wit. Instead, wit is shown to be a type of action because a witty remark has immediate physical repercussions on the characters' bodies (and not only on their metaphorical social standing). In *Ridicule*, the body's skill and elegance are just as important as the mastery of language and the latter can actually damage the former. Wit causes bodily harm and a fallen dancer is socially dead. In *Ridicule*, wit is neither a safety valve nor a metaphorical form of violence and, for the cultural critic involved in the current debates on hate-speech, the film's representation of the bodily effects of language are particularly significant. Because its images insist on what wit does to bodies, *Ridicule* makes a unique contribution to the issue of whether words (and in the 1990s we would be more specifically thinking of racist or homophobic declarations) can be said to hurt (Butler 1997).

The film does not argue that words and acts are one and the same thing. Like Judith Butler in *Excitable Speech*, the film refuses to suppose that each and every speech act will be 'felicitous', or that every witty remark will reach its objective (Butler 1997: 23). Leconte's interesting proposal, however, is that the representation of the power of language as bodily harm (here, a physical fall) is an *aesthetic* choice. In *Ridicule*, witticisms and falling are inextricably intertwined. When the verbal attack reaches its target, the camera records this as a moment when an individual is destabilized: it regularly focuses on bodies falling to the ground (especially during a ball) and equates the moment of the fall with the moment of final ostracization. People constantly fall in this film. During the opening scene, which sets the tone for the devious cruelty of the rest of the film, the Chevalier de Milletail visits M. de Blayac, an old aphasic man confined to a wheelchair (failed by both his body and his language), and to the spectator's surprise calmly, deliberately proceeds to urinate on the invalid. As he does so, Milletail remembers out loud that Blayac once dubbed him 'the Marquis of

Bangcrash' because he had fallen while dancing. As Milletail puts it: 'je ne m'en suis jamais relevé': 'I never recovered,' but also, literally, 'I never got up again.' Now, Blayac cannot stand up either, and Milletail does to the dying Blayac what he once did to him: he uses language to interpret the other's body in the most humiliating manner. As he leaves the room, he tells the servant: 'I fear joy may have caused Mr de Blayac to forget himself.'

Presented as prologue and prophetic warning, this unexpected revenge invites us, in retrospect, to remember that the end was predictable: this first scene announces the end of the film when Ponceludon will be violently excluded from the circle of the courtesans. Again, the symbolic social execution will be filmed as a physical fall: when the Comtesse de Blayac decides to discredit Ponceludon, she arranges for one of her allies to trip him during a ball while he is dancing with her. The fall is filmed in slow motion, the sound of Grégoire's head banging against the floor echoes his long scream of agony that signals the moment when language is replaced by the inarticulate expression of pain and disgrace. Ironically, the 'Marquis of Bangcrash', who had been forced into exile, now embraces the role of the executioner by dubbing Ponceludon 'Marquis des Antipodes', joking that, like the inhabitants of those far-off regions, 'he dances on his head'. Earlier, when Ponceludon had made it obvious that he was leaving the Comtesse for Mlle de Bellegarde, the Chevalier de Milletail had remarked: 'That was a faux pas.' Literally, Ponceludon had just tripped. And the film soon translates the 'faux pas' into a visual narrative. In *Ridicule*, a fall coincides with exclusion, exile, a moment of physical disappearance.

Leconte's aesthetic choices thus entail political and ethical decisions: an ambiguous heritage film, *Ridicule* redefines the genre by proposing to use a historical setting to ask very specific questions about our contemporary ways of relating to history, to words, to images, and, in the end, to the film itself. As a political parable, *Ridicule* needs a revolutionary *deus ex machina* to help Ponceludon and Mathilde out of their financial quandary. At the very end of the film, a few lines appear on the screen revealing that revolutionary politics achieved what Versailles had been unable to: the 'citizen' Ponceludon, with the help of funding from the Constituent, had started draining the swamps. This, of course, does not give us a clue as to whether *Ridicule* is implicitly recommending that we wait for the Revolution while resigning ourselves to the reality of contemporary plagues. Or perhaps it should be noted that these few lines are the most conventional moment of the whole film and that this is precisely the part of the story that Leconte had chosen not to tell us with images.

Notes

I would like to thank Bernadette Fort, Jean Mainil, and Wendy Michallat for their careful reading of the first draft and for their most helpful suggestions. Thank you to Yves Clemmen and Nancy Frelick for providing the opportunity to receive feedback.

1. The film was presented at Cannes, in May 1996, and on 6 June 1996 eight French television channels joined forces to produce the second Sidaction, a night-long television programme dedicated to fund-raising for the fight against AIDS.
2. Leconte is aware that his film is bound to be compared to Stephen Frears's much acclaimed *Dangerous Liaisons* (1988) with Glenn Close and John Malkovich but his *Ridicule* also belongs to a long list of French films set in the eighteenth century. In 1982, Andrzej Wajda directed *Danton* and later, both Robert Enrico and Richard T. Heffron's *La Révolution française*, and Pierre Granier-Deferre's *L'Autrichienne*, a film on Marie-Antoinette, coincided with the commemorations of the Bicentenary of the French Revolution (1989). Finally, Édouard Molinaro's *Beaumarchais, l'insolent* came out the same year as *Ridicule*. Interestingly, the French Revolution (many directors' favourite topic) is remarkably absent from *Ridicule*, which portrays events occurring right before and, as an epilogue, right after the event, leaving a curious void where the Revolution should be.
3. See for example Elisabeth de Fontenay's work, where the author insists that it is urgent to re-examine *Émile* and to scrutinize 'the assumptions, delayed effects and reverberations of this wicked enterprise' (Fontenay 1976: 1775; my translation).
4. According to Ginette Vincendeau, the film, even more ambiguously, 'sets out to criticize an order and mode of performance it cannot help but admire and which fundamentally sustains it' (Vincendeau 1997: 56).

8

Revisiting the Myth of the French Nation:
Les Visiteurs (Poiré, 1993)

MARTINE DANAN

COMEDY has been the most popular genre in France since the earliest days of sound films. Today, it is also the genre most capable of resisting the onslaught of American blockbusters (which have recently secured up to 60 per cent of the French market) and of challenging the new wave of globally oriented French super-productions. French comedies, for the most part, compete with American films on the list of best-sellers of the French market since 1956, as published by the CNC (Centre National de la Cinématographie). Among the newest additions to the list were two French comedies, Hervé Palud's *Un Indien dans la ville* (1994) and Didier Bourdon/Bernard Campan's *Les Trois frères* (1995), with 7.8 and 6.6 million spectators respectively (CNC 1997: 11). However, the success of Jean-Marie Poiré's *Les Visiteurs* (1993) has turned this comedy into the unchallenged box-office winner of the 1990s. With a sale of approximately 14 million tickets, it far exceeds the appeal of other popular comedies and, until *Titanic* (Cameron, 1998), even of recent American crowd-pleasers, such as the Disney animation *The Lion King* (Allers, 1994) or Steven Spielberg's blockbuster *Jurassic Park* (which attracted 10.1 and 6.5 million spectators respectively, according to the CNC list mentioned above). Of all films made in France, only one other French comedy, Gérard Oury's *La Grande Vadrouille*, filmed in 1966 at a time of much greater film-going attendance, surpassed *Les Visiteurs* at the box office with over 17 million spectators (CNC 1997: 11).

Les Visiteurs was transformed into a veritable cult film which clearly struck a chord with the national audience across social divisions. In this chapter, it will be argued that part of the national reconciliation brought about by this comedy may stem from the final restoration of the status quo despite conflictual relations among socially differentiated characters. Above all, this chapter will attempt to demonstrate how linguistic registers, signs of Frenchness, and carefully chosen historical references are likely to have played an instrumental role in leading the public to identify with a mythical image of France—the grand nation of noble tradition and lofty ideals impressed upon the French citizens' psyche by centuries of official nationalistic discourse and practice. By examining the numerous elements that transform an apparently innocent adventure comedy into an intrinsic part of the French myth, one may ultimately better apprehend the notion of a 'national' cinema and its role in the reproduction of an enduring traditional French identity.

By generating profuse discussions among the public and extensive coverage in the press, *Les Visiteurs* quickly became a social phenomenon rather than a mere box-office success. Throughout France, male and female spectators from all walks of life and of all ages praised the film while jokingly repeating some of the film's dialogue with the intonation used by the actors. Mainstream weekly magazines like *Le Nouvel Observateur* (in a four-page spread) and *L'Événement du jeudi* (in a lengthy, fourteen-page series of articles) compiled entire dossiers to examine responses to this film. Even *Cahiers du cinéma*, primarily concerned with films worthy of cinephiles' attention, devoted seven pages to it. Other specialized film publications like the *Mensuel du cinéma*, the mainstream weekly *France dimanche*, daily newspapers ranging from the communist *L'Humanité* to the conservative *Le Figaro*, regional papers from *La Voix du nord* to *Provençal*, all joined in to discuss the phenomenal success of *Les Visiteurs* and, at the same time, wholeheartedly recommended it to their readers.[1]

Not only the press, but also political parties united in their praise of this popular comedy. Although Jean-Marie Poiré and Christian Clavier declared that their primary goal in co-writing the film's scenario was simply to make spectators laugh, many saw a political message in the story of the twelfth-century knight Godefroy le Hardi, count of Montmirail (Jean Reno), and his faithful servant Jacquouille la Fripouille (Christian Clavier), whom a magic potion prepared by a senile magician mistakenly transports to the year 1993. In this travel-through-time adventure, ecologists observed a condemnation of our epoch, with its rapidly disappearing forests and ugly, noisy, polluted environment. The Right believed that the knight defended a traditional French heritage and chivalrous honour threatened by upstarts and the fast-changing values of our troubled times. As for the Left, the servant who emancipates himself at the end from the tutelage of his master represented the great egalitarian principles at the core of today's political struggle (Garcin 1993: 92, 94). But since all were comforted by *Les Visiteurs* in spite of their differences of opinion, the film succeeded, as a journalist noted, in reconciling the French nation (Garcin 1993: 94). If the consensus around *Les Visiteurs* is undeniable, the mechanism by which this reconciliation occurred still remains to be analysed.

Such a reconciliation may be all the more unexpected as the dramatic structure of *Les Visiteurs* seems to foster the opposite of harmony. Conflicts and desires driven by social tensions govern the characters' actions; upper-class types are confronted with common people, who nevertheless manage to triumph in the end in spite of their social handicap.

As Godefroy, accompanied by Jacquouille, lands in the home of his descendant, the upper middle-class Béatrice Goulard de Montmirail, the spitting image of his 'betrothed' Frénégonde (both played by Valérie Lemercier), the plot primarily revolves around Godefroy's desire to be recognized by the one he calls his 'great-great-great-daughterette', who insists on taking him for an amnesiac cousin previously presumed dead. It also involves his desire to return to his own epoch, which is apparently more civilized than our own ugly materialistic time ruled by narrow-minded bourgeois. Indeed, he is faced in his adventure not only with Béatrice's incredulity but also with the rigid attitudes of a number of bourgeois characters. He is confronted by Béatrice's overly down-to-earth husband, a dentist who believes Godefroy is a bothersome lunatic. He is irritated by the upstart Jacques-Henri Jacquart, Jacquouille's own descendant (also played by Christian Clavier), who tries (but fails) to act as the sophisticated new owner of the Montmirail family castle converted into a luxury hotel. This hotel is now a choice location for company seminars like the one organized by the conceited bank CEOs Edgar and Édouard Bernay. Imbued with their self-importance but lacking true nobility, these characters are prone to react hysterically to unpredictable situations that disturb their peace or threaten their possessions.[2] Obsession with social status and profit has replaced the old chivalrous values based on honour and generosity. This decadent obsession, it is implied, is responsible for the sorry state of the modern French nation, where nature is disfigured and social relations governed by pettiness. Even Béatrice ends up condemning her husband's materialistic short-sightedness and supporting Godefroy's desire to return to his past and fulfil his noble destiny.

The master's search to regain his identity is mirrored by Jacquouille's own search; he progressively learns to distance himself from his master. As Jacquouille's allegiance moves from Godefroy to 'Dame Ginette' (Marie-Anne Chazel), a self-proclaimed 'artist'/tramp who immediately recognizes Jacquouille as a peer and introduces him to the pleasures of modern life, the Godefroy–Jacquouille alliance turns into a conflict. Having learned to appreciate newly acquired freedom and the sense of justice, Jacquouille finally refuses to obey the one who in his eyes has become his equal and, ultimately, tricks Jacquart into travelling back through time with his former master to the Middle Ages. Satisfied with the present, the emancipated Jacquouille can then choose to partake of a more enjoyable life with his future spouse Ginette, who disregards social prejudice and pursues her own nonconformist form of happiness. Thus, Jacquouille emerges as the only character who betters himself, imposing his will and choosing his own modern destiny.

In spite of his struggle for emancipation, Jacquouille, the common man, is far from being a revolutionary. Although he claims his right to a proper place in a post-revolutionary society where all are theoretically entitled to freedom, equality, and fraternity, he only aspires to traditional bourgeois values, which the film's caricatural bourgeois characters, driven by greed, vanity, and power, have paradoxically forsaken. His desire to enjoy the 'freedom' of our modern world stems from having somewhat dishonestly cashed in on a hidden treasure, which allows him to partake in leisure activities (drinking, bowling) and indulge in luxury consumer goods (like his newly acquired Cadillac). His sense of equality means little more than his having access to individual property. And fraternity ensures that he finds his place within the national community, where he can comfortably associate with Ginette, also at the bottom of the social ladder, while being magnanimously tolerated in the most mundane situations (in Béatrice's home or at the luxury hotel, for example). Unlike Jacquart, the punished social usurper, forced to travel to the twelfth century where he pitifully wallows in the mud under the mockery of his new contemporaries, Jacquouille knows that he cannot step out of his own class and that he should be content with a subaltern role.

Although Jacquouille refuses to go back with his master, he nevertheless helps him return to medieval times, which will allow Godefroy to fulfil his destiny, marry Frénégonde, and secure his lineage. Godefroy's own emphasis on tradition, family, and duty legitimizes the very bourgeois society of which he was so critical, while a wiser Béatrice, now better aware of her noble ancestry, can none the less resume her middle-class family life in a comfortable modern home lacking the refinement of the family castle. Thus, once the conflict is resolved, Béatrice and Godefroy end up indirectly embracing bourgeois values and reinforcing the established order in a fraternal society united by traditional values but open to the possibility of better days—a recurrent conservative pattern in French popular comedies (Danan 1998). This serene, optimistic outcome to the modern-day adventure is reinforced at the end as the narrative returns to the past and closes with the final image of the reunited Godefroy and Frénégonde riding away, which provides the even more perfect, inevitable closure of a romantic comedy.

In the long run, therefore, life is as it should be, in spite of the apparent social criticism of *Les Visiteurs*. This criticism represents a form of 'vaccine', a constituting element in the rhetoric of bourgeois myths, which exposes the imperfections and injustices of a class institution before saving the 'avowed' evil in order to 'defend it from the risk of generalized subversion', according to Barthes (Barthes 1957: 45, 238). The bourgeois order may have its faults, but it still brings happiness to all those who accept it: *Les Visiteurs* presents the mythical image of a nation where every well-intentioned person can live happily.

Les Visiteurs' lesson in happiness seems a rather a simplistic sociological message. However, to be uncritically accepted and perform a cathartic function, this message must also trigger an emotional response among the public. Emotional involvement requires identification with complex characters constructed as individuals functioning with a certain degree of verisimilitude in their imaginary universe—as Brecht, after Aristotle, has shown (Brecht 1970: 226; 1972: 261, 291). Only a rich idiosyncratic language can express individuality, born of contradictory lived experiences and socially inherited beliefs. For characters to be credible, therefore, their language must reflect people's 'common sense', halfway between folklore and philosophy, representing a fossilized, fragmented view of the world on the one hand, and a critical, coherent mode of thinking open to change, on the other (Gramsci 1971: 323–4; 1985: 189–90, 420–1).

In *Les Visiteurs*, Jacquouille and Béatrice are the two characters whose language reflects the complexity of disparate viewpoints and who are most likely to give rise to multiple identifications among the public. In Jacquouille's case, his language evolves throughout the film as he learns to adapt to his modern environment and emancipate himself. At first, Jacquouille has a predictable role as a servant who obeys his master's orders, as well as a grotesque buffoon who can speak his mind, transgress bourgeois decorum with impunity, and cause physical catastrophes—a probable source of pleasure for the popular public. The physical resemblance between Jacquouille and the affected-sounding Jacquart, too eager to flaunt his newly elevated social status, helps highlight the servant's crudeness and total lack of inhibitions. Fascinated by his new environment, Jacquouille enjoys trying new technological wonders and imitating everything. Intrigued by foreign-sounding words like 'dingue' (crazy) and 'OK', he amusingly repeats them at all occasions while overstressing them (two of the patterns often imitated by the public after they saw the film), as if thrilled by their newness. But he also has the survival spirit of those who must fend for themselves and slyly seize opportunities as they arise. With the help of the newly discovered telephone technology, Jacquouille informs Godefroy of his refusal to return to the Middle Ages while expressing his emancipation linguistically as well: abandoning his usual 'messire' (My Lord), he addresses his master as an equal, calling him 'My Godefroy' (just as Godefroy called him 'My Jacquouille'). Thus, unlike the one-dimensional Godefroy, whose power belongs to the past because he is incapable of adapting, Jacquouille has discovered how to defend his rights verbally and embrace change in modern society.

Béatrice, too, knows how to use language to her advantage. With natural nobility and innate authority, backed by the Church, the police, and repressive medical personnel, she pays little attention to signs of obsequious respect from the 'common people'. She can take charge when necessary and expects no resistance to her wishes, even from her own husband who, after all, is only a commoner, a 'villein'. When she telephones Jacquart to request a snapshot of the last family picture hanging in the castle (to verify that Godefroy is in fact the amnesiac 'Cousin Hubert'), she actually does not ask Jacquart but *tells* him to do her a favour—which he clearly resents. She never loses her self-control and simply ignores Jacquouille's inappropriately noticeable body odours, flatulence, and belches, unlike Jean-Pierre, the husband, who is always yelling out of exasperation or disgust in a burlesque fashion. She tactfully addresses Jacquouille as 'Monsieur Ouille', to avoid the ill-sounding 'couille' (balls) of his original name—to the spectators' amusement. And her high-pitched intonation with artificially accented syllables and overly open vowels (especially 'a' sounds) also connote the haughtiness of a high-society lady (Sanders 1993: 46).[3] To paraphrase Pierre Bourdieu, Béatrice bears all the signs of 'distinction'.

But Béatrice's strength also resides in her power to adapt effortlessly to different situations and interlocutors. It has always been the privilege of the educated and higher classes to benefit from greater individual freedom of expression and use a wide range of linguistic registers, which are more marked in French than in English (Balibar 1985: 133; Sanders 1993: 27). With her fast delivery, varied facial expressions, and lively gestures highlighting the 'naturalness' of her speech, she can play the part of a 'regular' middle-class housewife as easily as she assumes her upper-class role. No longer residing in the family castle, she must deal with the domestic responsibilities of modern life, resorting if necessary to leftovers and convenience foods—like the 'leftover au gratin zucchini' and 'instant soup' she adds to her dinner menu to accommodate her unexpected guests. As if to stress her ability to renounce the privileges of nobility and embrace modernity, she swears mildly and uses everyday slang; she also frequently resorts to truncated forms (like 'Hub' for 'Hubert' or 'pola' for 'polaroid') and to hyperbole with her favourite 'hyper' prefix ('hyperchangé', 'hypermal')—two patterns typical of colloquial and especially adolescent speech (George 1993: 160–1). By easily switching from one register to another and drawing on multiple 'structures of feeling' (to use Raymond Williams's term), Béatrice may have given rise among the spectators to broad, shifting interpretations likely to facilitate multiple forms of identification.

Identification through the heroes' multifaceted language, leading to the French spectators' emotional involvement, also explains how the reassuring image of France represented in *Les Visiteurs* can function effectively as a myth. As Barthes pointed out, in order to come to life, a mythological concept must 'interpellate' subjects, in other words, address them directly and appear relevant to their lives (Barthes 1957: 210–11).

This interpellative aspect of *Les Visiteurs* is achieved not only through language, but also through multiple signs and allusions evoking a shared French culture. In particular, *Les Visiteurs* incorporates references to the film culture of the mainstream French public for whom this expensive Gaumont production (60 million francs) was clearly intended. The Godefroy/Jacquouille pair, for example, recalls the familiar master/servant relationship at the heart of many other popular French films, and especially the famous De Funès/Bourvil duo of France's most popular comedy, *La Grande Vadrouille* (see Danan 1998). *Les Visiteurs* draws even more directly on the pleasure of intertextual recognition through the obvious similarities between Ginette and another well-known character also played by Marie Anne Chazel. Ginette looks and sounds like the free-spirited Josette, a street character in *Le Père Noël est une ordure* (1982), directed by J.-M. Poiré and co-written with Le Splendid (a *café-théâtre* team known for its caustic satirical humour and spontaneous-sounding language), which became a young people's cult film in the 1980s (Frodon 1995a: 465). Like Josette, Ginette speaks in a colourful slang and drawled intonation reminiscent of the lower-class 'parigotes' played by Arletty (most famous for her 'Atmosphère... Atmosphère' line in *Hôtel du Nord*, Carné, 1938). But this amusing character also betrays her lower social status when she attempts to hypercorrect her speech in formal situations—a common occurrence among less educated speakers (George 1993: 167).

In addition to the filmic intertextual references woven into the plot and characterization, *Les Visiteurs* multiplies passing allusions to national cinema, television, and French culture in general. Since the medieval protagonists are unaware of contemporary customs and signs, they are victims of their naivety and become the butt of

the public's laughter. Their naive response to events actually introduces the modern narrative and draws viewers into the film, after
the historical prologue which unclearly mixes historical facts, credits, and subtitles. As Jacquouille and Godefroy venture onto a
tarred road and spot their first automobile, they viciously attack
this devil's cart with a mysterious emblem, easily recognizable to
French spectators as a frail Renault 4 postal car. But when the
heroes further mistake its black driver for a 'Saracen' or Muslim
arch-enemy, the public's laughter may have also stressed the
'Otherness' of a Frenchman who was not of 'pure' French descent.

Each viewing may reveal missed allusions to 'Frenchness', hence
the public's desire to repeat an experience which draws so much on
the people's common cultural heritage. Most objects, sites, and
names are unmistakably French.[4] But where exactly is the action
taking place? Godefroy's Montmirail castle seems to belong to the
Loire Valley or an area near Paris, although credits tell us that the
film was partially shot in the south, in Languedoc Roussillon.
Characters speak without a regional accent, and no road sign or
car plate is legible (although some may recognize the asylum where
Godefroy was originally interned as the Ivry hospital in the suburbs
of Paris). In fact, the absence of any real clue as to actual location
and the choice of Montmirail, a common enough name to be found
in various regions of France, highlight the quintessential
'Frenchness' of the story.

Godefroy himself functions more like an unequivocal sign than
a full-fledged character. Unable and unwilling to adapt to his new
surroundings, Godefroy reacts anachronistically in the same
manner he would have back 'home', according to a code of
chivalry that befits a nobleman. For example, jumping on his
horse, he brandishes his lance to chastize the rude innkeeper at the
Courte-Paille grill (a restaurant chain), or undauntedly takes on an
impressive group of CRS (the State Security Police), after yelling
the French knights' war cry ('Montjoie'), just as he would have
pursued the king's enemies in the twelfth century. Godefroy le
Hardi, whose name is reminiscent of historical characters like
Godefroi de Bouillon and Charles le Téméraire, evokes the history
lessons learned in primary school books. He is the Ancestor, who
helped found the old French nation and from whom all French
citizens derive their common origin. A faithful aide of Louis VI, he
fought alongside his king against England, France's perennial

external threat, which is briefly evoked in the prologue and high-lighted by a few subtitled English phrases. Subtitles are also used at the beginning to translate Godefroy's 'old French' and signify that he belongs to France's distant past. Yet, this past is still close to us, continues to live through us. In spite of a few archaic-sounding words and constructions, Godefroy's French basically sounds like modern French and is never truly incomprehensible. Through Godefroy, a likeable but archaic hero, all French people, bound by the same language in spite of different linguistic competences, can pride themselves in the glorious past and common origin of a pure, mythical France.

This comforting representation of a unified grand nation finds support in another historical period, by a direct reference to the lesson of the French Revolution. This reference is particularly revealing didactically because of its very superfluousness on the dramatic level, as Sorlin notes (Sorlin 1977: 173). Pushed by the sudden necessity of learning 'the history of the kingdom since Louis VI le Gros', Godefroy wakes up Béatrice in the middle of the night. At that point, with the assistance of the ultimate French reference book, the Larousse Encyclopedia, she teaches him that the family hero mentioned in all the history books is not *him*, but a certain Gonzague de Montmirail, who embraced the values of the French Revolution and was ready to divide up the land with peasants. Godefroy strongly dislikes this lesson, proudly repeated by Béatrice, while the eavesdropping Jacquouille takes good note of it. Later, Jacquouille will justify his own emancipation in the name of these revolutionary principles, yelling to Godefroy: 'I am no longer a serf. I am a free man. Long live the Revolution!'

Godefroy finally returns to the Middle Ages to fulfil his destiny, and the French Revolution is presented as a fait accompli instead of an ongoing social struggle. This narrative structure reinforces the fact that the French Revolution is an integral part of French society, which only an anachronistic character like Godefroy can still blatantly reject. Indeed, in French political life, the French Revolution serves as *the* reference point which all parties attempt to appropriate in a contradictory fashion, whether they accept the Revolution as a whole, like the Left, or whether they criticize the Reign of Terror, like the Right (Sorlin 1980: 42). As Étienne Balibar has suggested, myths of national origins and continuity rely on one historical moment because 'in the history of each modern nation, there can only be a *single* founding revolutionary moment' (Balibar 1990: 118). Thus, by presenting the message of the Revolution in the background, even if this message is only subconsciously perceived, *Les Visiteurs* contributes once more to a mythical image of France, a glorious country presumably forever devoted to the defence of liberty, equality, and fraternity. History itself becomes an ahistorical myth pointing out that the present conflates with the past and that nothing can or should be really chosen or changed in society (Barthes 1957: 239).

Through its use of history and culture as well as language and characterization, *Les Visiteurs* succeeded in capturing the very myth of the French Nation: in spite of historical transformations and differences among its citizens, today's France is still a grand nation which can be proud of its glorious past and of the revolutionary values serving as the foundation for contemporary society. Of course, contemporary society has its flaws, but these minor imperfections, once acknowledged, actually give greater credibility to France's overall positive image. Spectators are likely to internalize this image since they can identify with the congenial, natural-sounding characters and are constantly summoned by familiar cultural signs. All these signs ensure that the conveyed mythical concept is not too obscure, although it should not be perceived as too obvious either. As with most myths, viewers must simply believe that they are watching an 'innocent' story (Barthes 1957: 215–17).

Indeed, spectators who enthuse about *Les Visiteurs* are most likely to recount their favourite hilarious scene, focus on the numerous burlesque visual gags, or recall the verbal comedy resulting from the odd juxtaposition of different speech patterns previously described. But through the catharsis which laughter fosters, *Les Visiteurs* gives a particularly reassuring response to the anxiety invading contemporary French society, confronted with rising unemployment, intolerance to immigration, and the challenges of modernization in a globalized world. Against social injustice and France's changing environment, this film reproduces the unchanging image of national brotherhood and grandeur in the collective imaginary of its citizens. Five years later, with the long-awaited release in February 1998 of *Les Couloirs du temps: les visiteurs 2*, French audiences clearly hoped to relive this cathartic experience, since the sequel smashed opening-day box-office records. But there is no mechanical recipe for reproducing a myth, and by the second week, ticket sales had already sharply dropped (although the film still attracted eight million spectators by the end of 1998). The emergence of minority film voices challenging the notion of a homogeneous national identity, not to mention the French state's encouragement of lavish productions intended for an international as much as a national audience, may also echo the faster-changing world of the late 1990s. One may therefore wonder how long cinema will be able to perpetuate the French myth.

Notes

1. *Le Nouvel Observateur* (11–17 Mar. 1993), 54–7; *L'Événement du jeudi* (1–7 Apr. 1993), 92–106; *Cahiers du cinéma*, 465 (Mar. 1993), 83–9; *Le Figaro* (8–9 May 1993), 19; *Mensuel du cinéma*, 5 (Apr. 1993), 4–5. The other newspapers mentioned here are listed in the article in *L'Événement*, 92.
2. Jacquart's exasperated 'Mais qu'est-ce que c'est que ce binz?' (But what is this mess) has become a catchphrase.
3. This type of snobbish accent has been described by Carol Sanders as typical of upper- and upper middle-class Parisians.
4. Products were often provided by French commercial partners, like the fake Chanel no. 5 bottle emptied into Godefroy's bath. See, for example, Vachez 1993.

9

Right-Wing Anarchism and *Le Bonheur est dans le pré* (Chatiliez, 1995)

KEITH READER

> The important thing here is that the adventure has a happy
> ending, in the sunshine of a more or less leeward island, where
> all our scapegraces can live out their days happily.
>
> (Ory 1985: 129)

LE BONHEUR *est dans le pré* was Étienne Chatiliez's third, and at
the time of writing last, feature film, following on *La Vie est un
long fleuve tranquille* (1988) and *Tatie Danielle* (1990). *La Vie est
un long fleuve tranquille*, made on a shoestring budget using
largely unknown actors, was the surprise box-office hit of its year
in France, where its acerbic family romance in which two children
from families at opposite ends of the social scale are exchanged at
birth clearly struck a number of chords. The supposed political
sympathies of the film's two families, in a presidential election year,
were the subject of much debate in the French press, and their
names—'Le Quesnoy' for the *bien-pensant* Catholic *hauts bourgeois* and 'Groseille' for what might nowadays be called the 'underclass'—came to acquire virtually talismanic significance (see
Reader 1992). *Tatie Danielle* was more of a one-joke film, centring
on the apparently sweet but in fact profoundly malicious little old
lady played by Tsilla Chelton, and doubtless for that very reason
did comparatively better in the UK than in France. British audiences may well have recognized in the central character an echo of
Katie Johnson's Mrs Wilberforce in Alexander Mackendrick's *The
Ladykillers* of 1955.

 Le Bonheur est dans le pré marked a new departure for
Chatiliez, most notably through its use of major stars. His budget
for this film was between 60 and 65 million francs, compared to *La
Vie est un long fleuve tranquille*'s 15 million—an increase that

enabled him not only to field an impressive cast, but also to parody the intrinsically high-budget genre of the heritage film. Comedy, it is often forgotten, has right from the beginning of the sound era been the most consistently popular type of film within France, not least because it is constantly able to borrow new leases of life from other genres. Just as the military comedy or *comique troupier* parodied the war drama (as with Christian-Jaque's *Un de la Légion* of 1936), or Truffaut in 1960's *Tirez sur le pianiste* burlesqued the gangster genre in the film's most overtly comic passages, so *Le Bonheur est dans le pré*—like the other two comic films dealt with in this book—derives much of its impact from its references to the heritage film.

La Vie est un long fleuve tranquille had featured in a minor role Daniel Gélin, in his younger days a romantic lead for Jacques Becker (*Rendez-vous de juillet*, 1949) and Max Ophuls (*Le Plaisir*, 1952), but like *Tatie Danielle*'s Tsilla Chelton latterly much better known for his theatre work. *Le Bonheur est dans le pré*, on the other hand, uses four—or perhaps I should say five—big-name stars. Michel Serrault, who plays the harassed toilet-factory owner Francis Bergeaud, is one of France's best-known comic actors (largely thanks to Édouard Molinaro's *La Cage aux folles* of 1980), though at about the same time as Chatiliez's film he also starred in a more serious role for Claude Sautet (*Nelly et M Arnaud*, 1995). Sabine Azéma (Francis's upwardly mobile wife Nicole) reprises in a comic—some might say at times farcical—register the nervous bourgeoise type already familiar from Alain Resnais's *Mélo* (1986) and *Smoking/No Smoking* (1994). Eddy Mitchell, one-time claimant to the oxymoronic distinction of being France's best rock singer, appears as Francis's lubricious garage-owner friend Gérard in what, notwithstanding Bertrand Tavernier's *Coup de torchon* (1981), is his most successful screen role to date. Carmen Maura, who plays Dolores Thivart, is best known for her roles for the Spanish director Pedro Almodóvar.

The fifth star, of course, is Eric Cantona, the Rimbaud-loving former Manchester United soccer player who was able to appear only because he was at the time suspended from the Premier League for aiming what subsequently turned out to be a well-deserved karate kick at a racist heckler. Cantona plays a rugby player (Lionel), who despite being a married father of two is also expecting a child with one of Dolores's daughters, a role whose echoes of François Mitterrand's illegitimate daughter with Anne Pingeot would certainly not have escaped a French audience. I mention Cantona here simply because but for him so 'French' a film would in all probability not have been distributed in Britain. His role, like that of his brother Joël who plays his brother in the film, is a minor one—more than a cameo, but only just—so that the director's assertion that Cantona worried a great deal about his part may seem a trifle excessive.

The Cantona brothers fit into a theme that runs through this film as it does through *La Vie est un long fleuve tranquille*—that of the family romance, in *Le Bonheur est dans le pré* given a more idyllically rustic inflection than in its predecessor. At the end of *La Vie est un long fleuve tranquille*, the two children whose exchange has precipitated the drama are both in different ways clearly disturbed, and the doctor who was the unwitting agent of the exchange is wheelchair-bound and at the mercy of his former mistress. *Le Bonheur est dans le pré*, by contrast, ends with the formation of two happy couples and two strong same-sex friendships. Francis leaves behind his miserable marriage and old identity to assume that of Dolores's husband Michel, who went missing twenty-six years before and of whom Francis proves, when Dolores appears on a television show asking for news of his whereabouts, to be the exact double. Michel turns out to have been a bank-robber who was shot and pitched into a well near the family duck-farm, but this too is for the best, for Dolores has known all along that Francis was not her husband and has played along with his assumption of Michel's identity out of love at first sight for him. All thus ends happily ever after for the new couple, who benefit from Michel's ill-gotten gains without incurring responsibility for his death. Nicole, meanwhile, has found happiness in the vigorous embrace of Gérard and become fast friends with Dolores, while the male bond between Francis and Gérard—perhaps the emotional mainspring of the film—remains sturdily unaffected by the various heterosexual comings and goings. These latter also include the marriage of Francis's daughter Géraldine, the already-mentioned affair between Lionel and one of Dolores's daughters, and the other daughter's happily 'bigamous' relationships with Lionel's brother and another village youth.

The inspiration for the film is said to have come from an edition of the popular French television reality show *Perdu de vue*, which featured a 60-year-old farmer who, repelled by the idea of being obliged to grow kiwi fruit, left his native town for the first time and subsequently turned up on a cruise in Caracas. Kiwi fruit were a seemingly omnipresent feature of the 1970s and 1980s vogue for what was variously called *nouvelle cuisine* or *cuisine minceur*—a vogue which aroused the ire of (politically and gastronomically) conservative cookery writers, to the point of being seen as a threat to the integrity of France's culinary soul. The cavalier consumption of foie gras and Armagnac by which the film's Gascon sequences are marked is a clear riposte to the kiwi-fruit style of cooking, though it has to be said a somewhat belated one—by 1995 *nouvelle cuisine* was as dated as its intellectual twin *nouvelle philosophie* exemplified in the work of such as André Glucksmann or Bernard-Henri Lévy, and very nearly as impossible to find. Indulgence of bodily appetites, *Le Bonheur est dans le pré* tells us even in its title, is the route to happiness and freedom from guilt.

This is evidently true in the domain of sexuality too, for all the film's multiple, and except for Géraldine's marriage illicit, emotional activity takes place without a semblance of tension or unhappiness. The pastoral bliss announced in the film's title reigns unchallenged at its end, in a view of peasant life as heterosexual-ized Arcadia that is at the opposite extreme to the internecine vengefulness of Claude Berri's Pagnol adaptations *Jean de Florette* and *Manon des Sources*. Those films are set in Provence, often a much harsher region than its touristic reputation might suggest; *Le Bonheur est dans le pré*'s southern scenes, on the other hand, take place in the more consistently benign province of Gascony, home of Dumas *père*'s musketeer Porthos and of the gastronomic (over-)indulgence epitomized in the film by the foie gras produced on Dolores's farm and the Armagnac bottle always within reach. As Francis and Gérard cross France from east (their home town of Dole) to south-west to meet Dolores, they make periodic stops for gourmet meals—meals of the kind that, until his collapse in a restaurant, have provided Francis with his only consolation for an acrimonious personal and professional life. These episodes, which first announce the bucolic happiness of the film's title, are marked—are indeed rendered possible—by the total absence of women. Francis's life in Dole takes place in a persecutory gynae-ceum, beset by a snobbish wife and daughter at home and by a truculent, almost entirely female workforce at his strike-bound factory. The leisureliness of his southward drive with Gérard thus represents a sensually prolonged all-male idyll between one wife and the next, a rite of passage only after which can Dolores take her place in the meadow of his happiness.

Bertrand Blier had directed a far more overtly misogynistic variation on this theme in *Calmos* (1976). This film stars two of France's leading film comedians, Jean-Pierre Marielle and Jean Rochefort, who flee the world of women to take refuge in food and drink in the Beaujolais countryside. Their companion there is an elderly priest, reinforcing the idea that the joys of the table are enhanced by, if not actually dependent upon, the exclusion of women—a view endorsed towards the end of *Le Bonheur est dans le pré* by Nicole's vomiting after she has seen foie gras being prepared. *Calmos*'s two translations into English—as *Femmes fatales* or as *Cool, Calm and Collected*—are in this light less at variance with each other than we might think.

Among *Le Bonheur est dans le pré*'s other filmic intertexts are two films starring Gérard Depardieu—the earlier-mentioned *Jean de Florette* and Daniel Vigne's *Le Retour de Martin Guerre* (1982). The well into which Michel's body is flung is an ironic echo of that feverishly dug by Depardieu's Jean in the Claude Berri film, while the theme of the impostor 'recognized' by a wife who is in fact following her erotic and emotional impulses is common to Vigne and Chatiliez. An interview with Chatiliez and his scriptwriter Florence Quentin reveals that Depardieu was considered as a possibility for the role eventually taken by Eddy Mitchell (Diastème and Diastème 1995: 68). Given these allusions and Depardieu's notorious love of food and wine, the choice of the name 'Gérard' for this character is at least arguably a wink of homage.

As a family romance that also parodies the heritage film, *Le Bonheur est dans le pré* situates itself at the crossroads of two staple middlebrow genres. It played to mainstream audiences in France, but in Britain—if only because of the subtitles—was shown largely in art-house cinemas, and can thus be said to represent, like Jean-Marie Poiré's *Les Visiteurs* (1993), a kind of 'cross-Channel crossover' film. The 'Cantona factor' which almost certainly secured the film's distribution in Britain anchors it in what might be described as a culture of educated laddishness, in which copulation and alcohol thrive benignly, females and ducks alike know their place, and men will always be men, never more so than when there are no women around to complicate their jovial bonding.

The quotation from Pascal Ory with which this chapter begins suggests how this aspect of *Le Bonheur est dans le pré* also fits into a French cultural tradition particularly marked between the 1930s and the end of the 1980s, at which time the collapse or dilution of the forms of socialism on offer destroyed much of its polemical force: that of right-wing anarchism, associated with such names as the novelists Marcel Aymé and Louis-Ferdinand Céline or the screenwriter Michel Audiard. The *anarchiste de droite* tradition seems to be a peculiarly French one, I suspect because the role of the state in French society is much greater than in any other European country. For Pascal Ory (following Paul Valéry!), the basic position of the right-wing anarchist is that 'in the end, nobody gives a damn' (Ory 1985: 36), and he—the examples Ory gives are all male—can be culturally defined as 'the populist snob' (Ory 1985: 40) who 'speaks of the little man . . . in hatred of the big and in contempt for his inferior' (Ory 1985: 42). Scorn for anything that smacks of avant-gardism, mistrust of such notions as collectivity, equality, and perfectibility, and a concomitant hostility to any kind of social or intellectual system are the species's principal identifying marks. (Distinctively French the tradition may be, but it is not hard to see Lady Thatcher or Newt Gingrich finding themselves at home in it once the language problem had been solved).

Among film-makers, three stand out in the *anarchiste de droite* canon: Claude Autant-Lara, Jean-Pierre Melville, and Bertrand Blier. Autant-Lara's movement across the political spectrum, from Communist Party member after the war to National Front Euro-MP, appears in the combined light of his work and his life to be a cosmetic change of garb rather than the profound shift in attitude one might have expected. The irreverence of his 1956 *La Traversée de Paris* (based on a novella by Marcel Aymé), about two men smuggling a contraband pig across occupied Paris, is rooted in a hard-nosed individualism and a scorn for *connerie* that have far more to do with right-wing anarchism than with any ideology of solidarity. Melville—one of the founding fathers of that New Wave held in such bilious contempt by Autant-Lara—may be a surprising name to find on the list (notwithstanding his work with the flagrantly rightist Alain Delon), but the pared-down devil-take-the-hindmost nihilism of a film such as *Le Samouraï* (1967) is eminently in accord with the dandyistic aloofness and economic conservatism described by Frodon:

Publicly, Melville systematically denigrated the auteur cinema and supported the most conservative positions, joining the censorship body in the early 1960s when the vast majority of film-makers were demanding its abolition and noisily deploring the plundering of public subsidies to support art cinema . . . There was something of the dandy about the man who forged himself a silhouette composed of a Stetson, dark glasses, a trenchcoat and a Rolls-Royce—but a dandy in the Baudelairean sense, hiding tetchy despair behind his offhand loquacity like somebody out of sympathy with his time yet quite capable of shining in it. (Frodon 1995a: 98)

The final sentences strikingly evoke the style—in literature and in life—of the novelist Roger Nimier, another major representative of the tendency, whose disabused hussar Sanders famously pronounces at the end of *Le Hussard bleu*: 'Everything that is human is alien to me' (Nimier 1950: 434). Dandyism is hardly a quality one would associate with Bertrand Blier, yet the ubiquitous couldn't-care-less flavour of his work inscribes it firmly in a tradition that refuses any kind of ethical seriousness and views women, most egregiously in *Calmos*, as little more than objects of gratification.

When Ory describes *anarchistes de droite* as 'keen on hunting down technocrats and contemptuous of women (they're all gagging for it)' (Ory 1985: 79), the relevance of the term to *Le Bonheur est dans le pré* as well as to Blier becomes plain. The toilet-factory strike with which the film opens may appear to pit an assertive and unionized female workforce against the forces of economic rationalization, but its burlesque staging puts it at a far remove from the *gauchiste* world of Marin Karmitz's *Coup pour coup* (1971) or Godard and Gorin's *Tout va bien* (1972). The leader of the workers is also the lover of the local CGT organizer, with whom she is several times depicted in bed, and when a television crew arrives at the factory after Francis has supposedly been recognized on air the pickets forget their task in the stampede for autographs. When the film was released France was in the grip of large-scale strike action, so that the militancy it portrays and lampoons would have been very far from a joke for its audiences. The fact that Michel disappeared on 7 June 1968, at the end of what the television presenter describes as 'the dreadful events', a period which 'slightly upset

France', reinforces the sense that the film, in so far as it acknowledges the existence of movements for social change, treats them as matter for derision. The use of 'slightly' to undercut the impact of the 'dreadful events' seems to me characteristic of a right-wing anarchist rather than say an orthodox Gaullist approach, inflected as it is towards scorn and belittlement rather than clarion denunciation.

As for 'women [who] are all gagging for it', that obviously evokes the scene in which Gérard possesses Nicole across the bonnet of his car. The misogyny here resides less in that scene itself than in what precedes and follows it: Gérard's 'man-to-man' coarseness with Nicole in the restaurant before (he accuses her of always treating him 'as though my dick had a funny taste'), and his gleeful confiding in Francis afterwards, in which the woman is seen in classic Freudian or Lévi-Straussian fashion as object of jocose exchange among bonding males ('it cleared out her passages'; the French *écoutilles* meaning 'hatchways' in nautical terms, a homosocial frame of reference if ever there were). Gérard, we should remember, is a garage-owner—thus, Francis's approximate social equal, indeed from Nicole's point of view conceivably his superior since her husband 'earns "dirty" money' (Diastème and Diastème 1995: 67). The 'triumph' of his coarseness over her teetering pseudo-refinement is thus in no sense a class phenomenon (though the two characters' vocabularies may tempt us into reading it as such), but rather that of one kind of bourgeoisie over another, of the right-wing anarchist and 'past-master in human stupidity' ('maître-artisan en connerie humaine') (Ory 1985: 122) over the respectable cousin of *La Vie est un long fleuve tranquille*'s Le Quesnoy family.

For Ory, a further distinguishing characteristic of the *anarchiste de droite* is his implicit belief in the idea of race, which takes the form of a 'constant toing-and-froing between the biological and the cultural' (Ory 1985: 103). This sheds light on one curious subtext in the film—Francis's collection of African art, built up over twenty years and threatened with selling-off by Nicole in order to pay for their daughter's extravagant wedding. The family dog is called 'Bamboula', after the name of a Bantu dance or as my *Larousse Lexis* dictionary has it 'Blacks' dance' (!), and thus not inappositely translated in the film's English subtitles as 'Sambo'. It is during one of Francis and Gérard's conversations as they cross France—the same one in which Gérard advocates a clip round the ear for over-assertive females—that Francis dreamily says: 'You don't talk about Africa, you dream it.' We are here close to Edward Said's view of the Orient—a clear metonym for any colonized territory—as 'almost a European invention . . . since antiquity a place of romance, exotic beings, haunting memories and landscapes, remarkable experiences' (Said 1991: 1). Jean-Pierre Kérien's Alfonse in Resnais's *Muriel* (1963), reminiscing about a factitious Algerian past to which he supposedly gave the best years of his life, is part of the same discourse, one in and for which the colonial Other is reducible to raw material for utopian dreams and exotic wall-hangings. Nicole's wish to sell Francis's collection is on one level a straightforward example of bourgeois philistinism, on another the logical conclusion of that collection's very existence. Here again, Nicole is the focal point of the film's alleged anti-bourgeois thrust. Chatiliez describes her as somebody who aspires to the bourgeoisie but 'simply dreams of joining them' and reinforces this attitude with the observation that she 'thinks herself worthy of Paris, but if she walked down a street there, everybody would see straight away that she is a provincial' (Lavoignat and d'Yvoire 1995: 110). In the light of the film's much more indulgent presentation of Francis and Gérard, it seems safe to say that its choice of target is a matter of gender rather more than of class. For Ory, the *anarchiste de droite* perceives 'several kinds of eternal feminine', dominant among which are on one hand the 'stupid cow', on the other the 'horny bitch' (Ory 1985: 133). If Nicole can be said to 'evolve' in the course of the film, it is from the first of these categories into the second.

Dolores fits into neither category. Her all-understanding earth-motherliness laughs away possible tensions (as in the relationships of her two daughters), and is ultimately what makes the Edenic reconciliations of the film's ending possible. This, of course, is another 'eternal feminine', the (eventually) sexualized mother, distilling the homely virtues of rural life in at once soothing and arousing contrast to the strident Nicole—pasturing rather than posturing. Florence Quentin has spoken of the importance for the film of 'male friendship, the friendship of slightly rough-and-ready, vulgar people . . . And then there was always our fondness for the provinces' (Diastème 1995: 66). Chatiliez, from whose work Paris is almost entirely absent, is in some ways the provincial French film-maker par excellence, as his description of Nicole as a Parisienne *manqué* suggests. Happiness, salvation even, is in this film to be found as far from the big (or any) city as possible, in the depths of a provincial France unpolluted by technical and cultural change—what the French themselves, half-patronizingly, half-affectionately, refer to as *la France profonde*.

Ideological dissection of a 'feelgood' movie is always a risky task, laying one open to charges of misplaced not to say grouchy seriousness. (Frank Capra's films perhaps provide the textbook example of this in writing about cinema.) Chatiliez himself is at pains to deny any serious import to his humour, which he sees as 'half-way between Italian and Anglo-Saxon humour, not over-emphasizing things, skating swiftly over them' (Lavoignat and d'Yvoire 1995: 111). Bizarrely, he adduces David Niven as a role-model, though the thought of him rear-humping Sabine Azéma or owning a toilet factory is truly mind-boggling. Halfway between Britain and Italy, of course, is France, and Chatiliez's attempt at internationalizing his determinedly *hexagonal* humour fails through its very disingenuousness. More than any other contemporary French film-maker with the possible exception of Jean-Marie Poiré, he speaks to and articulates the values of *la France profonde*, summed up in the title of his film; yet that *France profonde* is as idealized and constructed as Alexander Mackendrick's Hebrides in *Whisky Galore* (1949) or indeed Capra's small-town America. *Le Bonheur est dans le pré*'s final epiphany is a Parisian weekend cottage-owner's vision of rural France, as the choice of actors makes all too clear. Serrault, Azéma, and Mitchell are very obviously Parisians 'on leave', while Carmen Maura's Spanishness cannot but dominate perceptions of her performance. Chatiliez's happy meadow is ultimately a toytown surrogate, all the better of course for its inhabitants, temporary or permanent. Here, as in the *anarchiste de droite* world emblematically summed up in the Ory quotation with which this piece starts, men can be boys and women have no choice but to be women.

Part II

INSCRIBING DIFFERENCES

10

Gender and Sexuality in *Les Nuits fauves* (Collard, 1992)

CARRIE TARR

LES NUITS *fauves* was an important film, not only for its controversial representation of sexuality and AIDS, but also for the way it highlighted differences in cultural criticism on either side of the Channel. In France, the film won four of the 1993 Césars: Best Film, Best First Film, Best Female Newcomer (Romane Bohringer), and Best Editing (Lise Beaulieu). It was acclaimed for its energetic and eclectic cinematic style, its daring treatment of a love story centred on a bisexual character with AIDS, its facilitation of public discussion about AIDS and safe sex, and its revelation of a new talent in Romane Bohringer. In Britain, however, the film was criticized for its failure to emphasize the importance of safe sex in the prevention of HIV/AIDS; Simon Watney in particular also attacked the film for not addressing the institutionalized homophobia which has allowed the spread of HIV/AIDS in France and for not equipping the bisexual central character with any awareness of a possible politicized gay response to AIDS (Watney 1993).

Cyril Collard's dramatization of living with and combating HIV-positivity and Kaposi's sarcoma undoubtedly injected a note of much-needed actuality into contemporary French cinema. A self-proclaimed bisexual, and one of only a very few French personalities to admit to being HIV-positive, Collard's multiple authorship of the film endows it with an undeniable authenticity. Not only was this his first (and last) feature-length film, he also adapted the screenplay from his own semi-autobiographical novel, wrote and sang some of the music, and gave a bravura performance in the central role of Jean (no other young French actor being willing to be cast in such a role). The film centres on the multiple sexual encounters of a 30-something HIV-positive camera operator in a recognizably contemporary Parisian setting. Add to the melodrama

inherent in the AIDS narrative the equivocal representation of the
main protagonist's bisexuality and the excitement of the fast
cutting, the hand-held camera, the original music track, and the
Pialat-style improvisations, and the film offers a potentially exhilarating experience of what one young French fan described as 'the
confusion of values and sexes' in contemporary French society
(Rouchy 1993: 20).

But exactly what values, and what sexes for that matter, are
being addressed in and by this film? In the drive to assess the political correctness or otherwise of the film's representation of sex
without a condom as the ultimate expression of love and trust
between a passionate young woman and an HIV-positive man, critics have perhaps been in danger of occluding the film's challenge to
normative representations of male sexuality through its simultaneous fascination with both heterosexual and same-sex desires and
pleasures. Given that AIDS and homosexuality have been such
taboo topics in French cinema, and that the implied (and mislead-
ing) link between homosexuality, sexual promiscuity, HIV infection, and death is one of the most potent ways in which western
society constructs homosexuality as perverse and pathological,
then an AIDS narrative which openly explores its central character's active bisexuality needs to be examined for the ways in which
it reinforces or challenges normative convictions about sexual identity and preference.

Collard's originality lies in refusing two of the most conventional forms of mainstream AIDS narrative. Despite the key role of
the 'innocent' female partner in this film, for example, the investigation of AIDS is not simply displaced onto the study of its effects
on the normative heterosexual population, stand-ins for the
presumed audience of the film. *Les Nuits fauves* can be usefully
compared with *Mensonge* (Margolin, 1992), in which a man's
bisexuality and HIV-positivity is constructed from the point of
view of the 'wronged' wife, and his furtive homosexuality represented as the source of his (and her) infection and a threat to the
nuclear family. Nor does it take the alternative liberal path of
constructing the man with AIDS as a tragic victim, as in
Philadelphia (Demme, 1993), which effectively desexualizes and
sanitizes homosexuality by playing up the similarities between the
politically correct, responsible gay couple and the 'normative'
monogamous heterosexual couple.

Instead, *Les Nuits fauves* offers an explicit investigation of alternative sexual identities and practices from the point of view of its main protagonist, Jean (Cyril Collard), for whom promiscuous bisexuality is a 'normal', if troubled, way of life. The film also confounds customary binary expectations by setting up as the objects of his desire: a young woman (18-year-old Laura, played by Romane Bohringer), a young man (22-year-old Samy, a Spanish immigrant, played by Carlos Lopez), and the groups of anonymous men who gather at nightfall under the arches of the highway running alongside the Seine. Arguably, the drama of AIDS works principally to intensify the drama of Jean's fragmented sexual identity. It is his inability to say no to the 'sirens' call' (as his sexual encounters are described in the film's opening song, repeated later in the film) which is the principal dilemma of this narrative of desire. What I want to investigate is the extent to which this dilemma problematizes normative understandings of phallic masculinity, and allows a positive representation of alternative 'feminized' masculine identities and pleasures. I will also consider whether the film's probing of masculine identity disturbs conventional hierarchies of sexual and ethnic difference, or merely works to valorize an enriched understanding of white, male subjectivity.

Collard's exploration of homosexuality in *Les Nuits fauves* is closely interwoven with and, arguably, subordinate to the heterosexual narrative of Jean's passionate love affair with Laura. A foregrounding of the heterosexual narrative may have been the price to pay for being able to treat the question of homosexuality at all in a successful commercial feature film. But the dominant reading of the film, supported by Collard's own statements, is that it is

Above all a love story with Laura. Then, . . . it's about the bloke's development: how a guy who is HIV-positive, so under threat, deals with this thing closing in on him, and finishes by opening up to the world, to other people, to her; he even manages to say 'I love you' to her, which he couldn't at the beginning. (Stern and Boujnah 1992: 15)

A typical synopsis of the film, then, suggests that the HIV-positive bisexual man can transcend incoherence and lack by learning to love a woman. In such a reading, Jean's homosexual desires are implicitly understood as deviant or regressive, rightly repressed in favour of normative adult heterosexuality. Brigitte Rollet has even argued that the film sets up a binary opposition between the 'unwholesome world' ('monde malsain') of the homosexual encounters and the 'purity' of heterosexual love represented through the role of Laura (Rollet 1994).

However, whilst there are certainly indications that the virus can help Jean to learn to love, and whilst Laura probably represents the view of the majority of the viewing public when she insists that *she* is the one who represents love and that gay sex is simply 'fucking' ('pour baiser'), nevertheless it is less clear that homosexuality is marked as deviant, heterosexuality as desirable, and Jean as actually able to make a choice between them. In fact, initially at least, a more significant distinction seems to be being made between sex within the couple, heterosexual or homosexual, and group homosexual sex.

The film's exploration of the couple offers close parallels between Jean's meeting with, seduction of, and relationship with Laura and Samy respectively. In each case, the objects of Jean's desire first perform for him to camera, caught up in his controlling directorial gaze. In each case, as a conventionally attractive young woman and a conventionally attractive young man who is also an immigrant, they exist in a relationship of subordination to Jean in terms of age, experience, income, and social status, and thereby signal Jean's privileged position as the successful, slightly older white male. The text regularly cuts from Jean with Samy to Jean with Laura, emphasizing the interchangeability of the two characters as well as their differences. And both Samy and Laura discover pleasures in their sexual relationship with Jean that they had not known before. For Laura, whose previous relationships with men have been unsatisfactory, this takes the form of orgasmic but unsafe penetrative sex (a key moment being her decision to throw away a condom, even when she knows that Jean is HIV-positive). For Samy, previously 'straight', it takes the form of the discovery of pleasure in sex with a man. However, here the film cuts away from showing the sex act (it shies away from any images of penis or anus), showing instead only mutually pleasurable stroking, so that the question of whether one or other (or both) of the participants is penetrated (and thereby feminized) is left unclear.

Interestingly, however, neither Laura nor Samy is able to handle their relationship with Jean or their disempowerment within the structures of domination generated by conventional notions of gender roles and sexual relationships. Laura leaves her mother for

Jean, but, as a result of Jean's inability to commit himself to her, then becomes hysterically jealous, possessive, and self-destructive, such that she has to be temporarily 'put away'. In turn, Samy leaves his girlfriend Marianne for Jean, but subsequently becomes increasingly committed to various disturbing sadomasochistic practices. His cult of the body and involvement with racist thugs leads not only to self-mutilation, but also to his seeking to mutilate others. But whereas Laura is motivated by an emotional dependency on Jean, the film allows the spectator to deduce that Samy is seeking punishment for the 'feminization/deviancy' produced in him through his discovery of pleasure in gay sex. The breakdown of the gay couple is confirmed when Jean rescues a young *beur* from a racist murder attempt in which Samy is a participant.

Laura and Samy's roles work to confirm the centrality of Jean's masculine subjectivity, his relative stability of character, and his physical attractiveness and powers of seduction over both women and men in spite of his HIV-infected body. But they can also be read as projections of inner fears and anxieties about Jean's problematic sexual identity. Heterosexual love as experienced in the relationship with an increasingly demanding Laura becomes a threat to his freedom and independence. Homosexuality as experienced in his relationship with Samy hints at the possibility of a normally forbidden feminized masculinity which the heterosexual relationship represented in this film does not allow: Jean is able to treat the wayward Samy with almost maternal protective tenderness, whereas his reaction to Laura's jealousy is to withdraw himself from her. However, both relationships in their different ways come to constitute a threat to Jean's need for control, which is a key structuring element of the film, whether he is shown maintaining his body in the fight against AIDS; zapping around the city in his red, phallic sports car; or making films which enable him to control and manipulate others. Jean's need for control is further dramatized through misogynist triangular configurations which allow him to 'win out' over a female figure, e.g. making fun of Laura's mother, humiliating Marianne, allowing Laura and former girlfriend Karine to fight over him, or rejecting Laura in favour of Samy. There is an obvious parallel here, too, with Collard's own controlling role as director, for he claims at times to have subjected his cast to unrehearsed improvisations in order to achieve his effects, as in the scene when Jean challenges his mother (Claude

Winter) to account for her lack of physical affection towards him as a child.

However, if the film displaces anxieties about Jean's sexuality onto the hystericized bodies of the gendered and ethnic Other (Laura and Samy respectively), and sustains Jean's overall position of control through a variety of other narrative and audiovisual strategies, Jean's fundamentally incoherent position as subject is further troubled (and with it, the positioning of the spectator) by the scenes of 'savage nights' which give the film its title. At three key moments in the narrative (just before he initiates the relationship with Laura, just after Laura decides to go away from him for a while, and during Laura's telephone persecution of him), Jean seeks oblivion through sexual gratification with groups of anonymous men beneath the arches beside the Seine. These scenes are certainly ambiguous, and can lend themselves to readings which endorse the view of homosexuality as deviant and perverse. For Anne de Gasperi, they represent 'the descent into hell' (Gasperi 1992), an image endorsed by Brigitte Rollet, who refers to the 'mass of men' meeting for 'furtive and sordid encounters in dark places' (Rollet 1994). The scenes clearly inspired the critics to search for expressive descriptions. For Serge Toubiana, 'men congregate [the French 's'agglutinent' is considerably more expressive], their bodies forming a tight, silent cluster or mêlée' (Toubiana 1992: 25). For a disappointed, and almost untranslatable *Libération*, they are 'operatic-operettish dives into queer muck, with their choreography of gay rutting between priests of the flesh' ('plongées opéra-pérette dans la bouse pédé, avec son lot de chorégraphie, du rut gay entre sulpiciers de la chair') (Seguret 1992: 38).

Certainly these scenes are encoded differently from the rest of the film, but it is less obvious that they need necessarily be read as 'hellish'. Collard himself wanted to avoid them being just scandalous or poetically sordid ('l'épate-bourgeois et la poésie de pissotière'; Collard 1992: 39), and describes the setting as 'a space of freedom, a place where there are no laws, no hierarchies, no power, where people can mix anonymously and let themselves go' (Lavoignat 1992: 119). Even if the *mise-en-scène* chosen as a backdrop to group homosexual sex is literally an 'underground' nighttime setting, out of sight of the world of normative bourgeois morality, the scenes are also marked out reverently through the lack of dialogue, the expressive lighting (much of the frame is in shadow and faces are picked out in pools of light), and the 'high art' music track which accompanies the first two scenes—first, a homage to Genet through a chorale-like rendering of 'Le Condamné à mort' by Marc Ogeret, then, a poignant violin solo. Instead of the fast cutting of much of the rest of the film, the camera positions the spectator to share Jean's search for pleasure through the use of slow panning shots around the churchlike space, and a hand-held camera which seems to want to join in the group sexual encounters in which Jean can abandon himself to desire. The scenes quite specifically avoid any explicit visualization of male genitals, acts of penetration, or hints of unsafe sex (and furthermore Jean takes care to inform his straight male friend—and thereby the viewing audience—that these encounters take the form of five-minute handjobs with no risks). Instead, the *mise-en-scène* of a group of men kissing and caressing provides a representation of an almost tender sexuality which can certainly be seen as 'feminine'. Indeed, the last of these scenes, when Jean lies down and asks to be urinated on, not only produces pleasure, as Jean surrenders his role as subject, but ends on touching and smiling between the three men involved, which suggests mutual affection and understanding. Not only are the scenes of group homosexual sex not necessarily to be read as sordid, they also challenge the common association between promiscuous homosexual sex and death. The spectator/voyeur is invited to experience these brief twilight encounters as both thrilling and safe, anonymous and affectionate, and by so doing *Les Nuits fauves* is at least potentially open to a reading which undermines the ideological supremacy of both the couple (heterosexual or gay) and normative phallic masculinity.

The scenes in which Jean is 'unmanned' are deliberately contrasted with the scene in which Jean makes love to Laura by day under the same arches, now empty and bare. This moment is introduced via a panning shot from an elderly couple dancing on a *bateau-mouche* amid a group of senior citizens, to the sound of Damia singing 'Tu ne sais pas aimer'. The sex act centres on the (unseen) thrusting penis, and Laura's sexual pleasure is inseparable from her commitment to the couple: 'Nothing will ever be able to take this away from us. It's above the law.' However, Laura may well be misreading the situation, and since Jean's facial expression is not shown, the spectator is invited to reflect on the multiple reactions such a moment might produce in him, since the pleasure of being the controlling partner in the committed heterosexual couple must inevitably be offset against the heady pleasures of freedom and self-abnegation represented by 'les nuits fauves'.

So, both homosexuality and heterosexuality are represented ambiguously in this film, and Jean's difficulty in making a choice between them is not surprising. What is perhaps surprising is that the film should have been read as so definitively pointing the way to transcendence through heterosexuality, since it ends, rather awkwardly, with Jean actually driving away from making any such choice. Facing the ocean near the lighthouse at Cape St Vincent (the most westerly point of Portugal and Europe), a transcendent Christ-like figure still clad in a skimpy T-shirt which shows off his HIV-positive but as yet undefeated body, Jean reaches a moment of pantheistic acceptance of his mortal human condition. Whereas, at the beginning of the narrative, his contact with the world and with others is through the intermediary of the video camera ('like an American tourist'), at the end he has broken through to a clearer vision, in which he feels at one with the world, saying 'I am in life' ('Je suis dans la vie'). But the price for such a vision is utter solitude. For even though the spectator hears Jean's voice on the soundtrack murmuring 'I love you' after a phone call to Laura, the phrase is significantly accompanied only by images of Jean himself. Laura is visually absent from the entire final sequence, and these words are not spoken directly to her (or to anyone else). Instead of moving beyond narcissism in order to engage in the world around him, as Cléo, threatened by cancer, does in *Cléo de 5 à 7* (Varda, 1961), the ending of *Les Nuits fauves* works primarily to confirm Jean's solipsism and need for phallic mastery. Jean turns to the sun setting over the ocean as the site of his final exercise of control. The sun goes down, only to rise again a few shots later from the same place, a magical resurr/erection produced by Collard's godlike ability as director to speed up and reverse the motion of the film. In fantasy, Collard as Jean is able to challenge the natural order and reassert his phallic masculinity in a scene which constitutes a stirring denial of death at the same time as it points to its inevitability.

Les Nuits fauves, then, maintains its ambivalent balancing act between heterosexuality and homosexuality by ducking out of making a positive commitment to either one or the other or both, and finally investing in Jean's solipsistic narcissism. Such a trajectory may be read as a positive reworking of the AIDS narrative, since it foregrounds Jean as heroic subject rather than as perverse object or passive victim. However, it is less constructive as a challenge to dominant hierarchies of sexual relations, since it fails to acknowledge the constructedness of gendered and sexual identities. In terms of its representation of women, for example, *Les Nuits fauves* repeats the familiar Gallic pattern according to which *amour fou* deprives a sexually independent young woman of her autonomy, and punishes her by rendering her dysfunctional: first, hysterical and mad, then silent and absent. The film does not explore femininity as embodied by women as a site of flexibility and change. There are no lesbian or female bisexual characters in Jean's male-centred world, and child-woman Laura represents a fixed patriarchal notion of what women want, namely subordination within the monogamous heterosexual relationship; her hysterical jealousy when she does not get it becomes a palpable threat to Jean's independence and lifestyle. If the film posits normative heterosexuality as an abstract ideal, then, it also shows the undesirability of the actual heterosexual couple and is unable to offer other successful models of heterosexual relationships. (Heterosexuality is shown at its most grotesque in the scenes in the brothel frequented by Samy and his rugby-club friends, and elsewhere produces fragmented families in which fathers are absent or silent, and mothers unable to give their children the support they need.)

In its representation of homosexuality, *Les Nuits fauves* is equally ambiguous. Although the 'savage' night scenes of group sex among consenting males can be read as positively subversive in their ritual celebration of feminized masculinity and in their demonstration that 'safe sex' and homosexual promiscuity are not incompatible, they are carefully separated out from the rest of the narrative and rather hastily closed over. In this, the film differs markedly from the novel, which comes to a close with Jean's realization that he has not left 'les nuits fauves' behind: 'as I go towards that point, an increasingly precise smell fills the air. A smell of urine which the strong wind cannot disperse. It is the smell of savage nights' (Collard 1993: 253). However, apart from Jean himself, there are no positive characterizations of individual homosexuals in the film. Although the relationship with Samy can be seen to demonstrate the continuity between male bonding and male homosexuality which is normally feared and repudiated, Samy's discovery of pleasure in sex with men comes to be pathologized, while other homosexual characters are merely comic stereotypes, like the camp 'travelo' who croons 'Mon homme' to Jean in the local bar and the masochistic M. André who likes to be beaten up by the men who want to use the brothel he runs.

Finally, then, any challenge that *Les Nuits fauves* is able to offer to normative convictions about AIDS and the nature of sexual identity and preference depends on the successful positioning of the audience with the character of Jean, as played by Collard. However, the fact that the film centres on Jean's troubled subjectivity has the effect of marginalizing the subjectivities of the sexual and ethnic Other (and in the process disengaging audiences who do not want to be drawn into Jean's narcissistic male-centred dilemma). *Les Nuits fauves* invites the audience to share Jean's appetite for life, his active sexuality, and his revolt against AIDS, including his refusal to feel guilt about or attribute blame for his disease. In the process, it also opens up a space for a more fluid conception of male sexuality. But it does so without challenging the hierarchical assignment of sexual and ethnic difference. The film's ultimate denial of incoherence and recuperation of a transcendental phallic masculine identity for its central protagonist can afford few pleasures for those who would like to see a more radical problematizing of gender and sexual identity.

Notes

This chapter was originally given as a paper at the conference of the Society of French Studies, Hull 1995.

11

Unruly Woman? Josiane Balasko, French Comedy, and *Gazon maudit* (Balasko, 1995)

BRIGITTE ROLLET

COMEDY, as Kathleen Rowe has recently pointed out, has for a long time been ignored by feminist film criticism. Only recently have American feminists, such as Tania Modleski amongst others, viewed comedy with different eyes and from different perspectives. When one considers Irigaray's rhetorical question which opens Rowe's book: 'Isn't laughter the first form of liberation from a secular oppression?' (Rowe 1995: 1), one wonders why laughter, be it transgressive or not, has been neglected for so long. My aim in this chapter is to consider French comedies made by one of the most successful female directors of such a genre, Josiane Balasko, in order to assess their level of 'transgressiveness'.[1] Keeping in mind that comedy is as gendered as laughter, I shall first briefly examine the evolution of a genre which was until recently a male-only cinematographic space. I shall then consider whether Balasko's work has modified the intrinsic content of comedy and/or the inherent mechanism of the joke.

In France, comedy is probably the oldest and the most popular cinematographic genre. It has also been for a very long period an almost exclusively male preserve, a feature it shares with the thriller, espionage films, and more recently heritage films,[2] to name the other genres most favoured by French audiences over the last fifty years. More than a century after the birth of the cinema, and at a time when French cinema-goers tend to prefer films from the United States, French comedies (and since the mid-1980s French heritage films) seem to remain one of the rare cinematographic genres able to attract not only French but also foreign audiences. A significant change in the last twenty-five years has been women's input to the genre. Although this aspect should not be overrated (comedy is still only favoured by a handful of female directors), it is worth noting that these comedies have often attracted attention (from both audiences and critics) that few 'women's films' had received before. Is this due to their success both in France (for example, Serreau with *Trois hommes et un couffin* (1985) is the only woman in the top twenty French comedies from 1958 onwards with 10 million spectators, and Balasko with *Gazon maudit* (1995) is the second woman in the top fifty with 4 million) and abroad (with the American remake of *Trois hommes et un couffin*)? Is it due to their gender? Or to the combination of both their success and their gender? It is true to say that women's participation and contribution to the genre before 1985, the date of *Trois hommes et un couffin*, was limited, although there were as many comedies before 1985 as after. Nina Companeez, Dolores Grassian, and Nelly Kaplan made comedies during the early 1970s, casting major stars of the time: Brigitte Bardot for Companeez in 1973, or Annie Girardot with Grassian in 1977. The chronic absence of women making film comedies from film encyclopedias and dictionaries of films (the Larousse, for example, does not mention Andrée Feix, Dolores Grassian, or Nina Companeez) reinforces the quasi-invisibility of women film-makers in the history of French cinema overall. The recent special issue of *CinémAction* devoted to film comedy does not often refer to women, except when male actors perform female roles. The comedies made by women since the 1970s are only briefly mentioned. It is as if the expression 'funny women' were considered an oxymoron, at least before the explosion of the *comique au féminin* originating in 1970s *café-théâtre*.

The fact that women could be funny was not new, however. There is the obvious example of the successful career in the second half of the nineteenth century of a female cabaret artist such as Thérésa (born Emma Valadon, 1837–1913). An indirect mother (or grandmother) of what French magazines refer to nowadays as *les marrantes*, Thérésa was in the 1860s, and according to Elisabeth Pillet, 'the first star of café-concert' (Pillet 1995: 29). Using her body in ways which did not conform to the criteria of the period for beauty and femininity, Thérésa displayed an early stage version of the carnivalesque typical of the female comedians of the 1970s. Pillet's comment that 'it is as if, in the limited space of the café

concert the comic show of women behaving as freely as men, func-
tioned as a catharsis' (Pillet 1995: 33) seems to reinforce this view.
What is interesting, however, is the fact that, unlike their male
counterparts, who in the early days of the French cinema came
from the circus and the music hall, women did not make it onto the
screen. Except for Alice Guy and Andrée Feix (the latter's name and
films having long been ignored and/or forgotten), women film-
makers never really succeeded in making comedies, at least during
the first seventy years of cinema. Could this be due to the extreme
conservatism of French comedy until the early 1970s, and therefore
to the difficulty for such 'unruly' women to succeed with what
were seen as sexual and social transgressions? Or could it simply be
explained by the inner mechanism of the joke and of humour overall?

It is accepted that 'comedy helps maintain the subordination of
some social (and sexual) groups through ridicule and reductive
"typing" ' (Kuhn 1990: 94). According to Freud, the joke needs
three participants in order to work: the joker (male), his victim
(female), and an accomplice (male). For the joke to achieve its aim,
it has to be shared by the two men at the expense of the woman, as
they bond together: 'The joke does not exist until the laughter of
the second man confirms it' (Rowe 1995: 68). What then are
women's possibilities for creating humour and laughter when most
of the traditional jokes are aimed at them, when they are more
often than not the butt of the joke and thus usually laughed at? In
his well-known essay on laughter, Bergson underlines the fact that
the worst enemy of laughter is feeling and that comedy needs what
he calls 'a temporary anaesthesia of emotion' (Bergson 1940: 4).
Although he is referring to the mechanism of the joke, the same
could be said of the reception of the joke as far as female spectators are concerned. As women in comedies are the objects and not
the subjects of the joke (just as they are more often than not the
objects and not the subjects of the gaze), 'women can engage only
through a masochistic identification with the female victim or a
transvestite identification with the male agents' (Rowe 1995: 6; she
is summarizing Doane's view). This point, as shown by feminists
from Mulvey onwards, is—and has always been—valid for all the
other cinematographic genres. The choice is consequently limited
for women directors or comedians willing to make comedies: they
can laugh either at themselves (which is what most of *café-théâtre*

actresses did in the 1970s), or at other women, which for Rowe means 'to occupy the "male" position' (Rowe 1995: 69). The mechanism of the joke can be and was indeed reversed by many *café-théâtre* female comedians such as Les Trois Jeanne and Marianne Sergent, who began to laugh at men. For Rowe, comic genres, when reappropriated by women, can be used to express a feeling which women have very little opportunity to articulate as men do: anger. For Ruby Rich in her definition of what she calls the Medusan film, comedy has 'a revolutionary potential as a deflator of the patriarchal order and an extraordinary leveler and reinventor of dramatic structure' (Rich 1985: 353). That reappropriation occurred most forcefully in and around May 1968 with the advent of *café-théâtre*.

May 1968 had a tremendous impact on all aspects of French society. Regarding the French cinema, it meant greater access to the other side of the camera for women. Although one should not forget that this participation of female film-makers was initially quite limited, the contrast with the previous decade is marked. What changed in and after May 1968 was a new conception of the genre, and the introduction of women (either as comedians or as directors) at the other 'end' of the joke. The place among others where a form of radical protest relying heavily on humour was to be found was in the *café-théâtres* which proliferated before, during, and after May 1968. The emphasis here will not be on a comparison between the cinema and the *café-théâtre* (although many stage events were later made into films), but rather on the close connections between the two means of expression in the French context, and on the way women used their one-woman show to voice their numerous and varied demands.

Café-théâtre was characterized by subversion and transgression, usually involving caricature of the French bourgeoisie. *Café-théâtre* gave comediennes the opportunity to express themselves on taboo subjects. According to Da Costa 'if the fashion was for feminism, the *café-théâtres* would present "feminine" plays . . . The themes of the moment were women's liberation, denunciations of their "alienation", their pregnancies, their menstruations, their orgasms, abortion, birth control' (Da Costa 1978: 199). The influence of satirical publications like *Charlie-Hebdo* or *Hara-Kiri* was obvious and strong in both tone and theme. In other words, what was being expressed on the stages of the Café de la Gare and the Splendid, to mention only two of them, is strongly reminiscent of carnival and of carnivalesque laughter, described by Bakhtin as 'a festive laughter [and] the laughter of all the people' (Bakhtin 1968: 11–12). *Café-théâtre* actors of both sexes rediscovered 'grotesque realism' through the presentation of the body and its physiological functions. Other features of Bakhtinian carnival characterize this women's humour: 'the celebration of the grotesque, excessive body, and of the "material bodily lower stratum", the valorization of the obscene and of "market-place" speech in language [and the] rejection of social decorum and politeness' (Stam 1989: 94). *Café-théâtre* became a space not only where women frequently staged their one-woman shows based on their own scripts, but also where they could defy an established order. The transgression was both sexual and social. Women of more ordinary physique were to occupy a new space, first of all on the stage, and sometimes on the big screen, since several of the plays mounted by Le Splendid became films. Speaking out was to acquire a new meaning here. Comediennes from the *café-théâtre* were using their bodies and the physiological functions associated with them as the very subject matter of their shows. This can be seen in Balasko's work.

Josiane Balasko (born in 1950) started her career in the early 1970s in the Café de la Gare, where she played alongside Coluche, Michel Blanc, and Gérard Jugnot. In 1976, she joined the Théâtre du Splendid, whose popularity grew fast in the 1970s, first on stage and later in films throughout the 1980s as the first film adaptation of one of their plays, *Le Père Noël est une ordure*, directed by Jean-Marie Poiré, became a cult film in France, marking the beginning of the troupe's successful cinematographic career. As with many French actresses of the time, including her contemporary Coline Serreau, Balasko's dissatisfaction with the female parts written mainly by male scriptwriters led her to start writing her own scripts. After playing the leading female part in Poiré's comedy *Les Petits Câlins* (1978), she wrote the script and dialogues of his next film *Les Hommes préfèrent les grosses* (1981), where she played the lead role. She directed her first comedy *Sacs de nœuds* in 1985. Although the film was not as successful as the other comedy made by another female director the same year (Serreau's *Trois hommes et un couffin*), Balasko continued her theatrical and cinematographic career both as actress and as director. Ten years after her first attempt behind the camera, she directed and played one of the two female leads (together with the Spanish star Victoria Abril) in her most successful comedy so far, *Gazon maudit*. Very different from Serreau's sometimes more timid and consensual attempts to counterbalance male comedies and humour, Josiane Balasko brought to the genre all the disrespect, crudeness, and excess inherited from the *café-théâtre* tradition which she skilfully integrated into the female-unfriendly and more traditionally male vaudeville.

The vaudeville tradition in French culture, on both stage and screen, is such that one can wonder whether there is any alternative for women film-makers. Deriving from the *théâtre de boulevard*, the French vaudeville on the screen was until recently, like its cousin on stage, a men-only genre (although Andrée Feix, with the help of Solange Bussi-Terac who wrote the scripts, did make two vaudevilles after the war: *Il suffit d'une fois*, 1946, and *Capitaine Blomet*, 1947). It is true to say that Labiche and Feydeau, to name two of the most famous nineteenth-century dramatists whose plays have been widely adapted for the screen, specialized in a form which fostered the accepted misogyny of French society. Sacha Guitry (1885–1957), a writer and director of such vaudevilles, epitomizes, amongst others, this penchant. Guitry is often seen as the embodiment of a particular type of Frenchman, with a debonnaire attitude to women. This makes the recent film of his play (and remake of his film) *Quadrille* (1997) by the female actress-director Valérie Lemercier even more surprising in so far as it could suggest that the cultural—male—heritage of the genre is endorsed by women themselves.

However, the first ever lesbian comedy, *Gazon maudit*, offers an alternative, subverted vaudeville which introduces the first cuckold in the history of French cinema whose rival is a woman. Playing the part of the lesbian troublemaker, Balasko transgresses social and sexual taboos and places the audience on her side. The film tells the story of Marijo (Balasko), a lesbian on holiday in the south of France who, when her car breaks down, meets Loli (Victoria Abril), the Spanish wife of a womanizer and homophobic estate agent. A love affair starts between the two women to the despair of the 'cuckolded' husband. After Loli's discovery of her husband's multiple infidelities, she decides to install Marijo in her house and bed. A rota system is established, with Loli sharing the week between her husband and her mistress, save for Sundays when

'everyone takes a rest'. Following a jealous outburst by Loli, triggered by the unexpected arrival of Marijo's ex-girlfriend (skilfully
exploited by Loli's husband Laurent), the devastated Marijo leaves
on condition that Laurent impregnate her. Learning about Marijo's
pregnancy a few months later, Loli and Laurent find Marijo in
Paris in the lesbian disco where she works. The shock of the meeting prompts the delivery. The final shots show Marijo and Loli in
bed with the baby between them, while Laurent, after kissing his
daughter good bye, meets the handsome Spanish landlord of the
house he is intending to buy for his larger family.

   Although the film's ending with the homophobic husband being
seduced by the attractive Spaniard undermines by its lack of realism the subversive charge of the film, it recreates a form of utopia
reminiscent of the 1970s, but whose added ingredients are the radi-
calism and subversion typical of the *café-théâtre* tradition.
Balasko's in-your-face humour (in both the concrete and figurative
sense, as she head-butts Laurent during the film after he punches
her) gives women the opportunity to laugh at men. This does not
mean, however, that a female audience's identification with her
character is unproblematic. She epitomizes in the film a social and
sexual 'Other', both by being a lesbian and by appearing to come
from a different social background from both Loli and Laurent.
Without going as far as saying that she represents a 'third gender',
she does, however, play with her gender and her sexual identity to
create laughter, and makes jokes where she is both object and
subject. For example, at the restaurant with Loli, her husband
Laurent, and his male friend, she is dressed in a very masculine suit,
and at one point leaves the table saying gruffly and, given her dress,
incongruously: 'I am going to powder my nose', before adding 'in
other words, I am going to go and have a piss'. We seem to be in a
no man/no woman's land.

   This kind of reversal applies not only to women in the film, but
also to men, as Balasko reverses the traditional roles within joke-
making, giving other women the power to use it as a weapon.
During the same dinner, after Marijo/Balasko goes to the toilet,
Laurent and his male friend continue to make jokes about gays.
Loli reverses the situation by asking them when they will sleep
together. Both men stop laughing, reacting badly to what she justifies as a joke, using the arguments and words they had previously
used to talk about lesbians. Laurent's final word is that 'it is vulgar

when said by a woman', which is no doubt what a part of the audience thinks of Marijo/Balasko's use of sometimes strong language. By demonstrating the men's double standards, Balasko places herself 'beyond' gender as far as humour is concerned. Despite her use of language to create humour, Balasko's unruliness is not only linguistic, since the film also relies on more basic comic ingredients such as slapstick and situation comedy, and has strong satiric edges by virtue of the lead actors, Victoria Abril and Alain Chabat, who are associated with the 'outrageous' Spanish director Almodóvar and the satirical television programme *Les Nuls* respectively.

Both actors connote the sarcasm and provocation reminiscent of the 1970s. This is not the only element inherited from the post-May 1968 period.The other interesting aspect of Balasko's humour is the way she has always managed to integrate a personal feminist agenda in her films and plays. As Balasko herself puts it, 'what I do for the image of women of the stage is something much more important than any speeches' (quoted by Lejeune 1987: 78). The generally positive reviews of the film published in the only French lesbian monthly publication *Lesbia* show that far from feeling laughed at and denigrated in the film, *Lesbia*'s journalists felt the director's sympathy, despite the way Marijo is heavily stereotyped as a butch. It was generally felt that between the fickle Loli and the serial womanizer Laurent, Marijo was the only trustworthy character. Both straight and gay female audiences reacted positively to her 'having a go' at men, even if they did not necessarily agree with the means used to achieve it, such as strong language and 'violent' behaviour. Laughter in Balasko's films and plays is indeed a form of liberation and she regularly emphasizes that provocation and transgression are part of the job by declaring on the one hand that 'What I like . . . is to take clichés and archetypes and demolish them', and on the other that 'I am accused of vulgarity. It's true that I have a provocative presence which upsets people' (quoted by Lejeune 1987: 78).

This provocation can also be found, although to a lesser degree, in Balasko's *Un grand cri d'amour* (1998), an adaptation of her eponymous play which ran successfully in Paris in 1996–7. The play tells the story of the making of another play supposedly written by an American playwright and also entitled *Un grand cri d'amour*. After the departure of the female star planned for the role, the producer asks Gigi Ortega (Balasko), a flamboyant has-been and former alcoholic actress, to replace her. Her male partner, Hugo Martial (Richard Berry, her brother-in-law in real life, who acted the same role in the play), was her former partner in life and on stage ten years earlier when they were both at the peak of their career. Time has passed and the relationship between the two has turned sour. The two actors, who, the audience is told, have previously performed Who's afraid of Virginia Woolf?, are violently confrontational. Unlike Gazon maudit, where the male protagonist Laurent was depicted as a despicable character, Hugo and Gigi appear more 'equal'. The contrast, as in Gazon maudit, relies more on the physical contrast between the two. Gigi Ortega/Balasko, appearing in the first scene heavily made up, with a leopard top, a red leather mini-skirt, gaudy jewellery, and carrying a small dog, epitomizes another form of provocation and outrage which is reinforced here by the sobriety of her partner's clothing and behaviour. This is not the first time that Balasko has played with her physical appearance, and her 'Madonne des pétasses' (the Madonna of the tarts), as she was dubbed by critics (quoted in Piazzo 1998: 13), is as credible as the butch Marijo. Her character also indirectly expresses Balasko's standing joke in interviews, that whatever her looks, she always ends up in bed with the sexiest men (Isaak de Bankolé, Daniel Auteuil, Christophe Lambert, and Richard Berry).

Un grand cri d'amour was indirectly publicized by 'Nom de code: Josiane Balasko', a two-hour long programme during prime time entirely devoted to Balasko, broadcast on TF1 (the private channel which has co-produced Balasko's latest films) on Sunday, 4 January 1998, a few days before the film was released. The guests included all the comedians of the former Troupe du Splendid, together with stand-up comedians such as Pierre Palmade and Muriel Robin. Paradoxically, given the excess and provocation which characterized the Splendid, Balasko and her friends were very well behaved, in their manners as well as their speech, suggesting that TF1, whose managers like to present the channel as a 'family channel', had decided to bowdlerize Balasko. However, Balasko used the platform to be more 'political', exploiting the presence of some singers to make 'committed' statements, underlining with one singer of the boys' band 2 Be 3 her similar foreign origin (she was born Balaskovic), and later alluding with the black rap singer MC Solar to the events surrounding the February 1997 call for civil disobedience (see the Introduction to this volume).

I would like to suggest in conclusion that, instead of referring to 'national humour', one could also speak of 'gendered humour'. Although it is no doubt true that the French do not necessarily laugh at the same thing or in the same way as other nationalities, there seems to be more of a consensus as to who laughs and at whom. Balasko and her equivalents in other cultures (such as Roseanne in the USA, or Jo Brand in the UK) are the exception, not the rule. Balasko demonstrates that there is a possible reappropriation of joke-making by women. She shows a way of reconsidering gender in a French society where feminism is seen by the vast majority of people as a thing of the past. Despite a number of French comedies by female directors in the 1990s,[3] Balasko is probably the only one who almost systematically destroys the boundaries of the socially and sexually accepted and acceptable behaviours. By using her sometimes 'grotesque body', in the Bakhtinian sense of the word, and by transgressing the norms of femininity, she could be seen as a worthy heir to Thérésa, an earlier unruly woman.

Notes

The author acknowledges the support of the British Academy for the writing of this chapter.

1. For a fuller exploration of women and comedy in France, see Rollet 1998.
2. The release in 1997 of two heritage films directed by women, *Artémisia* (Agnès Ferlet) and *Marquise* (Vera Belmont), could be seen as a sign that the genre is becoming more accessible for women.
3. *Le Jour des rois*, 1990, Marie-Claude Treilhou; *Ma Vie est un enfer*, 1991, Josiane Balasko; *La Crise*, 1992, Coline Serreau; *Elles ne pensent qu'à ça*, 1993, Charlotte Dubreuil; *Pas très catholique*, 1994, Tonie Marshall; *Personne ne m'aime*, 1994, Marion Vernoux; *Gazon maudit*, 1995, Josiane Balasko; *Les Fabuleuses Aventures de Madame Petlet*, 1995, Camille de Casabianca; *Les Gens normaux n'ont rien d'exceptionnel*, 1995, Laurence Ferreira-Barbosa; *La Belle verte*, 1996, Coline Serreau; *Romaine*, 1997, Agnès Obadia; *J'ai horreur de l'amour*, 1997, Laurence Ferreira-Barbosa; *Rien à foutre d'aimer*, 1997, Dominique Giacobbi; *Quadrille*, 1997, Valérie Lemercier; *Un grand cri d'amour*, 1998, Josiane Balasko; *La Nouvelle Ève*, 1999, Catherine Corsini; *Vénus beauté (Institut)*, 1999, Tonie Marshall; *Le derrière*, 1999, Valérie Lemercier.

12

Sleepless in Paris: *J'ai pas sommeil* (Denis, 1993)

CYNTHIA MARKER

CLAIRE DENIS'S *J'ai pas sommeil* revisits cultural conflicts alluded to in her earlier films: *Chocolat* (1988), the much acclaimed and loosely autobiographical story of a young French girl growing up in colonial Africa, and *S'en fout la mort* (1990), about the struggles of two immigrants, one West Indian, the other African, in Paris. Equally preoccupied with issues of race and identity, Denis's third feature film was inspired by the infamous 'Paulin Affair' which exploded in the French press in 1987 when two young Caribbean immigrants, Thierry Paulin (dubbed the 'granny killer' by the French tabloids) and his gay lover Jean-Thierry Mathurin, were arrested for robbing, torturing, and murdering more than twenty elderly women over the course of two years in Paris's peripheral eighteenth *arrondissement*. Instead of exploiting the sensationalistic appeal of this event, *J'ai pas sommeil* examines racial tensions that the Paulin murders brought to light in a nation increasingly divided over rising immigration quotas. Though Denis and her co-screenwriter Jean-Pôl Fargeau reset the story in 1990s France, the film's paranoid atmosphere summons up the racist campaign of the extreme Right leader Jean-Marie Le Pen, whose slogan, 'Let's keep France for the French' ('La France aux Français') won his National Front party a significant percentage of the vote in legislative elections the year after the Paulin scandal erupted. *J'ai pas sommeil* investigates the trajectory of three marginalized individuals forced to confront this mood of cultural paranoia. Through tactics of mimicry and masquerade, the protagonists combat prejudices inspired by a fear of cultural difference with regard to representations of the 'Other'. In the transformation of a true crime story (*un fait divers*) into a film noir, the filmmakers tap into a deep-seated restlessness in contemporary France.

The thematic restlessness expressed in the film's title is reinforced by stylistic and generic incongruities that attempt to subvert race and gender stereotypes. Abandoning a facile concept of 'Otherness' as merely the binary opposite of dominant cultural norms, *J'ai pas sommeil* promotes a complex investigation of ambivalent, and even indecipherable, postcolonial identities.

For Denis, who has co-written all of her feature films with Fargeau, story is intimately tied to visual technique and character development is central to the film's rhythm and pace (Lippy 1997: 85). The story of the serial killer, named Camille in the film and played by Richard Courcet, is combined with subplots of two other characters: Daïga (Katherina Golubeva), a young Lithuanian woman who comes to Paris with aspirations for an acting career, and Camille's brother Théo (Alex Descas), who plans to return with his son to his native Martinique over the objections of the child's mother, Mona (Béatrice Dalle). The perspectives of the film's immigrant protagonists overlap when Daïga starts cleaning rooms at a hotel owned by a friend (Ninon, energetically performed by Line Renaud) of her Russian aunt and crosses the path of Camille and his lover, regular patrons of the hotel. The complex representations of the Other in *J'ai pas sommeil* are saddled with Denis's interest in investigating the mixture of depravity and humanity in the make-up of the serial killer (Jousse and Strauss 1994: 27) in a screenplay which defies current trends of 'political correctness'. Making no apologies for the disturbing subject matter of her film, the director not only refuses to comply with the doctrine of 'politically correct' but also tries to disarm what she perceives as its 'reverse racism':

[The word 'correct'] has disturbed me for some time now because of the expression 'politically correct' or 'politically incorrect', which was constantly presented in the idea for this movie. I felt it was impossible to relate to this idea though questions were inevitably raised about this character who kills more than twenty old ladies, the most fragile members of society next to children, [this man] who is black, gay, and, one suspects, a drug addict (*vaguement drogué*). The absolute opposite of how black characters should be represented in films according to the tenets of 'politically correct'. . . .

It was best to completely rid the film of this idea. For me, it's just a corollary of racism. (Jousse and Strauss 1994: 27–8)

With respect to offended reactions to *S'en fout la mort* upon its release in the United States, Denis adds:

I think that we live in a society that is almost more backward than 1965, at the time of Malcolm X's death, when things were expressed with violence and rage, when words were pronounced. The strong emphasis on language today (*Le côté contenu, plus hurlé d'aujourd'hui*) gives me the odd impression that we're moving backward. I think it's important for people to be able to scream, yell in response to suffering, but the rough edges have been smoothed over with this idea of 'correct'. (Jousse and Strauss 1994: 28)

Resisting the tendency to 'smooth over' racial tensions, *J'ai pas sommeil* reintroduces the issue of violence in the construction of the marginalized Other. Departing from the typically surprised reaction of an arrested murderer's family and friends—captured in the film at the moment when Ninon says of Camille and Raphaël, 'They're lovely boys, lovely' ('Ils sont gentils, mais gentils!')—the script investigates disorienting reversals of behaviour in characters who defy one-dimensional psychological portraits. Dismantling binary oppositions that typify film noir archetypes, Denis's protagonists are both gentle and violent, kind and calculating, engaging to varying degrees in a masquerade which complicates a facile labelling of their identities.

In this respect, Camille's passion for cross-dressing is a clear inversion of gender stereotypes (Butler 1990), and the frank portrayal of his homosexuality warrants consideration of Denis's film as a significant 'queer text' of contemporary French cinema. So many moments point to Camille's infatuation with disguise: the zooms and slow pans on his black fingernail polish, fishnet hose, and tight-fitting leather outfits, the modelling photos Daïga finds of a nude Camille in a variety of sexy costumes and seductive poses, the professional portrait Camille gives his mother for her birthday in a scene suggesting the ironic inability of the parent to identify the monster in her own son. The contrast of Camille's violence and kindness is presented when he first appears chasing and beating up his lover in a Parisian street before being pictured, moments later, in a tender shot with his young nephew in Théo's apartment.

Equally unsettling is the association of Camille's violence and sexuality. His most seductive scene takes place in a gay nightclub when he dances in a low-cut, black velvet dress against deep blue neon lights and lipsyncs the highly synthesized song playing in the background while a row of men watch in silence. Interestingly, Denis's direction for Richard Courcet was to appear both seductive and menacing. Camille's character maintains this masquerade throughout the film as he is alternately violent with his lover and seductive in the nightclub, generous with his family and the maids at Ninon's hotel and monstrous in the emotionless and ritualistic murder of his elderly victims. The shadows of Camille's monstrosity are powerfully illustrated during a love scene with his accomplice Raphaël which evokes simultaneously a loving tenderness and a fearful loathing. Raphaël is submissively reclined on his back on the hotel bed, whimpering that he wants to go away, and avoiding looking in the eyes of his oppressor. Meanwhile, Camille sits over his lover, gently caressing him as a slowly advancing camera travels around their intertwined, softly lit bodies. With his face approaching Raphaël's and hidden from the camera, Camille whispers threateningly, 'You can't get rid of me. You know that?'

Echoing the complexity of Camille's character, Daïga is presented as simultaneously naive and tough. Naive for believing the overtures of the French theatre director Abel who enticed her to Paris with promises of an acting career, she unemotionally confronts the economic and cultural adversities of her move to Paris, eventually taking revenge on Abel by hunting him down in a traffic jam and repeatedly ramming into the back of his car. Her natural beauty in contrast with her 'tomboy' attire (jogging pants, oversized shirt, and dingy jacket) offers an androgynous image that reverses that of the sexy, seductive Camille as cross-dresser. In addition, her Lithuanian heritage, repeatedly referenced in a subplot that involves her aunt's vain attempts to integrate her niece into the immigrant Russian community in Paris, suggests the precarious and irreducible quality of Daïga's character. In her resistance to the role of Other both French society and her compatriots attempt to prescribe, Daïga undermines the marginalized status of 'female immigrant'. Refusing to submit to the will of those who would like to tame or control her, she becomes a symbol of hope and vitality for the burgeoning multicultural identities of newly formed nations in the aftermath of the USSR's dissolution.

In the film's opening sequence, the heroine immediately rebels against the stereotype of the vulnerable foreign woman male characters try to impose on her. In the minutes following the opening titles, she is stared at by two men driving beside her with a dog in their back seat, insulted by a café owner for not speaking French, and harassed by two police officers for her Lithuanian licence plates. In these instances, the idea of not speaking the language is central to the complexity of her character. Channelling an inability to communicate into a refusal to succumb to an objectifying gaze, she transforms an initially perceived linguistic weakness into a culturally defiant act. Through subversive mimicry, Daïga returns the oppressive male gaze literally by staring back at the men in the car and symbolically by cursing at the policemen in her native Lithuanian, replacing the burden of incomprehension on those who mock her and refusing to speak their language. The most powerful sign of her resistance to sexist stereotypes comes when she is walking through a sex shop district at night and runs into a porn theatre to escape the overtures of a passer-by. As she walks to an open seat in the theatre, the penetrating stares of the exclusively male audience recall the obtrusive stares of the men in the car in the earlier sequence. In the next shot, Daïga's inquisitive look towards the movie screen is contrasted with the lecherous look of the man sitting beside her. Suddenly, Daïga starts giggling loudly. The laughter continues as the camera pans from insipid shots of the naked woman on screen to Daïga and her neighbour, who appears disturbed by her outburst. This scene is a significant reversal of the film's opening shot which displays policemen laughing inexplicably in a helicopter over Paris. Like her resistant gaze, Daïga's disruptive laughter subversively strips the men in the porn theatre and, by association, the laughing police in the earlier scene, of a purely symbolic patriarchal authority that eroticizes the female body.

Like Camille and Daïga, Théo's character offers a complex, elusive portrayal of the Other. Camille's brother is stonefaced in scenes when he works as a carpenter and beatific when playing Caribbean music on his violin. His gentle, playful scenes with his son and intimate moments with Mona clash with the silent violence of his response to a client's offensive implication that he is an illegal immigrant. Angered at the racism he constantly encounters in France, he mocks Mona's mother for asking incredulously how he will get by in Martinique:

In the morning I'll take my canoe to go fishing, Mona will pound manioc for my lunch. She'll fetch water from the river, one kilometer from the house. It's all there for the taking, the bamboo hut, bananas, avocados... Clothes? Why bother? You live nude all day there. Money? No need. I'll barter. It's paradise.

This mimicking of racist stereotypes characterizing the Caribbean as lazy and primitive is reminiscent of Daïga's subversive reversal of sexist stereotypes.

However, in addition to offering another example of an irreducible concept of Otherness, Théo, in the role of Camille's brother, provides an inverted reflection of the serial killer. Whereas Camille is outwardly kind and secretly monstrous, Théo is seemingly callous but privately gentle. Also, while Théo exhibits a strong personal connection with their native Martinique, there is no evidence that Camille shares the attachment to their heritage. Their differing attitudes towards family surface when each son dances with his mother at her birthday party. Théo's respectful, warm embrace precedes Camille's stumbling, drugged stupor. In this and other moments, the total lack of communication between the brothers is palpable. They say little to one another, do not look at each other, and avoid physical contact. The camera estranges them from one another by isolating them in separate one-shots rather than framing them together. The opportunities presented for a reconciliation between the two are fleeting. At one point, a visibly distressed Camille stops by Théo's apartment saying he must speak with him before abruptly excusing himself and acting aloof and annoyed when Théo follows him to the metro station to see what is wrong. Later, at Théo's concert near the end of the film, they exchange a prolonged glance. Noticing Camille smiling in the audience, Théo sees in the next shot that his brother has left in the middle of the performance. The Caribbean melody plays loudly during the brothers' distant and final encounter before Camille is arrested in the following scene.

The failed communication between the brothers highlights the theme of the familiar as strange. This message is conveyed in the exchange between Théo and an officer at the police station, where Camille's family is waiting to be questioned about the murders. In response to the suggestion that Théo should have suspected something since Camille was his brother, Théo replies, 'My brother's a stranger to me, just like you.' The thought that one would not be able to recognize the monstrous nature of a sibling reinforces the reference to insecurity in a scene following the enactments of the murders. As a high-angle shot floats over open windows on the top floor of an apartment building, a man's voice emanating from an indoor radio offers this ominous reflection: 'Security means being in a place where you're safe and knowing it, or believing it at least. It means being reassured. Therefore, it's very subjective: who can claim to be safe from death?' This observation, while directly linked to the pursuit of the serial killer, symbolically alludes to the film's daring portrayal of cultural difference. The insecurity inspired by the idea of a killer on the loose and so effectively evoked in the title underscores the insecure concept of identity posited by atypical representations of the marginalized Other.

The incongruities and complexities of the main characters reverberate in other images of confused identities and reversed stereotypes. A comical example is seen in the sequence with the karate class the hotel owner Ninon teaches; the sight of the elderly women gleefully responding to Ninon's order to 'kick their aggressor in the balls' defies the stereotype of the old, defenceless ladies victimized by Camille and his lover. A more unsettling reversal of stereotype is, however, evident in the portrayal of the French police, alternately seen as society's protectors and bullies. This confusion arises in the first image of the film. As the titles appear, the loud engine of a helicopter drums, mixed with the sound of rising, uncontrollable laughter. A close-up on one of the two men in the helicopter reveals his policeman's uniform. Their laughter continues over subsequent titles as the camera pans from an extremely high-angle shot through the clouds and descends into the streets of Paris, eventually settling on Daïga's moving car. The unidentified reason for the officers' laughter creates an immediate uneasiness, evoking the abuse of a godlike power, as though the officers were mocking a world dependent on their protection. In addition, the uncontainable laughter conveys a loss of control, undermining the image of police as guardians of security. Subsequent scenes increasingly represent officers as predators and harassers—ridiculing Daïga for not speaking French and Camille for 'having a girl's name'.

The scene of Camille's arrest plays on viewers' expectations in a particularly odd way. As Camille is pictured walking down an abandoned street after leaving Théo's concert, the camera pans to a car following him with a man staring at Camille from the open window in the back seat, suggesting an anonymous sexual encounter. Only then does the camera pan down to the insignia of the police car. This postponed revelation is the clearest indication of the confusion between the police as protectors and predators. The image of sexual predator curiously likens the suggested bestiality hidden under the officer's uniform to the monstrous aspect of the serial killer's behaviour.

The blend of bestiality and social conformity is further explored in a subplot involving the young couple living next door to Théo. In one scene Théo hears the woman crying and screaming and goes to knock on their door, asking the husband in a threatening tone, 'Is everything OK?' Later, Théo runs into the couple in the elevator as they are escorting two men with a dog to the front door of the building (recalling the men and the dog in the car that pulls up beside Daïga in the opening sequence, thus positing the dog as a mnemonic device for scenes investigating the theme of a hidden bestiality). When Théo goes upstairs, he finds the neighbours' door open and walks in their apartment, past the figure of the dog's head on the door knocker into a room where a table is cluttered with empty bottles of champagne and dirty plates from what looks to have been a sumptuous repast. The point-of-view shot follows Théo's gaze into the open bedroom where magazine covers featuring photos of dogs are strewn across the floor next to the bed; the studded dog collar and leash on the fully made bed are strongly suggestive of sexual bondage instruments. When Théo turns to leave, his eyes meet those of the wife who has returned alone to the apartment and who smiles meekly, averting her gaze and murmuring, 'It doesn't matter' ('C'est pas grave'). Invoking the disturbing violence in Camille's menacing love scene with Raphaël, these decadent images indicate the hypocrisy of a society that lives according to respectable social appearances masking an inner monstrosity. This hypocrisy is particularly ironic in light of Théo's marginalized status in French society. Though a responsible role model for his son, he is forced to confront racist stereotypes in France based on his external appearance, the colour of his skin. Meanwhile, his white, middle-class neighbours' closet sadism goes unnoticed due to the outward, socially acceptable appearance of their bourgeois lifestyle.

The concept of a lurking evil effectively resurfaces in the provocative encounter between Daïga and Camille in a café before Camille attends Théo's concert. After Daïga recognizes Camille's photo in the police station (where she is led after causing the car accident with Abel), she follows him from Ninon's hotel to the café where she joins him at the counter while he finishes a glass of wine. After Daïga smiles and their hands gently brush as she reaches for

PLATE 1. Etienne Lantier (Renaud) in *Germinal*

PLATE 2. Eliane Devries (Catherine Denueve) and Camille (Linh Dan Pham)
in *Indochine*

PLATE 3. Albert Dehousse (Mathieu Kassovitz) in *Un héros très discret*

PLATE 4. Maggie Cheung as herself in *Irma Vep*

PLATE 5. Madame de Blayac (Fanny Ardant) in *Ridicule*

PLATE 6. Comte Godefroy de Montmirail (Jean Reno) and Jacquouille (Christian Clavier) in *Les Visiteurs*

PLATE 7. Francis Bergeade (Michel Serrault) and Gerard (Eddy Mitchell) in
Le Bonheur est dans le pré

PLATE 8. Jean (Cyril Collard), Samy (Carlos Lopez) and Sylvie (Marine Delterme)
in *Les Nuits fauves*

PLATE 9. Marijo (Josiane Balasko), Loli (Victoria Abril) and Laurent (Alain Chabat) in *Gazon Maudit*

PLATE 10. Romuald Blindet (Daniel Auteuil), Juliette Bonaventure (Firmine Richard) and family in *Romuald et Juliette*.

PLATE 11. Vinz (Vincent Cassell) with the stolen police gun in *La Heine*

PLATE 12. Camille (Charlotte Gainsbourg) and Joel (Anouk Grinberg) in *Merci la vie*

PLATE 13. Michele Stalens (Juliette Binoche) and Alex (Denis Lavant) *Les Amants du Pont-Neuf*

PLATE 14. Chloe (Garance Clavel) and Djamel (Zinedine Soualem) in *Chacun cherche son chat*

PLATE 15. Julie (Juliette Binoche) in *Trois Couleurs: Bleu*

the sugar, he pays for her coffee. No words are exchanged except for Daïga's 'merci'. But that moment of contact, Daïga's smile, and their briefly exchanged glance indicate a successful communication, and even a collusion, between two of the film's three marginalized protagonists. This suggested camaraderie is, however, immediately undermined in the subsequent sequence when Daïga rummages through Camille's hotel room to retrieve the stolen money, then packs her bag to leave the city. What initially appears a single, uncompromised humane gesture turns out to be a calculated ruse on the heroine's part in a film intent on examining an underlying monstrosity in human nature. The momentary escape from the film's restlessness in the hopeful and silent exchange between Camille and Daïga is revealed as just that—a brief pause from the overwhelming paranoia at the heart of the incongruities and confusion that characterize the film's representations of identity.

The sense of restlessness conveyed by the story's indecipherable and complex portraits of the Other is also represented on a stylistic level. Denis claims to have been inspired by the image of Peter Lorre as the child murderer in Fritz Lang's *M* (1931; Pascal 1994: 1131). The urban setting, darkly lit *mise-en-scène*, numerous refracted mirror images, and murder mystery in Denis's film conspire to produce the dominant mood of paranoia. In this respect, *J'ai pas sommeil* can certainly be described as:

A modern film noir, that is to say, a contemporary film, without any sign or fetish of the era. Film noir in the sense that, based on a murder mystery, it proposes a very original urban vision, both profound and transparent, and that it is transformed by the shifting rhythm of interchangeable days and nights which end up canceling each other out. Film noir also because Claire Denis seeks to penetrate society's dark shadows, that cursed section inhabited by outcasts who haunt the city's corners and deepest recesses. (Jousse 1994: 22)

However, in addition to 'modernizing' film noir, Denis subverts the classical genre with a playful allusion to stock characters, a bright colour scheme, and a disarming film structure. The androgynous aspects of Daïga's and Camille's characters play an important role in deconstructing noir archetypes. In the first sequence Daïga drives into town at dawn, a loner amidst the dispersed traffic and a veritable incarnation of the conventional noir hero—à la Jean-Paul Belmondo driving on an isolated country road at the

beginning of Godard's *A bout de souffle* (1959), a satirical tribute
to the American film noir. Opposite Daïga, Camille is the closest
embodiment, especially in the nightclub scene, of classic
Hollywood cinema's femme fatale.

The gender reversal of stock characters is matched by a striking
composition that subverts conventional noir's chiaroscuro effect
through a heightened use of the primary colours red, blue, and
yellow. These bright-coloured hues dominate the *mise-en-scène* to
such a degree—from the neon back-lit exteriors of the balcony at
Théo's apartment to the similarly soft, colourful lighting in
Camille's dance sequence—that interior shots appear indistinguishable from exteriors. The visually collapsed barrier between inside
and outside once again raises the theme of an impossible security
in a society where evil remains misunderstood and easily disguised
(an idea expressed in Camille's final confession to the police: 'I am
not a monster. No one likes to suffer. It's the world that's gone
crazy').

The notion of a physical insecurity mirroring the film's representation of insecure, irreducible identities is heralded by radio
broadcasts and newspaper headlines (like 'La France a peur')
reporting the latest updates on the 'granny killings'. Nevertheless,
Denis's story is surprisingly devoid of the structural suspense in
classical film noir. The two murder scenes that occur unexpectedly
towards the middle of the film are, in fact, chilling because totally
unpredicted. In direct contrast with a sensationalized display of
violence, Camille and Raphaël's murders are a banalized routine.
There is no musical crescendo but absolute silence and a troubling
effortlessness in Camille's method of strangling his victims. The
only identifiable moments of suspense are contained within the
actual murder scenes—when Camille and his lover wait on an
upper landing for the victim to open her door, when the delivery
boy rings the doorbell after the murderers leave, and the victim
moves suddenly under the coat Camille throws over her after
mistaking her for dead.

This exceedingly restrained use of suspense, along with other
technical deviations from the noir genre, renders *J'ai pas sommeil*
a contemporary film noir that resists being a film noir—a film that,
in essence, masquerades as a genre it is in the process of subvert-
ing. This concept is aligned with the masquerade performed by the
central character and the masquerade of evil in the film's dominant

images and themes. Just as the disorienting images and complex characters do not allow viewers to trust what they see or to fall back on an easy stereotyping (i.e. good vs. evil, masculine vs. feminine, same vs. other), the elusive film style precludes facile generic categorizations.

The ultimate implication of the thematic and stylistic masquerade in *J'ai pas sommeil* is that there is no possible separation of the mask and the identity the disguise conceals. There is, therefore, as the *mise-en-scène* attests, no distinguishable boundary between inside and outside with regard to identities the film imagines. Instead, the story seems in search of 'in-between', culturally negotiated spaces (see Bhabha 1990: 291–322; Chambers 1991; Pratt 1991: 33–40) where one may explore the more slippery notion of an indecipherable and irreducible 'Otherness'. This 'in-between' stage is evoked in the first and last scenes of the film which present Daïga entering Paris at dawn and leaving the city shortly after dusk. Nothing better communicates the complex rendering of marginalized identities than the film's symmetrical structure, opening and closing at those absolutely indeterminable moments of human consciousness—between sleeping and rising, night and day.

13

Comedy and Interracial Relationships: *Romuald et Juliette* (Serreau, 1987) and *Métisse* (Kassovitz, 1993)

DINA SHERZER

LAND of asylum or garbage can ('terre d'asile ou poubelle') are two labels given to France depending on one's point of view on immigration. Since the nineteenth century and until the 1950s, with the influx of Italians, Poles, Spaniards, Portuguese, and Yugoslavs, France has been a land of asylum, absorbing and integrating these European populations. During the 1960s a new wave of immigration displaced men from the former colonies, mainly the Maghreb and black Africa, to the French mainland, where they were imported to work in road and building construction, car factories, and garbage collection. These men lived in communal lodgings with fellow workers, met in cafés, sent money back home to their families whom they visited once or twice a year, and kept to themselves, apart from the French population. In 1981 the socialist government under President Mitterrand proclaimed that these workers had the right to live with their families and to reunite with them on French soil, thus creating a second generation of immigrants who have been raised in France. The presence of a sizeable Asiatic population mainly in Paris and its suburbs is the consequence of the various waves of immigration brought about by the Indo-China war, the Vietnamese war, and the exodus of the boat people from communist Vietnam, as well as immigration from China. An important population from Guadeloupe, Martinique, and Réunion lives in France where there is more employment than on the islands.

Indeed, since the 1980s France has become increasingly multi-ethnic, and various ethnic groups live side by side mostly in big cities and their immediate surroundings (*banlieues*). Hence the term France=garbage can, used by the extreme Right represented by Le Pen and his followers. Unemployment, poverty, drugs, violence, and racist incidents have drawn attention to the complexity of the situation, and to the necessity of finding solutions. This demographic, sociological, and political configuration has given rise to a keen awareness of identity and ethnicity which expresses itself semantically. Now the distinction between French-French (*Français de souche*, i.e. children from French parents) or French-Non-French (children of immigrants, *beurs*, naturalized citizens from any country), and Non-French (immigrants), is frequently alluded to, and xenophobia, hatred, and racism are countered by pleas for tolerance and acceptance of difference (SOS Racisme). The notion of hybridity (*métissage*) is more widespread, referring to cultural manifestations, artistic trends, and individuals born to interracial couples who are becoming an important segment of the population.[1]

France is criss-crossed by many discourses engaging with these issues. Journalists, sociologists, politicians, historians, and novelists write or speak about them.[2] For instance, Jean-Marie Le Clézio, Marie N'Diaye, Daniel Pennac, Leila Sebbar, and Michel Tournier invent characters who live in multi-ethnic settings and experience cultural difference, rejection, and problems of identity.[3] Many film directors have contributed to these discourses on identity and ethnicity as well, and cinema has been, in the words of one critic, a mirror (Gaston-Mathé 1996: 9–12). *Tchao Pantin* (Berri, 1983), *Police* (Pialat, 1985), *Le Thé au harem d'Archimède* (Charef, 1985), *Black Mic Mac* (Gilou, 1986), *Un, deux, trois soleil* (Blier, 1993), *Hexagone* (Chibane, 1994), *Douce France* (Chibane, 1995), *Raï* (Gilou 1995), *La Vérité si je mens* (Gilou, 1997), *Bye Bye* (Dridi, 1995), *La Haine* (Kassovitz, 1995), and *L'Autre côté de la mer* (Cabrera, 1997) portray French and Others in dramatic situations and bring into view the reality of life in immigrant communities, focusing on clashes between generations, unemployment, drugs, ethnic difference, and racism.

Practically all these films involve an interracial love affair or relationship which pairs a French and a *beur*, a French and a Black, or a Jew and a Gentile, and such relationships are presented as common occurrences for today's young people. However, it is significant that the outcome of the relationships is not successful, because of normal difficulties encountered by young adults, such as unemployment, lack of understanding of parents, a feeling of not fitting in society, or disagreements in the couple, but also because of problems of ethnicity, cultural differences, and racism. Interracial affairs in postcolonial French films are accepted and legitimate, but they are discouraged, and presented as not viable at this time.[4]

Two exceptions stand out. Coline Serreau in *Romuald et Juliette* (1987) and Mathieu Kassovitz in *Métisse* (1993) make the interracial relationships the centrepiece of their comedies and propose a positive, optimistic outcome. Serreau and Kassovitz are directors intending to revitalize traditional French realist cinema, notes Austin (1996: 171); yet in these films they offer utopian solutions. They also use comedy, a genre most prone to stereotypes especially on questions of race and gender, as Hayward aptly states (Hayward 1993: 184). How do Serreau and Kassovitz, who are known for their open-mindedness and sensitivity to race, Otherness, and gender, engage with these issues? What strategies do they deploy to convey their messages?

Serreau's film is a rewriting of *Cinderella* and *Romeo and Juliet* in postcolonial and feminist modes, so that the prince and the step-daughter/maid of the fairy tale are now the white CEO of the yogurt factory and the black cleaning lady. The Capulet and Montagu families are now the white upper-class family from the sixteenth *arrondissement* of Paris and the black family living in a tenement house in Saint-Denis, a working-class, multi-ethnic suburb north of Paris. As in comedies the film ends happily with a double marriage, a double pregnancy, and multiple friendships. As in fairy tales and Utopias, the CEO and the cleaning lady are united, overcoming barriers of class, race, and economics.

In addition Serreau creates many situations during which black and white individuals are in close proximity, thus punctuating the film with subliminal messages which show positive interracial mixings. Repeating with variation the scene where Juliette finds her small children in her bed, she puts Romuald in bed with the black children so that the black children and the white man are shown in an intimate closeness. Romuald is also seen in his car with his chauffeur and all the black kids, and he comforts Juliette's older son, greets him outside the jail, like a father would, by putting his arms around the adolescent's shoulders. The scene at the new house completes and expands this mixing, since now even Romuald's children are paired with Juliette's. The new baby will be called Caramel, a name fitting his mixture of blackness and whiteness. The soundtrack enhances the message of the film as it is composed of American jazz performed by black musicians such as Duke Ellington and a white musician, Stevie Ray Vaughan, playing lively triumphant pieces in happy moments, blues in sad moments or love scenes.

How does Serreau make this improbable and unconvincing story acceptable so that spectators are willing to suspend disbelief? How can a black cleaning lady get close enough to a CEO to marry him? It all hinges on the representation and the construction of the most unlikely character, the black cleaning lady. This begins with the plot. First, Serreau introduces a foreign body into a smooth-running system. It was the baby in Serreau's earlier film *Trois hommes et un couffin*; here it is Juliette and she is appropriately named Juliette Bonaventure.[5] In a postcolonial and feminist move Serreau makes Juliette, the black cleaning lady, usually a secondary character, invisible and forgotten, the most important protagonist, who rescues Romuald from deceits, impostures, and cuckoldry.[6] But Juliette does more than just solve the crisis; she and her family transform Romuald's personality. From ruthless, selfish, arrogant CEO, he becomes a thoughtful man who cares about his children and ex-wife, and Juliette and her children. The *mise-en-scène* reinforces Juliette's important role since she occupies centre frame most of the time and is photographed with medium shots, thus giving an impression of power and stability.

Serreau endows Juliette with qualities which make her a likeable character. She is intelligent and remarkable for her perseverance, perspicacity, and sagacity. She has a healthy, sculptural, matriarchal beauty . At first, she seems to fit the stereotype of the single black mother with five children living in a housing project, but then Serreau counters this stereotype and makes Juliette a hard-working woman, not a mother living on welfare benefits. Even though she has had five husbands and a child with each, she is not constructed as promiscuous. Whereas Romuald and his wife have illicit affairs, Juliette is divorced and does not want to have affairs. She is proud of, and takes good care of, her five children, who have significant names: Aimé, Félicité, Désiré, Claire, and Benjamin. The stereotype is that African men are polygamous and repudiate their wives. Here it is Juliette who kicked out her husbands.

Romuald et Juliette is not only entertaining, playful, and witty comedy. It also displays a keen awareness of contemporary issues debated in French society. In *Trois hommes et un couffin* Serreau underscored what it means to be a working mother, to perform all the chores associated with taking care of a baby. She also indirectly interrogated the western conception/stereotype of masculinity which discourages men from being sensitive, and pokes fun at their sensitiveness. In *Romuald et Juliette* she focuses on class and race. With parallel editing, she contrasts the upper-class life of a white family with the life of a working-class single black mother and her five children. Thus spectators see a spacious elegant apartment in a bourgeois building contrasted with cramped rooms in a housing project; the car driven by a chauffeur taking the white children to school and the CEO to work, contrasted with a bus stop or the subway used by the black family; the elegant party at Romuald's apartment, with jazz, champagne, and lavish buffet, contrasted with the lively party with colourful African clothes and music in Juliette's apartment. Serreau foregrounds differences of speech, clothing, and wealth. The elegant, educated French of Romuald contrasts with the uneducated popular way of speaking and the Antillean accent of Juliette; the slim, well-dressed CEO with the stocky cleaning lady in ordinary clothes who hides her money in her bra as is common in the Antilles and in fact among women of colour more generally; the generous sum of money the CEO gives his teenage children with the little money the cleaning lady denies her children because she is late to pay her rent. Thus the fairy tale is also a sociological, political lesson which documents life for radically different social classes.

If in the fairy tale the black and the white characters get along very well, paying attention to dialogue gives a different picture. During many verbal interactions the black characters display their awareness of difference, division, and racism, and statements revealing anxiety about race punctuate the film. Truth comes from children's mouths says a French proverb, and in the film this is precisely what happens. Juliette's youngest boy, who has been told by his mother, 'Nobody sleeps in my bed,' discovers Romuald in it, and rushes to his mother to tell her, 'Mommy there is a gentleman in your bed,' to which Juliette answers 'So what,' and the child responds, 'But Mommy he is white.' Later on he asks again why the white man is still in the house, thus underscoring the awkwardness and unexpectedness of a white man's presence in the family. One of the former husbands has the same reaction on seeing Romuald in Juliette's apartment and he enquires, 'You sleep with this white man?' to which she answers, 'you are crazy'. Romuald, who has heard this interaction, reports to her, 'He thought we were together,' and Juliette answers, 'Do you realize how crazy he is.' Juliette states several times that she, and her children, are black. She refuses to marry Romuald because, she says to him, 'you are white', and when Romuald brings his children to Juliette's apartment she says, 'I am sure he did not tell you we are all black.' Clearly, black characters do not feel it is natural, normal, to be close to white people. At the marriage ceremony, where all the guests are white, we hear one of them asking if Romuald is marrying his secretary, which would be a plausible and possible ancillary marriage. It would certainly not come into their minds to ask if the secretary is white. What is implied here is that it is an aberration, an unimaginable possibility that the CEO marry a black cleaning lady.

Serreau points out instances of racism to which black people are subjected in everyday life and their awareness of being treated as different. When Juliette brings a message to the tennis club, Romuald's son asks her who she is. She answers: 'in fact I am nothing.' She knows she does not count for these people, because she is black and a cleaning lady. During a crucial interaction in Romuald's office, Romuald's secretary behaves in a condescending fashion to Juliette. Although she does not say anything overtly insulting, the child feels her hostility and asks his mother: 'Why is the lady nasty?' Aimé, the oldest son, who gets involved with drugs and is sent to jail, expresses his despair by rejecting the white world of his mother. He tells her, 'your money stinks whites' housekeeping', to which she responds, 'your money stinks the whites' clink'. These dialogues capture the harsh contemporary reality of racism in France, undermining the fairy-tale ending of the film.

Kassovitz's film is a French postcolonial rendition of Spike Lee's *She's Gotta Have It* (1986). The African-American Nola, her black male lovers, and the eventual female lover are transformed into the Martinican Lola and her two lovers, a Jewish pizza-delivery boy and a black university student. Nola invites her lovers to Thanksgiving dinner and Lola summons hers to her apartment in order to announce that she is pregnant, wants the child, and her two lovers. *Métisse* ends with an idyllic scene in the hospital. Lola, the creole girl who already represents a blurring of racial boundaries, is now united with the black and the white man and their child. *Métissage*, or racial mixing, wins out.

This light comedy, which advocates sexual freedom and the possibility of having an interracial *ménage à trois*, is more than just a lively and entertaining film. Intelligent, full of energy and warmth, it also addresses issues of identity and ethnicity from a variety of perspectives. Kassovitz foregrounds the multi-ethnicity of the world young people experience in France today. Félix invites Lola, a Martinican creole, and Jamal, of African descent, to meet his Jewish French family, immigrants from Central Europe. At the pool, on the basketball court, in the gym, in discos, in bars, and in courses at the university, the film displays ethnic diversity. In the hospital the nurse is black, the doctor is Asiatic. Félix's grandparents speak Yiddish, Lola's grandmother speaks creole, and the university professor speaks with a Central European accent. Félix works for Jewish relatives who make pizza. Interracial relationships are frequent occurrences. Jamal is dating Lola the creole, but also Julie the blond girl; Félix and Jamal realize that at different times Lola went on vacation with both of them, but with others as well. Kassovitz uses comic situations deriving from the *ménage à trois* to show black and white characters in close proximity, for example the two men in an elevator or together in bed with Lola, one on each side of her. Thus the plot and the various activities present multi-ethnicity and racial mixings as already taking place. They give 'another vision of things', the characters are 'not afraid of hybridity, of bastard children', and 'respect varieties of skin colour', attitudes and behaviours which the rap song framing the film calls for insistently. Furthermore, the music of the film is performed by multi-ethnic groups Assassin and Zap Mama, and Kassovitz, the Jewish-French director, pays homage to Spike Lee, the black American director. In a playful interfilmic construct, like Spike Lee, Kassovitz plays a pizza-delivery boy, complete with accident-prone bike and glasses.[7]

As in *Romuald and Juliette*, below the utopian surface of *Métisse* lies a complex network of attitudes, feelings, and behaviours about race and ethnicity. Like Serreau, Kassovitz contrasts two ways of living, one associated with upper-class French individuals and the other with working-class ones, but he uses the comic technique of role reversals to draw attention to prevalent clichés and stereotypes.[8] He attributes to Jamal, the black man, characteristics which French society would associate stereotypically with a well-to-do white youth: he is a university student, comes from a well-to-do family of diplomats, speaks elegant and correct French, does not make inordinate gestures, controls his kinesics and his body appearance, drives his own car with the inscription CD (*corps diplomatique*) on it, wears expensive shoes, lives in a tastefully decorated apartment, has a black maid, tips taxi drivers generously, and invites Félix to a Jazz Club. Adding another twist to this, Kassovitz has Jamal work in a fast-food restaurant so that he fits the stereotype of the black youth doing menial work, which he thinks will please Lola. Félix, on the other hand, is constructed as a coloured youth from the working class, and fits the stereotypes that people have of black or *beur* youth. He is noisy, boisterous, cocky, provocative, gesticulates all the time. He delivers pizza on a bicycle, invents and sings rap songs, lives in cramped quarters, wears jeans and sneakers, and speaks *verlan*.[9]

Stereotypes about penis size are also played on in the film. First, Kassovitz sets up an interaction during which the stereotype of the sexual power of the black man is stated. In the gym, Félix, who complains that his rival, Lola's other lover, is black, is told by a black friend, 'You are not in luck,' implying that the girl will prefer the sexually potent black man. Then we see Jamal in bed with Julie. His performance does not conform to the stereotype, and Julie reassures him by saying: 'don't be troubled by a technical deficiency.' A third interaction offers yet another perspective on this issue. This time it is Lola herself who whimsically and knowingly tells her girlfriend, who enquires who was better in bed, the black or the white man: 'It does not depend on the size of the boat, but on the power of the roll (*roulis*).'

Kassovitz's foregrounding of stereotypes with role reversals and sexual jokes works very well to amuse the spectators, but at the same time it deconstructs these stereotypes and shows to what degree the identity of the Other depends on artificial and mechanical constructions of racial difference.

As in *Romuald et Juliette*, in *Métisse* the characters utter remarks, insults, clichés, and sayings which reveal their racist attitudes. They repeatedly display their awareness of difference, the awkwardness of dealing with an Other, and their intolerance towards the Other's race and religion. When Félix and Jamal meet for the first time at Lola's, the interaction is not too friendly; Félix says to Jamal, 'we did not watch pigs together', a very commonly heard French expression meaning we are different, we belong to different ethnic groups, we have nothing in common. During the jail incident, Jamal is better treated than Félix because his father is a diplomat. Félix tells the policeman behind the desk: 'I thought it was better to be white and poor than black and rich. Traditions are disappearing,' again a common saying. And when characters lose their temper, racist insults fly: 'dirty nigger', says Félix to the black guy who implies his penis is too short; 'Muslim macho', says Lola, furious at being ordered around by Jamal; 'it's not a family, it's an Arab telephone', complains Félix when his relatives ask him about Lola.

Colour is an issue which preoccupies several characters. Jamal tells Julie the blond girl that he cannot continue their relationship because she is too white. He tells Lola that Félix dates her because it is fashionable to have a black girlfriend. Lola confides to her grandmother that Jamal is too black, thus voicing a common feeling in the Antilles that to be light-skinned is more desirable than to be dark. The conversation during the dinner party at Félix's house is bitterly ironic because it displays the racism of people who have themselves been victims of racism. The mother asks Jamal: 'So you are black?' Then she adds, 'there are black Jews in Ethiopia', but Jamal answers, 'I am not Jewish.' Turning to Lola the mother asks: 'and you?' Lola answers, 'My mother is Christian.' 'Too bad,' says Félix's mother. To Lola she declares: 'all the same you are good looking.' Since this is a comedy, the mother redeems herself partially when she tells Lola: 'Colour or not, it is not serious, you did wonders for my son.' Félix expresses his anxiety about the colour of the baby's skin. He asks Lola: 'and what if he is black?' His dream reveals his anxiety and fear, as it involves a baby carriage with Jamal as the baby in it. And at the hospital the first question he asks concerns the baby's colour, a question never answered, since the nurse only says the baby is pink with green stars. The film ends with each character proposing a name for the baby, a Muslim name, El Khebir, a Jewish one, Jacob, and a French one, Clothaire. With these names, the characters reaffirm their ethnicity and difference and their desire to impart it to the baby. In the cradle, the baby's identity is already sealed by his name.

Kassovitz, like many contemporary directors such as Kurys in *Coup de foudre* (1983), Belmont in *Rouge Baiser* (1989), and Lelouch in *Les Misérables* (1995), makes a point of giving historical depth to his film, reminding spectators of traumatic events linked to the Holocaust. Félix asks his father what will be his grandmother's reaction to his *ménage à trois*. The answer is 'your grandmother was in Buchenwald. She has seen much worse.' In addition Kassovitz refers to slavery. He has Jamal tell Lola that she should prefer him to Félix, because 'our grandparents were slaves together'. Thus the Holocaust and slavery, which epitomize racism, difference, and division, are conjured up in the film, linking past and present. Albeit presented in a comic mode, in all of these instances crucial issues and preoccupations about race and difference are brought to the fore and, as in Serreau's film, break the illusion and foreground the mechanisms of racial division and racism.

Serreau's and Kassovitz's films have a fast-paced action and a lively soundtrack. They amuse with their witty repartees, puns, and euphemisms, their pairing of contrasting characters, their repetitions, and their role reversals. They offer optimistic and generous responses to social problems. Katsahnias captures exactly the mood of the happy ending of *Romuald et Juliette* when he writes that the meeting of the CEO and the cleaning lady takes on the fullness of a 1968 mythic hippie scene reviewed and corrected by SOS Racisme (Katsahnias 1989a: 50–1). This remark applies also to the reunion of the three lovers with their baby at the end of *Métisse*. Both films advocate compromise and social integration and, as comedies do, aim at creating a sense of pleasure and euphoria. They avoid contributing to racism and xenophobia by exposing and deconstructing the complex issues of identity and ethnicity. They inscribe stereotypes and racist attitudes which are created by reactions to Otherness, and by so doing they show that racism is prevalent in all the groups, a darker subtext which undermines what the comedy asserts. Indeed Serreau and Kassovitz seem to have invented a new genre which Moulet has aptly labelled 'neo-irrealism' (Moulet 1994), i.e. a blend of realism, idealism, and irrealism in postcolonial France.

Given Serreau's and Kassovitz's personalities and their achievements to date, it is safe to speculate that this neo-irrealism is a concerted strategy aimed at communicating a generous and positive message. Both directors chose comedy because it entails the creation of a state of liminality,[10] where the in-between status gives licence to transform everyday behaviour, and to show interracial relationships which succeed. By providing a positive way to imagine Otherness and coexistence, comedy here becomes a subversive instrument which teaches while it entertains. Comedy is also a response to the question: how can one engage with political and social issues? It is a way to enter into direct resonance with French social reality, and to work on individual and collective subjectivity. Furthermore, *Romuald et Juliette* and *Métisse*, as well as *La Haine* and *Hexagone*, frame and foreground ways of speaking (*verlan*, contemporary slang, and intonations), ways of dressing, and ways of gesturing and moving which are part of urban youth culture, and as such they contribute directly to bringing about awareness and understanding.

While these films challenge racial homogeneity and invite spectators to think of a French space where mixing is possible, and the Other is accepted, they nevertheless convey troublesome and regressive messages. In *Romuald et Juliette* it is the white man who steps in to re-establish the family unit. Both films end with the creation of traditional, though not quite nuclear families, and both show overtly that money can buy everything. And while both films show interracial mixings, they are between a white man and a black woman, thus continuing the pattern of slave-owner/colonialist sexual appropriation of black women, and the fear of black men's sexuality. Still, these films are telling explorations of today's France's ambiguous, contradictory feelings and attitudes toward identity and race: land of asylum or garbage can.

Notes

1. See Sherzer 1998. For a recent study of the different ethnic groups which constitute today's French population, see Roze 1995.
2. See Maffesoli 1996 and Taguieff 1996. These two articles provide extensive and informative bibliographies. For an analysis of the construction of Otherness in France see Todorov 1993 and Todd 1994.
3. Sebbar 1982, 1984; Tournier 1986; Le Clézio 1980; N'Diaye 1990; Pennac 1987, 1990; Hargreaves 1991.
4. Such films as Annaud's *L'Amant*, Wargnier's *Indochine*, Denis's

Chocolat (1988), Roüan's *Outremer*, and Giraudeau's *Les Caprices d'un fleuve* (1996) show and glamorize interracial love affairs or attraction in colonial times, and in distant lands, but again the message is not altogether positive (see Sherzer 1996).

5. See Katsahnias 1989*b*.
6. On the significance of the subaltern taking power, see Rosello 1996*a*: 52–80.
7. In this interfilmic relationship between the two films, to which should be added several films by Woody Allen, the director/actor plays the role of the schlemiel/trickster who always gets (and then often loses) his woman.
8. Kassovitz imitates Spike Lee, who uses stereotypes of black men in *She's Gotta Have It*, and Woody Allen, who plays with stereotypes in most of his films, in particular in *Annie Hall* (1977). For an excellent study on stereotypes in films, novels, and comics in contemporary France, see Rosello 1998. In particular, she points out the significance of Kassovitz's foregrounding of Jewishness in *Métisse*, an identity which has been silenced in French culture (1998: 8–9).
9. French words spoken backwards used in songs and in everyday interactions in the *banlieues*.
10. For this notion of comedy and liminality, see Horton 1991: 5.

14

Which Mapping of the City?
La Haine (Kassovitz, 1995) and the *cinéma de banlieue*

MYRTO KONSTANTARAKOS

A NEW type of film has emerged in France, which, for the first time since the Western, takes its name from a geographical feature: the *banlieue* film. *Banlieues* are at the outskirts of large cities, but the term cannot be translated by 'suburb', because it lacks the bourgeois cosiness of the English term. Although *banlieue* only means any area at the periphery of town, in recent years it has come to designate more specifically the working-class parts of it (Thorns 1972: 71). Many attempts have been made by British and American journalists to translate into English the emotionally charged French terms of *cité* and *banlieue*: paradoxically, the *banlieue*'s spatial opposite, 'inner cities'—which is the translation one of these films, *État des lieux*, was given in America—would better render the deprivation of some housing estates at the periphery of big French towns such as Paris, Lyons, and Marseilles which have seen a number of very violent riots between youth and police since the 1980s.

The styles of these films are all very different, the only point in common being their location. Five of them actually mention a spatial indication in their title: Jean-François Richet's *État des lieux* (1995) and *Ma 6T va crack-er* (1997); Malik Chibane's *Hexagone* (1994), *Douce France* (1995), and *Nés quelque part* (1997); Paul Vecchiali's *Zone franche* (1996). The title first given to Mathieu Kassovitz's *La Haine* was *Droit de cité*. The representation of space in these films is therefore of paramount importance and I shall investigate further its treatment by exploring the stark division between centre and margins. After Jean-Luc Godard's *Deux ou trois choses que je sais d'elle* (1967), there were a number of films in the 1980s that were set in the *banlieue*, but most have appeared in the mid-1990s. In the limited space of this chapter, I will concentrate mainly on the hugely successful *La Haine*, which won the Best Director award at the 1995 Cannes Film Festival, but reference will be made to the other *banlieue* films.

Although Kassovitz, *La Haine*'s director, would have liked the film to be controversial, it was much admired and taken by the media and the government, who were instructed to see it, as a true portrayal of societal woes in France, almost as a documentary. Opinions diverge, however, on the importance of the setting of these films. Kassovitz and Richet both deny their subject matter is the *banlieue*: the latter purports to have made his film, *État des lieux*, about a factory worker who loses his job because of his political activity, and Kassovitz constantly repeats in interviews that his film is about police blunders, thus putting it firmly in the realm of hip-hop culture, pervaded by strong anti-police feelings.

Nevertheless, the films are symptomatic of the old tradition of centrality, typical of France. Just as Paris is central to French literature, so it has been a popular setting since very early in the history of cinema. It is certainly one of the most filmed cities in the world (Hillairet et al. 1985): in 1995 no less than sixty films—half of French production—were shot in the capital. René Clair and Jacques Prévert in the 1930s and 1940s set their characters in its poor quarters and its working-class outskirts, rebuilt in the studio with great precision by Alexandre Trauner. The Nouvelle Vague took French film into the streets of the capital. Meyer has shown how literature overturned the traditional representation of centre and periphery with Céline's *Voyage au bout de la nuit* in 1932: 'For the first time, the angle of vision would be reversed: from now on, the *banlieue* would not be scrutinized from the high points of the inner city; instead Paris would be examined from the *banlieue*' (Meyer 1994:17). Now run-down *banlieues* are the subject of French films, or, to be more precise, the city in relation to its margins is the main topic of this new genre. Mahoney argues that *La Haine* represents 'the possibility of reclaiming or re-imagining the space of the city', for 'texts which set out to inscribe experiences of the city previously marginalized or marked as "other" do implicitly or explicitly challenge traditional discourses on urban space' (Mahoney 1997: 183).

Studies have shown that, to inhabitants of the periphery, the centre of activity is no longer the local market and the local bars, but Lyons or Paris town centre, and that this contributes to the loss of identity of the *banlieues* (Hargreaves 1995: 74). *Hexagone* is the only film in which there is an inverse movement: a Parisian comes to the *banlieue* to visit a friend and go to a party. Usually, it is the other way round: the protagonists embark on a journey to the city centre in search of money or sex.[1] In most of the films in question—except in Richet's—the characters go from the periphery to Paris. This trip is never easy, as if the distance between the two places were immense: in *Hexagone*, the protagonists cannot find a ride to Paris because their friends' cars are all broken down or out of petrol. Conversely they may have trouble returning from the city centre: in *La Haine*, the police keep them in custody until the trains have stopped for the night, and in Thomas Gilou's *Raï* they do not have enough money for petrol. The mobility of the male characters and their ability to use transport seem therefore to be prevented: in *État des lieux*, the protagonist's motorcycle breaks down. As movement between centre and margins is made so difficult in all the *banlieue* films, so the perceived distance between the two increases and appears as much greater than it is in reality. The significance here is that, whereas various elements of plot and, as we shall see, cinematographic techniques are used to separate *banlieue* and city centre, it has been suggested that the cause of recent delinquency might in fact be the bringing together of the two through fast means of transport such as the RER underground train (Maspéro 1990: 171). Poorer inhabitants of the *banlieue* have thus been brought to within twenty minutes of the affluent parts of Paris like Les Halles, where the central scene in *La Haine* is shot. Indeed, the most violent *banlieues* are to be found near big cities, in which the inhabitants are confronted by wealth as soon as they step outside their neighbourhood.

Given the effort to show the separation of outskirts and city centre, the following remark by Oscar Moore (1995) shows a complete misunderstanding of the spatial significance in *La Haine*: 'Kassovitz is at his street-wise best in describing the volatility of this trio but loses his grip when the story veers into a long digression in Paris, only in the final reel does the story get back on track for its explosive climax.' Rather, the point is that *La Haine* is constructed entirely around the opposition between Paris and periphery. The film is divided in two, the first half being shot in the *cité*, the second in Paris; Kassovitz even wanted to shoot one episode in colour and the other in black and white, one in 35 mm and the other in 16 mm. Instead, he shot the *cité* by day and Paris by night, the *cité* with ample travelling shots and Paris with a small crew (by foot and with a hand-held camera); the *cité* in stereo and Paris in mono. Short focal distance was used for the *cité* scenes, in order to integrate the characters in their surroundings, whereas Paris is shot with long focal distance to detach them from the background (Vassé 1995). The result is that, as soon as the protagonists get to Paris, the whole atmosphere and sound changes and they feel out of place and strangers (Favier and Kassovitz 1995: 96). Kassovitz also explains that he carefully constructed the part in the *cité*, whereas the episodes in Paris could be presented in a different order.

Having ascertained that the films have emphasized the spatial division between centre and periphery, one must ask what characteristics of the different areas have been used to map the city. In his review of the year 1995 in French cinema, Keith Reader (1996) sees in the *banlieue* films the direct expression of the Mitterrand years but, at the same time, he believes *La Haine* to be inspired by the films of Spike Lee and John Singleton. He reiterates the statement made when the film came out in Britain, that this is the greatest impact American cinema has had on that of France since the Nouvelle Vague (Reader 1995: 13). Indeed the Anglo-Saxon tendency is to compare these films to American 'ghetto films' and to see them as enactments of racial conflict. The titles of the articles and essays about them also emphasize the importance of the comparisons with the "hood movies' in America, to quote just a few: 'Boys in the banlieue' (Reader 1995), 'garçons in the 'hood' (O'Shea 1995) and 'Arabz N the Hood' (Nesselson 1994). In France, the tendency to view the films in terms of race has been compounded, where *La Haine* has been a word much used when referring to Jean-Marie Le Pen and to the racist thesis of the Front National political party (it has been observed that the 'n' of FN pronounced in French sounds very similar to 'haine', hate). Direct reference to racism is also made in Kassovitz's film when three protagonists encounter a group of skinheads—one of whom is played by the director himself.

Comments about the soundtrack have contributed to the apparent similarity between American "hood movies' and *banlieue* films, for, like the American projects, the outskirts of French cities are the birthplace and subject matter of recent films and rap music. So expected is rap music on the soundtrack of these films (as it is in the American ones) that many critics and scholars have actually 'heard' it in *La Haine* (Mars-Jones 1995: 11; Mongin 1997). To be accurate, there are three very short diegetic rap songs, actually played by characters, and, alongside the soundtrack, a collection of eleven French rap songs also called *La Haine* was released, but it must be stressed that these songs were *inspired* by the film script and are not actually *in* the film.

The link with the United States is not limited to music, for many cinematographic references that are made are American. In most of the *banlieue* films characters discuss or go to see an American film: two black characters on the staircase recall *Harlem Nights* (Murphy, 1986) in a very funny scene of *État des lieux*; in *La Haine*, youngsters discuss the make of the gun of *Lethal Weapon* (Donner, 1987) on the roof, and Vinz goes to the cinema whilst his friends are in police custody: he gets in without paying from the exit and wanders from screen to screen, pausing only to watch Hollywood films with big stars referred to in the film script as Stallone, Clint Eastwood, Arnold, and Bambi, all dubbed into French. Moreover, Kassovitz officially acknowledges the influence of American cinema, namely from Spike Lee and Scorsese: Vinz's scene in front of the mirror is from *Taxi Driver* (Scorsese, 1976), one of the three protagonists, Hubert, is a boxer, and Vinz goes to see a fight in Paris. These, in addition to the use of a sound effect at the beginning of *La Haine* found also in the central fight scene of *Raging Bull* (Scorsese, 1980), are clear homages to Martin Scorsese. No doubt street fights are a tribute to Spike Lee's *Do the Right Thing* (1989). As Tarr has pointed out, and as Sherzer reminds us in her chapter in this volume, Kassovitz's debt to Spike Lee is also acknowledged in his first feature film, *Métisse* (1993), in which the long opening scene of him riding a bicycle through the streets of Paris is a direct homage to Spike Lee's character in *She's Gotta Have It*, Mars Blackmon (Tarr 1997a). Furthermore, the two films have been compared by critics for their similar subject matter: a young woman who refuses to choose between her lovers.

Nevertheless, the American influences on the music and the style of the *banlieue* films should not be mistaken for an imitation of the subject matter of the ''hood movies'. Rey argues that the fear of the *banlieue*—and of its music—is in a way the fear of the United States, of ghettos ruled by gangs and ethnic conflicts: there is a fear that America is only anticipating what will eventually happen in France (Rey 1996: 11). However, Alec Hargreaves points out that: 'In the US it is not uncommon for large neighbourhoods to be almost entirely mono-ethnic' whereas 'there are very few sizeable estates in France where French nationals are in a minority . . . areas containing relatively large concentrations of foreign residents are almost always multi-ethnic' (Hargreaves 1995: 74). The two urban experiences are indeed radically different (Wacquant 1992) and my contention is that though the French films are influenced by Hollywood, they are not about racial hatred nor about the racial mapping of the city, hence the choice of ethnically diverse protagonists: in *Raï* and *Douce France* there is a friendship between French young men and second-generation North African immigrants; in its Parisian first part, Zaïda Ghorab-Volta's *Souviens-toi de moi* (1996) presents us with the same 'integration' in a feminine version. *La Haine* goes even further by showing black policemen, while the central characters are a trio from different backgrounds—'*black, blanc, beur*' (Arab in backslang). Their circumstances and the situations in which they find themselves are characteristic of all races.

As with the choice for racial backgrounds for the protagonists, the music is expressing the *métissage*, or blending, of different cultures in the *banlieue*: in Thomas Gilou's *Raï*, Slimane complains the driver of the car is playing too much ethnic 'raï' instead of American music, and in the powerful scene of *La Haine* in which the camera becomes the rap spinning over the *cité*, the words abusing the police turn themselves into—or are covered by—Édith Piaf's 'Je ne regrette rien'. The two cultures blending together are in these instances less African and French, Afro-Caribbean and French, Jewish and French, than they are American and French (Hargreaves 1995: 107).

However, because *banlieues* have an important proportion of immigrant population and the first wave of these films in the mid-1980s were made by North Africans of first or second generation, the so-called *beurs*, some of whom are still making them, this label has been attached to these films. How does a film qualify for this label? Is the origin of the director and/or the characters the defining factor, as Christian Bosséno (1992) argues? Also, because we saw how tempting it is to view this new and very popular genre in French film-making as being directly influenced by the 'ghetto films' of the United States, critics and scholars sometimes believe these films express a search for identity between French and Muslim cultures: Tarr, for instance, speaks about those made by *beur* film-makers as 'representation of "new ethnicities" ' (Tarr 1993: 321). Clearly, multiculturalism, the centre, the in-between, the lack of identity, and integration can be used to sell products, but is it not ultimately ethnocentric voyeurism? How important is the film-maker's nationality? Does it not contribute to the victimization of immigrants when only ethnic films are considered 'authentic'? My contention here is that the label of *beur* is nowadays less significant than when the first films appeared in the mid-1980s. Furthermore, this is not a label happily endorsed by those it is supposed to designate, whether film-makers or not (Rosello 1996*b*).

Irrespective of the directors' origins, we witness with most of these films the projection of the official discourse on 'segregation' and 'assimilation' onto the screen. *La Haine* constructs a national identity of 'assimilation': the family of the *beur* character is the only one not to be shown, so as not to single them out as different, and there is no mention of Islam at all. This playing down of religion is all the more significant if we bear in mind that 'Islam' is cited as the main reason for the 'non-assimilation' of this particular wave of immigrants as opposed to the previous ones. Also, it renders surprising the fact that, in response to the publication of the list of the Pope's top ten recommended films, a set of religious leaders from various denominations got in on the act and the Muslim religious leaders listed *La Haine* in their top ten (Malcolm 1996). The premiss of *La Haine* and most of the *banlieue* films seems to be that 'integration' can only be achieved by cutting off any link with the community of origin, hence doing away with any pleasure of hybridity.

If the mapping of the city is not racial, it is social: poor whites and second-generation immigrants are excluded from the capitalist circulation of money/work/consumption. This is also Bosséno's reading of the *beur* films: 'It matters little what colour their skin is or whether they are *beurs*, blacks, Portuguese, Italians, Turks or (white) French, rockers, punks or rastas: they all suffer the same raw deal to an equal degree' (Bosséno 1992: 52), not only because they are excluded but also because they are young. Michel Wieviorka (1993: 131) argues that the inhabitants of the *banlieue* lack identity as much because of their age as for racial or social reasons. *Douce France* is the only film in which the characters are slightly older, between 20 and 30; the others all feature adolescents with no prospects in life. Bosséno points out that already in *Le Thé au harem d'Archimède*, the director Mehdi Charef 'is careful to connote racism not as anti-North African but as an outlet for resentment against young people' (Bosséno 1992: 50). The negative image of the *banlieue* projected by French society provokes a crisis of identity in the youngest inhabitants who do not seem to fit in anywhere. In *La Haine*, the youngsters' crisis of identity manifests itself in a number of ways. The first few minutes of the film are punctuated by the names of the protagonists. These are introduced with the appearance of the characters and are not only uttered but written down: as a tag on a police van sprayed by Saïd; as a close-up of a big ring on Vinz's finger; and printed on a boxing poster in Hubert's gym. Underpinning these labels is the audience's knowledge that these are also the names of the actors. It is as if they were trying to taking possession of space by writing their names on it. This is more evident when in Paris Saïd modifies the advertising board reminiscent of Al Pacino's palace in *Scarface* (de Palma, 1983) from 'Le monde est à vous' to 'Le monde est à nous', the world is yours to ours. However, it is made clear that Paris does *not* belong to these young men when the old routine, often found in European films, of clicking one's fingers to switch off the lights of the Tour Eiffel from far away repeatedly fails.

The great number of mirrors in the film has been focused upon by Michel Estève (1995), who interprets them as support for the spectacle of the characters. However, he concedes that mirrors have a different role in the Parisian toilet scene, where they allow the characters to be in shot together neither one in front of the other, nor next to each other, but separated, isolated. I would suggest that mirrors have a further significance: when Narcissus saw his reflection in the water, he did not recognize himself straight away. There is a gap between the gaze and the acknowledgement of identity. Indeed the scenes of *La Haine* in which characters are in front of mirrors are scenes entirely devoted to the exploration of the youths' identities: Vinz, a Jew, imitating Robert De Niro or cutting Saïd's hair 'the American way' and uttering: 'I do not want to be the next Arab boy to be killed by the cops'; and the scene in the public toilet in which an episode illustrating Jewish persecution during the war is narrated to them.

In the city centre, the characters of the *banlieue* films lack identity for lack of space. Because they have no job and no money, they have nothing to do other than to walk endlessly, without any obvious purpose or intent. The youngsters are in perpetual motion and are not only ejected from localities (the flat of Asterix) but also prevented from entering: for instance, the taxi and the nightclub (interestingly, this scene is to be found in all the *banlieue* films). While the characters experience alienation in Paris, one must ask whether they feel more at home in its periphery. Whereas Mongin (1997) believes this to be the case, there is evidence to the contrary: the protagonists are incessantly driven away from the places to which they go, such as the roof where the barbecue is taking place and the hospital in which their friend Abdel Ichaha is dying. Despite the aesthetic opposition in the representation of the two localities in *La Haine*, the periphery does not present the characters with a healthier environment than the city centre: they are 'enfermés dehors', 'locked outside', both in the *banlieue* and in Paris.[2] As Bachelard (1957: 194) would put it, the prison is outside: the characters in *La Haine* are excluded from all the spaces, from any location, for they do not have a place in society because of their age and social class.

As a result, in common with the American ''hood movies', salvation implies escape and it seems that for many of the characters the solution is to go away, to change space. The title of Karim Dridi's *Bye Bye* is significant in this respect and *Raï* ends with the departure of the female protagonist. Personal morality is not enough: one needs to get out of the *banlieue*, to change space, in order to change social predicament. There is a strong will on the part of the youth of the periphery to get out from it, from marginalization and exclusion. But escape to where? We have seen the city centre did not offer a more welcoming environment and in fact the only space which seems to have a potential for happiness is the countryside. Indeed there is a tendency in contemporary French cinema to return to the great historical opposition between the countryside and the city and to attribute positive and escapist connotations to the former. The so-called 'heritage' genre, comedies such as Étienne Chatiliez's *Le Bonheur est dans le pré* (1995), and films of a more committed type, like Manuel Poirier's . . . *À la campagne* (1995), *Marion* (1996), and *Western* (1997), all express a nostalgia for a healthier life in nature, amongst 'simpler' people, reminiscent of the contrast between urban and rural settings which was fashionable in the 1960s with the call to go 'back to nature' of the hippie movement.

Nature does not appear as such in *La Haine*, but, excluded from urban space, it creeps back: in the name of the *cité*, Les Muguets, which recalls the real troubled area of Les Minguettes in Lyons, but also translates as 'lily of the valley'; in the name of the *banlieue* in which the film was shot: Chanteloup les Vignes (often *banlieues* have rural names: e.g. Le Val-Fourre, le Mas du Taureau); and in the cow of which Vinz keeps having surreal visions in the housing estate (as if to express the impossibility of representing the inaccessible, the unknown, the total Otherness of the countryside).

In a few of the *banlieue* films, nature is not just *opposed* to the city, as in ''hood movies' and gang films—Spike Lee's *Clockers* (1995), for example (which ends with its protagonist finally redeemed from drug-selling, saved from prison and the sickness that was invading him, by escaping outside the projects, in a train crossing the desert into the sunset), Francis Coppola's *The Outsiders* (1983), F. Gary Gray's *Set it Off* (1996), and Dough McHenry's *Jason's Lyric* (1994) set in bucolic Dallas—but actually reappears *within* the urban setting, like the horse in *Raï*. For the *banlieue* is still the city, but at the same time it is outside the city, at its edge, halfway between the city and the countryside: still urban, but with some rural elements resurgent in it, not wanting to let go and reclaiming their territory. Nature is the city's unconscious, located on its outer edges, but thirsty for revenge.

Having established, I hope, that the *banlieue* films are more concerned with social and youth issues rather than that of race, my contention is that the importance of these films lies principally with the creation of a new genre in French film. Beyond the burning topicality of the subject matter, Kassovitz's and Richet's works represent also a true manifesto for a new type of cinema. The *banlieue* films aim to address one of France's major social preoccupations at present, something that France has not done for a long time, since the militant films of the 1970s. In this, these films are much less influenced by the French cinematic tradition than by Italian neo-realism and by one of its great heirs, Pier Paolo Pasolini, poet of the deprived Roman periphery of the 1960s: 'Marginality, after falling out of favour somewhat, has once again become a central concern of the French cinema' (Bosséno 1992: 56). Like Victor Hugo in *Les Misérables*, Kassovitz's avowed intention is to lend his voice to those who cannot express themselves.

Committed cinema is also what Kassovitz's father does, as a militant of May 1968 who used to work with Chris Marker. However, he belongs to another generation, does not understand his son, and wonders why he wears trainers and listens to rap music all day long. Mathieu admits that his intention was to show his parents, who live in the fifth *arrondissement*, on the Left Bank of the capital, that the police can still kill. We can therefore detect a wish to re-establish a dialogue with the previous generation via the film. This is why Kassovitz senior plays the artist who, in the private viewing in Paris, is compassionate and tries to understand *le malaise des banlieues* as he puts it. This is also why, I suggest, the footage of riots on which the credits appear at the very beginning of the film is not shot in the periphery, as the narrative would have us believe, but during student riots in Paris, probably in 1986, when it took the death of a student to stop the then Prime Minister Chirac making drastic reforms in education. By this initial scene, the link is made with the revolt of 1968 and with Marker's *Le Joli Mai* (1962).[3]

When film-makers were the first to react against the Jean-Louis Debré law on immigration in 1997 with a petition to advocate civil disobedience (which extended then to other professions in show business), they were criticized for not making particularly committed films. I have to disagree. Films like the ones discussed here are part of a Renoiresque return to political concerns of French cinema, which *Cahiers du cinéma* saluted, calling it *le retour du politique*.

Notes

1. Movement between the centre and the margins structures the French genre, whereas, with the exception of Spike Lee's *Jungle Fever* (1991) and *Set it Off* (Gray, 1996), in which the 'career' of the characters takes them to other parts of town, we are usually not shown other neighbourhoods in the so-called American 'ghetto films'.

2. 'The *banlieue* is presented as a desert, with no feeling of public space

and precious little private space either; Paris, where Vinz, Saïd and Hubert spend almost half the film, is rejecting and alienatory' (Reader 1995: 14).

3. Richet's films make this filiation with committed cinema of the late 1960s and 1970s even more explicit with their Marxist terminology (Tobin 1995: 29).

15

Ethnicity and Identity in the
cinéma de banlieue

CARRIE TARR

DESPITE the presence of increasing numbers of young French people of Maghrebi origin on screen and behind the camera during the mid-1990s, their voices have been obscured by a critical discourse which either situates their film-making under the umbrella term *cinéma de banlieue* or associates it with Algerian cinematic concerns. The first strategy includes them but renders them invisible, the second excludes them as Other to French cinema proper. Both refuse a perspective generated by the hybrid status of people whose double culture makes them both insiders and outsiders in relation to dominant French culture. Insiders by virtue of being brought up in and resident in France, insiders also in the hybrid multi-ethnic youth culture of the *banlieue* (France's grim outer city housing estates), French people of Maghrebi origin are also outsiders, not just because of institutionalized state racism and the racism of those who target 'Arabs' and Islam as the scapegoats for France's socio-economic difficulties, but also because of the republican definition of integration. For the French approach to integration is to assume that ethnic minority Others must assimilate to the dominant culture rather than acknowledging and accepting minority cultures within a multicultural society, cultures which, given the historic relationships between France and its former colonies, also have a diasporic dimension. French people of Maghrebi origin are in a position to manœuvre in and between 'territorial, local, diasporic, national and global cultures and identities', as Marie Gillespie describes the cosmopolitan state of mind of young British Punjabis in Southall (Gillespie 1995: 21). However, a *cinéma de banlieue* which represents the *banlieue* as just a 'melting-pot' of marginalized and excluded young people risks ignoring these multicultural dimensions. To cite Mireille

Rosello, ' *"La culture des banlieues"* is . . . an interestingly de-ethnicized and de-essentialized paradigm of coalition between communities and a reassuringly reuniversalized entity for the dominant culture, the Republic' (Rosello 1998: 68). Cinematic representations of French people of Maghrebi origin, then, are significant to the extent that they recognize not just the right to integration but also the right to ethnic diversity.

Representations of France's postcolonial ethnic minorities have been largely confined either to the stereotypical, marginalized roles of dominant cinema (Tarr 1997*b*), or to the more subjective expressions of concern about the identity of second-generation Maghrebi immigrants, voiced in the handful of films of the 1980s known as *cinéma beur* (Bosséno 1992; Tarr 1993). In the mid-1990s, however, Mathieu Kassovitz's stunningly inventive second film, *La Haine*, with its central '*black–blanc–beur*' trio of unemployed youths, brought the representation of the *banlieue* and *la fracture sociale* (the increasing disparity between haves and have-nots in contemporary French society) to the centre of the cinematic viewing experience (Reader 1995; Tarr 1997*a*). In the same year, the multi-ethnic youth culture of the *banlieue* provided the setting for Jean-François Richet's *État des lieux* and Thomas Gilou's *Raï*, as well as for *Bye Bye* by Karim Dridi (a Franco-Tunisian director, who made the award-winning *Pigalle* in 1994), *Krim* by Ahmed Bouchaala (a director of Algerian origin whose previous work was in music videos and advertising), and *Douce France* by Malik Chibane (also of Algerian origin, whose first low-budget film, *Hexagone*, had been hailed in 1994 by the French press as 'the first film by a *beur* for *beurs*' (Tarr 1995)). For the critics, this *cinéma de banlieue*, with its concern for social realities, not only formed part of the 'jeune cinéma français' (Trémois 1997), but also seemed to establish a new, popular French genre (see Konstantarakos, this volume). However, the slippage from *cinéma beur* to *cinéma de banlieue* risks effacing the specificity of ethnic minority experiences and, indeed, the clear thematic links with the *cinéma beur* of the 1980s were generally ignored. For example, Yann Tobin in *Positif* refers back only to *Black Mic Mac* (Gilou, 1986), *La Thune* (Galland, 1991), and the later *Hexagone* (see Tobin 1995), while Thierry Jousse in *Cahiers du cinéma* mentions only *Laisse béton* (Le Péron, 1983) and *De bruit et de fureur* (Brisseau, 1988). At the same time, the unexpected success of *La Haine* limited critical consideration of the other five films. Yet, if *La Haine* and *État des lieux* emphasize the significance of *la fracture sociale* across ethnic lines and the commonality of experiences of a predominantly male underclass, the film-makers of Maghrebi origin handle the same or similar material in rather different ways. This chapter examines the different representations of ethnicity and identity (and by extension, integration) in the six *banlieue* films of 1995, and establishes a comparison between the three 'white'-authored films (*La Haine*, *État des lieux*, and *Raï*) and the three films by film-makers of Maghrebi origin (*Bye Bye*, *Krim*, and *Douce France*). It takes into account the narrative function and degree of subjectivity accorded to the characters of Maghrebi origin, the representation of the *banlieue* as a site of violence, the values ascribed to the culture of the parents' generation, and the construction of gender and sexuality.

La Haine mobilizes a trio of young men from different ethnic backgrounds, Jewish, black, and *beur*, and insists on their common bonding within a hybrid oppositional youth culture, based on the language of the *banlieue*, music, drugs, petty crime, unemployment, hatred of the police, and social exclusion, in a world where white, black, and *beur* youths are all victims of police violence. The film follows the trajectory of the three youths through a day in their lives in which events spiral out of their control. Nevertheless, the characters of white, Jewish Vinz (Vincent Cassell) and black boxer Hub (Hubert Kaoundé) are more fleshed out than Saïd, the Maghrebi-French character (Saïd Taghmaoui), and both have more significant roles in the narrative structure and final tragedy, where one is killed, the other about to kill or be killed. The ineffectual Saïd can only close his eyes in horror. *État des lieux* centres even more firmly on a white working-class character, Pierre (Patrick dell'Isola), though class solidarity across the racial divide is depicted through interracial encounters which are shot through with humour. The opening scene foregrounds a chorus of primarily black youths complaining direct to camera about their socio-economic situation, using a language inspired by Marxist rhetoric. Later, in a scene at Pierre's workplace, a workmate tells a long story about trying to get his friend Ahmed admitted to a nightclub and ending up in a brawl with the police. *État des lieux*, like *La Haine*, takes for granted the presence of ethnic minorities in the social spaces of the *banlieue* (and on the film's soundtrack), but gives more space to black youths than to youths of Maghrebi origin, and marginalizes the latter in terms of its narrative concerns. In *Raï*, on the other hand, as the reference to Raï music suggests, the *banlieue* is particularly associated with *beur* culture through a group of young, aggressive, predominantly *beur* males, which nevertheless includes Laurent (Tara Romer), a token 'white' boy. The film centres on Djamel (Mustapha Benstiti), who has a job as caretaker of the local swimming-pool, his brother Nordine (Sami Naceri), a drug addict, and Sahlia (Tabatha Cash), whom Djamel is in love with, the sister of the volatile Mezz (Micky El Mazroui). The spectator is encouraged to sympathize with Djamel, but Djamel's narrative trajectory, like Saïd's in *La Haine*, is equally ineffective. He loses Sahlia because he does not understand her sexual desire and need for autonomy, he loses his brother whom he is unable to save from drugs, and when he finally throws in his lot with Mezz and the gang, in a climax of violence against the police, he does so out of despair rather than conviction.

The action of these three films takes place primarily in the sort of Parisian housing estate which is better known from television reports on crime and violence in the *banlieue*. *La Haine* opens with scenes of a riot transmitted by television. Its narrative then depends on the fate of Abdel, the hospitalized victim of a police assault, and on the police gun found by Vinz, with which he plans to get his revenge if Abdel dies. A series of scenes show confrontations with on the police and the abuse of police authority (even if this is mitigated by the presence of a Maghrebi cop and a new recruit who is horrified by the violence). The film is sympathetic to its central trio who do not initiate violence, despite their macho posturing, whose resort to drugs and petty crime is a product of their impossible social situation, and whose justifiable anger does not merit the excessive police violence of the ending. The violence of the state is rendered even more explicit in *État des lieux* through a series of negative encounters between Pierre and various authority figures— his boss, the employee at the employment agency, the police—each of which leads to an explosion of anger. Although, like Vinz, he is unable to change his worsening situation, he does not give in to it, and finds consolation in his political beliefs, his boxing, and in secret, explosive sex with his (white) friend's wife, shot in a protracted scene which brings the film to a close. In *Raï*, however, the youths (with the exception of Djamel) are more proactive in initiating violence and the reasons for their behaviour are less clearly attributable to their desperate socio-economic situation. The film opens with the group operating a scam to steal money from a couple of naive white hitchhikers, proceeds through the activities of Nordine, in particular, to procure drugs (the film's most entertaining moments being provided by his theft of a race-horse actually destined for the knacker's yard), and ends with a full-scale riot, initiated by the youths in protest against the shooting of Nordine by a (white) policewoman, after he has been seen threatening the crowd in a shopping centre with a gun. However, Nordine clearly provokes his own death by insulting the police-woman and pretending to draw a gun on her (which the spectator knows he no longer possesses), and the ensuing riot therefore seems hardly justified, as Djamel at first acknowledges. Instead of under-lining legitimate grievances (as in *La Haine*), *Raï*'s repeated scenes of muggings, shootings, car burning, looting, and violence against the police play into majority fears about mindless violence and aggression on the part of ethnic minority youths.

In *La Haine* and *État des lieux*, there is no representation of the family backgrounds or living spaces of the Maghrebi-French youths and no interest in first-generation immigrants. Saïd's contin-ual intrusion into and ejection from the spaces of others demon-strate his lack of place in society. In *Raï*, however, the predicaments of Sahlia, Djamel, and Nordine are attributable to the immigrant family rather than to their socio-economic situation. Mezz's honour depends on him preventing Sahlia from leading her own life, and Sahlia's resistance to marriage with Djamel, prematurely arranged according to tradition by the two mothers, leads her to walk out on her family and the estate. Djamel's superstitious mother favours her drug addict son and relies on a fetish from a marabout (a Muslim holy man) to protect him from harm, while Nordine attributes his drug problem to his feelings of inadequacy at being expected to take over his dead father's place. Meanwhile, one of Nordine's attempts to procure drugs reveals an entire Maghrebi family involved in parcelling them up. *Raï* thus unapolo-getically attributes the alienation and violence of young people in the *banlieue* either to the immigrant Muslim family's outdated valuing of female purity, belief in arranged marriages, and super-stitions, or, alternatively, to their involvement in crime. Despite its foregrounding of the immigrant family, then, *Raï*'s representation of Maghrebi culture plays into the stereotypical prejudices of the majority culture and suggests that the only future for the second generation lies in leaving the *banlieue* (and Maghrebi culture) behind, like Sahlia, or sinking into violence, like Djamel.

In all these films, the masculinity of the central characters is in crisis. In *La Haine*, it is clear that the central trio are incapable of communicating with women, and the formation of the couple, mixed race or otherwise, is not seriously entertained. In *État des lieux*, Pierre's wordless sex scene with his friend's wife may provide him with a sense of his identity as a man, but the black characters' relationships with women remain at the level of macho verbal posturing. Again, it is *Raï* which is most concerned with ethnic minorities and the representation of gender, but here again, the film plays into racist stereotypes. Above all, it suffers from the casting of former porn star Tabatha Cash as Sahlia, and the decision to display her body as the object of a voyeuristic gaze. Her revolt against the patriarchal constraints of Maghrebi family life and Djamel's misplaced idealization of her could have called into question conventional assumptions about masculine and feminine identities and gender roles. But a revolt which has Sahlia first try (unsuccessfully) to seduce Djamel, then sleep with Laurent, then erupt into the dance the gang has organized on the estate, wearing a blonde wig, tight skimpy skirt, and thigh-high boots, smacks primarily of the fantasies of the film's white, male director. Sahlia is the only character able to leave the *banlieue* at the end of the film, but her role offers little hope for the formation of either the mixed race or Maghrebi-French couple.

Even though *La Haine* and *État des lieux* are cinematically exhilarating films which express a healthy anger at the injustices and inequalities of contemporary French society, they do not highlight the specificity of the situation facing second- and third-generation Maghrebi-French immigrants in France. As for *Raï*, though it foregrounds this specificity, it does so in a way which, however unintentionally, plays into racist stereotypes of an alien immigrant culture, spawning an irresponsible, violent youth culture. *Raï*'s representation of the *banlieue* can be usefully compared with Chibane's *Hexagone* (for which Gilou had been an adviser), which is also centred on two brothers, one of whom is a drug addict who meets his death, the other a dutiful son with a girlfriend who rebels against traditional Muslim family values. *Hexagone* handles its subject matter in a sensitive, low-key, realist manner, allowing the central characters an unusual degree of subjectivity, and highlights the characters' problematic positioning in relation to both French and Maghrebi culture, rather than focusing on Maghrebi culture as the cause of violence and alienation (Tarr 1995).

Bye Bye, Krim, and *Douce France* address the situation of ethnic minorities in France through narratives which move beyond the semi-autobiographical bases of much *beur* film-making, like *Le Thé au harem d'Archimède* and *Hexagone,* and the later *Souviens-toi de moi* (1996) by Zaïda Ghorab-Volta, the first feature film about the *banlieue* by a Maghrebi-French woman (Tarr 1997c). In *Bye Bye,* Karim Dridi evokes the multi-ethnic Panier district of Marseilles through the eyes of two second-generation Maghrebi-French brothers, Ismaël (Sami Bouajila) and Mouloud (Oussini Embarek), who are travelling south, prior to Mouloud being sent back to join his parents in North Africa. In *Krim,* Ahmed Bouchaala constructs a melodramatic world of obsession through the story of Krim (Hammou Graïa), who is released from prison for murdering his wife and goes back to Lyons after sixteen years' absence to search for his long-lost daughter (a story based on a *fait divers*). In his second film, *Douce France,* Chibane uses comedy to explore the interracial friendship of Moussa (Hakim Sahraoui), the son of a harki, and Jean-Luc (Frédéric Diefenthal), a white youth, and their relationship with three very different young Arab women. It is immediately noticeable that these films do not centre on the multi-ethnic gang of unemployed youths typical of many *beur* and *banlieue* films. In each case, the central (male) Maghrebi-French character is older (aged 30 rather than 20) and has put crime behind him. The films focus rather on interpersonal and intergenerational relationships within the Maghrebi-French community, and the central character's problematic relationship with French society.

In *Bye Bye,* a series of flashbacks indicates that Ismaël is haunted by memories of the death of his handicapped brother in a fire for which he may have been responsible. His integrity, sensitivity, and despair are rendered through a series of lingering close-ups, a relatively unusual technique in the construction of a Maghrebi-French character. Ismaël is responsible for sending Mouloud back 'home', but the film first explores the brothers' family of relatives and experiences of life in Marseilles. Mouloud gets led astray by his cousin Rhida, refuses to go back to North Africa, and gets embroiled with a local North African drug dealer as well as becoming the target of a group of racists, thanks to his spraying of graffiti on their car. Ismaël drifts into work as a dockside labourer alongside his uncle, makes friends with his white workmate Jacky (Frédéric Andrau), who saves him from drowning, but falls for Jacky's Maghrebi-French girlfriend Yasmine (Nozha Khouadra) and becomes the object of Jacky's abuse and Yasmine's contempt. He finally assumes responsibility for Mouloud, escapes with him from the drug dealer, and decides not to send him away. Having outstayed their welcome in Marseilles, the two homeless brothers set off in their 2CV, and the film ends on their reconciliation, even if the breakdown of their car means that they will have difficulty finding somewhere else to go.

In *Krim*, the central character is a former boxer, who has spent sixteen years in prison for murdering his wife, sharing a cell with an older father-figure (of uncertain ethnic origin), Eugène Parodi (Philippe Clay), his mentor and friend, an artist whose paintings represent his dreams for the future. On his release, he records the sounds and feelings of freedom to send back to Parodi, his experiences rendered through elaborate fragmentation of the image and the intercutting of unmotivated shots of a distressed young woman, who eventually turns out to be his niece, Nora (Elisabeth Rose). When Krim discovers that the block of flats where he once lived is due to be demolished and that his daughter has committed suicide, he cannot bring himself to tell Parodi the truth, and his tape-recorded lies cause a disillusioned Parodi to dismiss him as just 'un bougnoul' (a racist term of abuse). Haunted by his past life and the loss of his daughter, he squats in the deserted flat and attempts to recreate the past, rejecting the friendship of a drunken white layabout, formerly his friend. Just as he is about to give up, his sister Samia (Zakia Tahiri) asks for help with Nora, who has become a drug addict. Krim accepts the task, and tries first to force Nora, then to persuade her, to kick her habit. After a major setback, he is ready to abandon her, but Samia then confesses that Nora is actually his daughter Yasmine. Krim's love for Nora enables her to pull through, and the film ends with Nora's voice-over on the tape to Parodi, who has at last regained confidence in his friend. Like *Bye Bye*, *Krim* invests the Maghrebi-French male with a new sense of responsibility towards the younger generation, though the father–daughter relationship perilously resembles the traditional incestuous duo of classical French cinema (Vincendeau 1992).

Douce France operates in a different register from *Bye Bye* and *Krim*. Moussa and Jean-Luc are able to transcend their condition as unemployed young men in the *banlieue*, thanks to a plot device in the opening sequence which has them discover a cache of stolen jewellery. Consequently, they are able to set themselves up in business, Moussa by taking over a bar frequented by North Africans (called L'Impasse), and Jean-Luc by setting up his solicitor's office in the back room. The film thus evades the pessimistic realism of more typical *banlieue* films, and is able instead to explore with humour the duo's interactions with the local community, and particularly with women. Jean-Luc tries to win back Souad (Séloua Hamse), a thoroughly modern young Maghrebi-French woman, while Moussa sets his sights on her sister Farida (Fadila Bellkebla), who has chosen to adopt a strict Muslim identity. Moussa's pursuit of Farida, which requires him to frequent the mosque, is put at risk by the revelation that his mother has already arranged a marriage for him with an Arab girl from back 'home' (Algeria). When Myssad arrives, her sophisticated, liberated attitude confounds stereotypical expectations, and her decision to walk out on a marriage which is not based on love leads to the final sequence in which the three young women drive to the airport together, and Farida eventually throws away her headscarf. The ineffectual Moussa may be at an impasse, unable to stand up to his mother himself, but, as in *Raï*, the young women end up clearly rejecting the values and traditions of their parents in so far as they affect their lives as women. *Douce France* thus operates a significant shift from the male characters to the female characters as the agents of integration and change.

In terms of cinematic space, these films extend the representation of a multi-ethnic France from the Parisian *banlieues* of Saint Denis in *Douce France* to Marseilles in *Bye Bye* and Lyons in *Krim*. But their *mise-en-scène* also foregrounds the domestic spaces of the Maghrebi family and refuses to focus on the *banlieue* as site of violence and clashes with the police. In *Bye Bye*, Ismaël finds himself at a crossroads, confronting the claustrophobic spaces of his uncle's apartment, the uncertainties of the workplace, the open-ness of the seascape where the ferryboat heads for North Africa, and the streets of Marseilles which are the site of drug-dealing, racist violence, and sexual temptation, but also of a more utopian vision of a multi-ethnic working-class community, as in the scenes of the open-air dance and the marriage between a white woman and a black man. In *Krim*, the wasteland of abandoned, decaying tower blocks represents the emotional disorder of Krim's mind, from which he manages to escape through his utopian vision of a little house in the country for himself and his daughter, as figured in Parodi's paintings and the brightly coloured wallpaper pattern of his daughter's bedroom, which he uncovers in the ruined flat. At the end of the film, Krim has left behind the city with its ex-cons and prostitutes, and the *banlieue* with its drunks and drug addicts, signs here of a degenerate white French culture, and the ruined *banlieue* towers collapse in glorious slow motion. Both these films end, then, with the Maghrebi-French character leaving the *banlieue* in search of a new way of life, however impossible. *Douce France* chooses another strategy to avoid the clichés of the *banlieue* film. Instead of impersonal tower block settings, its characters live in small suburban houses or modern flats, and are seen at work, like Souad's father selling merguez outside the makeshift mosque and Souad herself working in a Quick burger bar. The film repeatedly draws attention to racism and ethnic difference as issues, but defuses them through comedy, as when the police shooting of a drunken immigrant becomes an opportunity for Jean-Luc to build up his business, or when a drunken Moussa finds himself accidentally in bed with a neighbour whose racist husband had earlier pulled a gun on him, or when Farida's sophisticated command of French leads to her teaching it to little Jewish children. Whereas the central characters of *Bye Bye* and *Krim* can find no future in the *banlieue*, *Douce France* assumes that the *banlieue* can accommodate people of different ethnic backgrounds and ends with Souad and Farida returning from the airport, hopefully in order to exercise some control over their lives.

These three films value the Maghrebi culture of the older generation, even if they also show that the second generation is capable of refusing or questioning aspects of that culture. *Bye Bye* invests heavily in the sympathetic protrayal of the extended immigrant family, presided over by the silent but encouraging figure of the great aunt. In *Bye Bye*, the uncle (unusually) has a job but still worries about the loss of his paternal authority, and the warm-hearted aunt helps her daughters with their homework and smokes the odd cigarette in secret. In contrast, the more rigid, authoritarian attitude of Ismaël's father, evidenced in his telephone calls, demonstrates why Mouloud refuses to go back to North Africa. The affectionate banter between the two brothers at the end of the film gives a positive image of Maghrebi-French youths, whose family ties enable them to combat both racism and crime. *Krim* evacuates the older generation (Krim's parents apparently died of shame at his crime), and positions Krim as alone in the world except for the friendship of Parodi. But Krim desires to assume his position as head of the family, and berates his sister Samia for her acceptance of 'francaoui' (French) values. (Samia works in a beauty salon, has dyed her hair blonde, and is eliminated from the narrative at the end, even though she dyes her hair black again.) *Krim* thus puts its trust, not in adaptation and integration, but in the acceptance of traditional values, and the purifying of the new second-generation Maghrebi family is symbolized by the scene in which the father bathes the daughter in a tin bath outside the flats. In *Douce France*, Moussa spends his time trying, unsuccessfully, to escape from the influence of his violent harki father and his sick mother, who blackmails him into accepting her plans for an arranged marriage (in contrast to Souad, who leaves home to assert her independence from her parents). The community gathering for Moussa's wedding is primarily an excuse for local colour provided by the spectacle of traditional Algerian costumes and dancing. But the future of the second generation is shown, here, to depend on the refusal of traditional Muslim values, and Moussa's predicament is resolved by Myssad's rejection of a marriage which is not based on love. *Douce France* goes further than *Bye Bye* in displaying the Islamic culture of the parents' generation (whose new mosque has been designed without minarets so as not to disturb the indigenous French), but it does so in order to demonstrate that this culture does not impede the process of integration among the second generation.

As in *La Haine* and *Raï*, the masculinity of the Maghrebi-French male is at stake in these films, given the impotence of their central characters, but the question of gender roles is addressed more extensively. *Bye Bye* attempts to redeem Ismaël's impotence by allowing him to have sex with Jacky's girlfriend. However, Ismaël's inability to accept responsibility for his act leaves Yasmine in the thankless role of object of exchange between men, and the film ends on a regressive return to a 'safe' all-male world. In *Krim*, the overly masculine Krim, whose violence has already caused the death of his wife, avenges his powerlessness by having sex with and then humiliating a prostitute who had taken pity on him, and rejecting his French-identified sister. His possessive attitude towards his wayward teenage daughter is a sign of his inability to enter a world of adult sexual relationships, even if the film itself endorses the formation of the father–daughter couple. In *Douce France*, Moussa is assumed to be capable of forming a heterosexual relationship, but there are no images of the couple and he is last seen discovering Myssad's absence. However, *Douce France* is different from the other films in that the female characters provide the film's narrative impetus and the final image shows Souad, literally, in the driving seat.

The differences between the two sets of films discussed here are significant. The white-authored films express the anger and alienation of young people in the *banlieue*, regardless of their ethnic origin, and focus in particular on violence and hostility between male youths and the police, a violence which is even more pronounced in Richet's follow-up film, *Ma 6T va crack-er* (1997), and, in a more stylized form, Kassovitz's *Assassin(s)* (1997). The films by directors of Maghrebi origin are careful to avoid or defuse scenes of confrontation with the police and other authority figures, and are more interested in exploring individual problems of identity and integration, and addressing changes within the Maghrebi community in France, including the question of women's place within that culture. This does not prevent them from reaching different conclusions. Whereas integration is considered possible in *Douce France*, it is far more problematic in *Bye Bye* and *Krim*. And while *Douce France* consolidates the theme of interracial friendship and signals the importance of women in the process of integration, both *Bye Bye* and *Krim* refuse interracial friendships (apart from Krim's ambiguous relationship with Parodi) and seek to contain the female characters they construct.

Nevertheless, even if *Bye Bye* and *Krim* are pessimistic about the integration of French people of Maghrebi origin, it is clear that the three films considered here are more sensitive to questions of ethnicity and identity than the first three films. Without them, the representation of Maghrebi-French characters would remain marginalized or even invisible (as in *État des lieux*), undeveloped (as in *La Haine*), or verging on the stereotypical (as in *Raï*). Their more diverse, individualized, and challenging representations show the importance of ethnic minority contributions to the representation of contemporary France as a multicultural society. The shared hybrid culture of young people represented in a white-authored *banlieue* cinema should not mask the significance of ethnic difference, and the difficulties it presents for an assimilationist understanding of integration, represented in Maghrebi-French-authored *banlieue* cinema.

16

Zapping without Mercy: *Merci la vie*
(Blier, 1991)

RUSSELL KING

Merci la vie is a zapper's film; the director is telling five or six stories at the same time. . . . I adore zapping; otherwise we'd be bored stiff.

(Blier in Toubiana 1991: 26)

Zapping allows the viewer to construct a viewing experience of fragments, a post-modern collage of images whose pleasures lie in their discontinuity, their juxtapositions, and their contradictions. This is segmentation taken to the extreme of fragmentation and makes of television the most open producerly text for it evades all attempts at closure.

(Fiske 1991: 105)

BLIER'S easily recognized and oft-repeated 'style' of violence, surprise, and provocation is aggressively announced in the opening scenes of *Merci la vie*, in his preferred manner: 'I like opening sentences in books; films that attack. It's my aggressive nature: I need to grab people by the throat; I can't begin gently' (Toubiana 1991: 22). *Merci la vie* begins in this way, with a short scene, before the credits appear, showing a young woman (Joëlle/Anouk Grinberg), dressed as a bride, being brutally kicked and punched by a young man who then drives away in a sports car. The spectator is cued to accepting this establishing scene as one that somehow begins the narrative and introduces thematic motifs. Who are they? Why is the young woman dressed as a bride? Why is the young man beating her up? The bride's dress will later connect with another bride and Joëlle's visit to a bride shop and her reappearance as a bride; though this instance of brutality is never explicitly explained, it will form a pattern of violence within the film, and, though the spectator may hypothesize explanations which the film will neither confirm nor disconfirm, total closure will always be denied.

Most spectators endeavour to focus on the way the story is a vehicle for illustrating certain themes, teasing them out and ultimately reaching some plausible interpretation of the film. This approach is amply illustrated by two studies of the film: Guy Austin analyses its historicity, whilst Michel Mesnil interprets and 'naturalizes' *Merci la vie* as a narrative constructed around a fantasy scenario. Mesnil argues that the only 'real' scene is the final one, the arrival of the family—mother, father, daughter, and boyfriend—at the seaside resort in July for the summer vacation. The daughter, Camille, may have been there a few months earlier, in the empty resort, alone, preparing to resit her baccalaureate. The film is therefore an enactment of her fantasies: her desire for a friend who is both an experienced, sexually promiscuous instructor and/or a fantasized alter ego, and her anxieties about sex which she may or may not have experienced, with a local decorator preparing holiday homes for the summer, who becomes the boyfriend in the final scene.

As Mesnil suggests, according to this scenario, *Merci la vie* is a kind of *Alice in Wonderland*, in the era of AIDS, or even, given that the film is a kind of female road-movie, a *Wizard of Oz* (Fleming, 1939). In some respects Blier's films resemble those of Buñuel in that they provocatively play with the slippage between the real and the non-real, without the traditional signals of change and switch. In many of his films, there is a basic event, an incident, a situation, around which a fantasy, a 'what if' scenario, is constructed. In the preceding film, *Trop belle pour toi* (1989), the opening scene would be construed as the 'real' scene, in which a temporary, plain-looking secretary arrives to work for a BMW dealer. When the hero (Depardieu) looks at her, the rest of the film is quite plausibly the fantasy that springs from the hero's imaginings at that moment. Once alerted to this constantly repeated structure, of slipping from the real into the unreal, into fantasy, into dream/nightmare scenarios, Blier's earlier films become much more accessible. Failure to recognize this pattern accounts in a large measure for the constant reference among spectators and critics to surrealism, to the absurd, to narrative anarchy. What we must ask, however plausible we may find the Mesnil thesis, is this: are we satisfied that this reading accommodates the formal complexities, the interpretative difficulties, the resistances to closure?

Another common way the thematic-narrative spectator approaches this film and Blier's earlier films is to examine the characters who people and inhabit the auteur-director's perverse universe: dysfunctional females, represented by a misogynistic director, even more dysfunctional males, and these breaking taboos and forming relationships and families which implode and explode. For example, to return to the opening scene of *Merci la vie*, what we find to be particularly shocking, especially for female spectators, is the violence against women. Where is it coming from? How do we react? Is there a point of view? Is it there simply as an illustration of male aggression towards women? Is it calculated to appeal to the (male) spectator who sadistically derives pleasure from the sight of women being beaten? On the other hand, by a complete shift of focus, one could argue that the core of Blier's concern resides in the representation of inadequate, dysfunctional male characters, whether they be young men, as in the opening scene, or old fathers, as in the final scene which depicts a pathetic, abandoned father, sitting, pants soiled, motionless, gazing out to sea, whilst wife and daughter go off to their apartment and the boyfriend to the local Mammouth supermarket. Is he the ultimate picture of fatherhood/patriarchy, disempowered, as conceived and represented by a pessimistic and cynical Blier? The term misogynist has been constantly applied to Blier and his films and the subject has been fully and explicitly examined elsewhere; it is not, however, the subject of this study.

My approach to Blier's film is to focus on one formal characteristic, and to base my reading on specific points made in an interview between Blier and Serge Toubiana. What is especially new and unusual about *Merci la vie*, proclaimed in the film's first two scenes, is the manner in which colour is established as the film's principal form of punctuation.

| SCENE 1 | 50 secs. | A young man beats up a young woman (Joëlle) dressed as a bride, and drives off. | Sepia-tinted black and white. |
| SCENE 2 | 1 min. | Camille pushes a shopping trolley, with seagulls sitting on it, along a road, from the beach. | Colour, daylight. |

SCENE 3	45 secs.	Camille meets Joëlle lying in the road.	Return to sepia-tinted black and white.
SCENE 4	1 min. 35 secs.	A series of shots as Camille and Joëlle return to Camille's holiday apartment: they walk down the road; Camille takes Joëlle in the trolley after she collapses.	Return to the colour of scene 2.
SCENE 5	1 min. 7 secs.	After Joëlle runs outside, a conversation in which Camille explains that Joëlle is 'the friend she has always been wanting'.	Sepia-tinted black and white.
SCENE 6	17 secs.		Colour, but darker, more sombre as it is sunset.
SCENE 7	1 min. 24 sccs.	Camille and Joëlle are on the apartment terrace.	Blue-tinted black and white.
SCENE 8	18 mins. 52 secs.	The decorator and night watchman.	Largely monochrome, at night, with a blue filter and spotlight producing for much of the sequence an almost expressionist blue colour with splashes of colour and at other times a blue-tinted black and white. The use of the blue filter and spot light produces considerable variations within this sequence.

This brief analysis of the punctuating changes of colour typifies the entire film. The three general categories are now in place: first, black and white with its variants of sepia and other tints; for example, the first scenes with the doctor Marc-Antoine will be in a greenish tint, and a short interior of the bridal shop will be in a pink tint; second, colour; and, third, a strong blue expressionist tint which sometimes allows splashes of colour. The spectator accustomed to the traditional use of switches from colour to black and white to indicate a shift from reality to unreality, from present to past, will suspect that these may no longer be applicable here, or certainly not the sole explanation, as they not only seem too random, but also sometimes fail to follow other forms of punctuation such as shot and scene. For example, the war scenes at the railway station near the end of the film are filmed in colour and various tints. These colour switches establish the fundamental, defining visual character of *Merci la vie*; they underscore the film's segmented and fragmented look.

Let us now return to the Toubiana interview, part of which was used as an epigraph to this chapter:

The film is a kind of pop video lasting two hours instead of three minutes. . . . *Merci la vie* is a zapper's film; the director is telling five or six stories at the same time; and it so happens that the five or six films showing that evening spoke of the same things: what luck! that gives you an idea; then suddenly it's in black and white; there's the war, and since the subject is eternal, there we are right in it. I adore zapping; otherwise we'd be bored stiff. (Toubiana 1991: 26)

The surprising effect of incorporating this TV principle of zapping into script construction and film-making is quite different from the earlier principle, apparent in almost all his other films, of setting traps for spectators: in an interview with Haustrate, Blier spoke of his constant desire to 'trap the spectator', not to give him what he expects, to set up a scene and do something outrageously different, unexpected: 'I call a trap-film one which disconcerts the spectator. When I start working on a film-script, I imagine ways which will allow me to surprise. I particularly like using clichés and classic dramatic structures, using them as a starting point. Then I turn them inside out' (Haustrate 1988: 115).

I am arguing that the principle of zapping is not merely a continuation and variation of a desire to provoke, surprise, break taboos, do something different. The notion of zapping belongs to television, and not television production, but television viewing. I propose to examine four ways in which zapping shapes the way spectators may wish to consider *Merci la vie*:

1. segmentation and fragmentation of the narrative;
2. control of the film's rhythm and the speed of viewing;

3. construction by the spectator of his or her own text;
4. characteristic activity of youth.

What film allows so easily is the juxtaposition of scenes or parts of scenes, from disparate sources, to create the effect of hallucination and fantasy. Thus, like the zapping from one TV channel to another, various narrative elements can be stitched together. The distinction I make between segment and fragment is this: a segment, as a part, implies being part of some actual or hypothetical unified or unitary whole; thus, in a more conventional narrative, shots, scenes, and sequences are all segments of what will become the whole, unitary film. On the other hand, a fragment always implies something which has been broken, and which will never be part of a whole, with the emphasis not on the whole to which it belongs or belonged, but on its brokenness.

This provides a convenient way of considering the narrative structure(s) of *Merci la vie*. In this film, the primary story/segment concerns inexperienced Camille and experienced Joëlle as they meet and set out on the road. It combines with the story/segment, initially shown in a greenish tint, of Marc-Antoine, the doctor who is going to exploit venereal disease amongst his local patients to increase his business. There is a return to the past, much of it in sepia-tinted black and white, to witness one's own parents and one's own conception, by means of artificial insemination. Camille's father, now crippled in a wheelchair, has, it would seem, had a miserable, sexually and emotionally frustrated marriage. What greater gift could she, Camille, make than to offer her beloved best friend to him, to offer him the love he never had. Thus narratives are entwined, abandoned, and resumed. We jump from one historical moment to another: since the past is the past, since Camille's conception and war both happened in the past, the times become confused (despite a seventeen-year gap in reality), with her mother consorting with a German officer; there can be an imaginary flashforward to Camille joining Joëlle as a film actor, and, together, they can return to the past, and appear in a war film. It will allow the young and old mother to hold a conversation. Further segments include at least two films within films: the first, the Fellini-like one with the balloon, with one director, gradually gives way to the one in which Joëlle stars, with Camille alternating between spectator-companion and co-actor within the film. The film of the second director is entitled *La Vie*, which reflects and parallels Blier's own *Merci la vie*. Neither the spectator of *Merci la vie* nor Camille and Joëlle know whether they are 'real' (*Merci la vie*), or in *La Vie*.

In a sense, this self-conscious fragmented cinema goes back to Blier's very first film, *Hitler, connais pas* (1963), which is constructed around a series of separate interviews with young people, about their experiences, desires, anxieties. These interviews are cut, mixed, and edited together as if the interviewees had been interviewed together. The extraordinary editing transforms this conventional, interview-based documentary into a kind of virtuoso film.

Zapping (constant changing of TV channels) and zipping (fastforwarding a video) result in, and derive from, a sense of impatience and speed, a desire for speedy viewing, for not missing out on other available viewing possibilities. The modern audience, according to Blier, wants this:

I take them for a ride in the TGV, without giving them time to look at the landscape outside; we have to go fast. There's one thing I learnt about cinema and that is that you mustn't think too much. You must go quick. What's great about TV is that you can look at films: one scene is being set up, and, meantime, you have time to switch to another one which had been set up and finally is now really under way. You see two or three scenes, and so you can watch three films at the same time just by skipping all the dull bits. Sometimes, you get caught up, so you put the remote control down, and watch and it's great. Why? Because it's a good film. For the rest of the time, average films provide a kind of rhythm. (Toubiana 1991: 26–7)

This is precisely what happens in the opening ten minutes of *Merci la vie*. Each of the segments, punctuated by the change of colour and tint, and never lasting more than one and a half minutes or so, suddenly settles down to the decorator/night watchman sequence, which also contains within it a series of inserts in blue tints. Thus an alternation is established between the resolutely short segments and longer ones which might hold the attention for a longer period.

Most, but not all, colour switches represent, in some measure, a change, if not always of people, at least of tone, story, or place. The paradox, of course, is that this TGV ride of a film, lasting just seven minutes short of two hours, begins to drag and even become repetitive.

What zapping achieves is that the spectators, armed with the remote control, in fact control the text: they create their own text to a certain extent, by switching films. They create what is, in Barthian terms, the writerly text. However segmented and fragmented it is, it resembles a composite anthologized text. Of course, *Merci la vie* is not a text produced by the TV-zapping spectator mingling three films, but a single film made by Blier, who denies that the spectator has total freedom: 'A film is a work of art; so there's no need to know why there is this or that. You can discuss it later. Everyone has a theory. I guide people; I don't leave them totally free with their own creation. It's not like Godard who requires that everyone make his own film: that's great' (Toubiana 1991: 25–6).

The Blier film is, in terms of authority of interpretation, a compromise between authorial supremacy—the director guiding and manipulating the spectator—and reader/viewer power. For example, the spectator is at liberty to invoke Freud in the female Oedipal scenario: displacement of the mother, and offering one's friend/alter ego to the father. ('Everyone has a theory,' as Blier says in the quotation above.) Likewise the film's potential symbolism— shopping trolleys or eye compress—can be taken as significant or insignificant instances of symbolic play. Blier argues that there is a necessary link between the demands of making a film and the spectator's desire for speedy viewing, not pausing to reflect too much: 'When you write a novel, you work at it all day, and can step back and start again. When you write a film, especially one like this, there are commitments, dates; it's heavy work. It either works or it doesn't. There are some things I don't understand about this film, and I will find out about them by the way spectators judge it' (Toubiana 1991: 23). Blier's assertion in the same interview that the film is a composite of five or six films and that the 'five or six films showing that evening spoke of the same things' implies that the underlying subject is *La Vie*, title of the film-within-the-film, and catch-all title which accommodates anything and everything which can befall two young people hitting the road, and being initiated into the adult world.

According to Blier, young people are exemplary modern spectators; they are master zappers: 'Children do that [zapping] wonderfully well. They even put on a video when they make a phone call.

Afterwards they can criticise, tell you what they saw. It's a kind of spectator gymnastics' (Toubiana 1991: 27). He suggests that the science fiction/action movies of Hollywood have largely created this modern youth audience:

I was amazed by the script of *Total Recall*, which is hallucinating in its complexity. To think that American kids look at that while chewing gum or eating popcorn is encouraging; it means that they can follow very complicated things. They are really sharp viewers, afraid of nothing, and if they don't understand, it doesn't matter; they've got their own explanation. American cinema has done a lot for the viewing public. Of course you can deplore the lack of content, but at the level of form, it's important. Spielberg has really broken new ground. (Toubiana 1991: 26)

It is this youth audience that Blier wished to attract. He wanted—but admits to having failed—to make a film which would in some way be addressed to his daughter, to her generation:

The idea for this film came from the fact that I have a daughter who is growing up, and that one has anxieties about children. I wanted to make a film for young people—which I have not done—because my daughter asked me to: you've got to make a film for us, so we can have a good laugh. . . . What's fun, when you have children of 14 to 15, is that they become wonderful spectators. That fascinates me. I ask them what they like and why, and they answer: we saw such and such a film and it was great. We ask them why it was great, and they reply, 'because it's great'. (Toubiana 1991: 22–3)

Modern youth is sophisticated in that it can understand plots as it zaps from channel to channel, but paradoxically its knowledge base is fragmented, with a precarious hold on history. It is this aspect which informs the way the war, the Occupation, and the treatment of Jews are represented in *Merci la vie*: for example, trains transporting clothed Jews to concentration camps and naked Jews being led to gas chambers become conflated in Camille's mind:

It's a mixture of what's true and what is not, the idea being the Occupation as seen by kids of today who have vaguely heard about it. I tried to use the confusion that exists in the minds of kids: Hitler, the Nazis—they killed Jews, but you are not too clear... The idea was to make a sort of rock 'n' roll film about that, as seen by kids who suddenly say that it must have been horrible. Children are precocious, but in fact they don't know much about anything, including sex. (Toubiana 1991: 24)

This may well explain why—and here we may feel unease—
Camille and her fantasies sometimes seem to be localized outside of
Camille and Joëlle, but by the director-auteur-scriptwriter, Bertrand
Blier. Mesnil points to the way the narrative is structured around
the blending of the adult male narrator, who views the world as a
tragic farce, with the interior monologues and adolescent fictions
of a female teenager (Mesnil 1991: 132).

What is surprising about *Merci la vie* is that, though it may be
formally influenced by the TV viewing habits of contemporary
youth, it is a film that is resolutely about the cinema. This is
reflected by its overwhelming self-referentiality. Thus, after about
thirty minutes of film, Joëlle becomes or reveals herself to be a film
actor. We now remember that when the decorator ran down to the
beach earlier, he had been accompanied by a theatre spotlight,
pointing to the unreal/theatrical nature of the scene. From now on,
clapper boards, intertitles ('Distress with Tears'), addresses to the
camera, dialogue with the 'he said' and the 'she said' intact,
Camille asking Joëlle if 'that is what's called a flashback', slow
motion, in other words, all the baggage of self-referentiality, dominate the narrative, gaining momentum as the film progresses,
achieving a climax in the storm scene with the levitation of Joëlle
and the floating lamp changing shape like something from a surreal
painting. For this reason, the 'back to reality' of the final scene is
all the more striking and discordant.

Blier's clear intention is not to incorporate TV into cinema: 'TV
could be an extraordinary support to cinema, but that isn't the
case. They only do stupid things' (Toubiana 1991: 27). Blier's
attraction to TV certainly does not reside in its content, but in three
factors: (1) that TV shows films, (2) the viewing practices of youth-
ful audiences, and (3) the way knowledge is acquired through TV.

It is apparent in both theory and practice that Blier is dissatisfied
with the conventional story-led nature of conventional cinema. What
is needed now, according to him, is a new experimental cinema:

Yes, that is part of my concept of cinema. I am there to try things, to till
new ground (*défricher*). If it's to make the eternal sex comedy that's a bit
risqué, I have shown that I could do that. Now we must go further. We are
in a really interesting period in which the public is intelligent, open, which
means that we can launch experiments, try things... If spectators don't go
to the cinema very often, it's because they are bored: there is no reason to
go to see in the cinema what you can see on TV. (Toubiana 1991: 24)

And for Blier the enemy of this boring, conventional cinema is its double dependence on story and realism:

Increasingly I couldn't care less about stories; what matters is having an interesting theme, and that is played at the level of form, the way the story is told. . . . When you are an author, the job consists of freeing yourself from structures, to burst open the story, time, the stupidities which make the cinema boring, and which make you a prisoner of realism: when it's daytime, it's not night-time: impossible that it can be both at once. (Toubiana 1991: 24)

Blier's admiration for American films, and in particular Spielberg, whom he calls a great pioneer ('défricheur'), is important in this need to escape from the rule of realism: 'If there is any coherence [in *Merci la vie*] it is a form of cinematographic coherence, and not one based on the story. You are not preoccupied with asking if something is life-like. That's not what cinema is for; it's there to make films' (Toubiana 1991: 26).

The film Blier has made this time is a departure from his previous ones. It is made for a different audience, the young, sophisticated/ignorant audience of the 1990s. I argue that to 'recuperate', 'naturalize' the film, in the manner of Mesnil, to treat it largely as an enigma to be solved, is to miss the point. Colour switches punctuate the film, just as the young spectator zaps from one channel to another: the content ('life') may be similar, but the texture is constantly changing. One moment we are watching an old film in sepia, then we are watching a contemporary colour film, then we switch from one tint to another. What Blier has achieved is precisely the same feel of a visual medley of colour textures as the spectator zaps from one more or less old film to another in front of the small screen. This is the playful pastiche of postmodernism, respectful to an audience formed by TV, but one that is contemptuous of the content of TV. Blier aspires to a form of cinema and spectatorship freed from the shackles of realism and the desire for a well-constructed story with a beginning, a middle, and an end, in that order.

Part III

DEFINING THE 'NATIONAL'

17

Representation, Masculinity, Nation: The Crises of *Les Amants du Pont-Neuf* (Carax, 1991)

GRAEME HAYES

THREE years in the making, dogged by accidents, vastly over budget, and constantly delayed, *Les Amants du Pont-Neuf* was finally released in 1991. Reviews were mixed. Some, particularly the *Cahiers du cinéma*, championed Carax as 'the most gifted film-maker of his generation' (Taboulay 1991: 15), his view personal, poetic, brilliant; others were less impressed. Many of these contrasted the excess of the film-making—the budget, the reconstructed set of Paris, the casting of Juliette Binoche as a down-and-out, the quasi-epic time-span of the shooting—with the raw subject matter; the treatment of homelessness as a spectacular love story produced criticism that the film was nothing more than a hollow, even immoral, self-indulgent lifestyle movie.

My purpose here is to try to separate some of these readings from the textual strategies at play within the film, by exploring the ways in which myth and intertextuality (the quotation of or allusion to other texts, filmic or otherwise) operate in the text in terms of representation, identity, and identification. Primarily, I shall attempt to show how *Les Amants du Pont-Neuf* articulates a crisis of masculinity; crisis, because by laying open the process of the construction of masculine subjectivity the film is implicitly 'raising the question of what it takes to be a man' (Cook 1982: 44). Masculinity is not, however, the only crisis played out by the text; for the film links this crisis with those of representation and national identity, to which I shall turn in the second part of my argument. The relationships, territorial and emotional, played out between the characters and the bridge itself will be vital in any attempt to draw these different strands together, and it is to these structures that I will turn first.

Constructed on the Île de la Cité, the Pont-Neuf stands geographically at the heart of Paris. Despite its name, it is the oldest surviving bridge in Paris; idiomatically it is a metaphor for strength and well-being (Reader 1993). The history of the Pont-Neuf parallels that of Paris: it was the first bridge in the city to break with the medieval tradition of constructing a row of houses along each side and marks the first attempts at coordinated city planning. Further, representations of Paris are central to the development and projection of French culture; the Pont-Neuf by implication thus also lies at the cultural heart of Paris, and indeed at the heart of French cultural representation. Given its historical, cultural, and political significance, therefore, the Pont-Neuf itself will be central to any reading of Carax's film.

Les Amants du Pont-Neuf is Carax's third feature film and the final part of his 'Alex trilogy', completing the series begun by *Boy Meets Girl* (1983) and *Mauvais Sang* (1986). In each of these films, the Parisian space inhabited by Alex was metaphorical rather than physical. In *Mauvais Sang*, the characters operate in a highly artificial, theatricalized space; in *Boy Meets Girl*, Alex's marginalization from society is signalled by the map of Paris in his bedroom: he lives under, not within, the city. The same is true of *Les Amants du Pont-Neuf*: closed for repairs, the bridge is cut off from the rest of Paris, placed outside the time and the space of the city. The noise of the city does not penetrate its bounds; the cars and buses we see around it are distant and vague; physically, it is blocked off by corrugated iron fencing. For Alex in particular, the bridge is a sanctuary; for the rest of Paris, its presence is symbolized by the yellow and black 'Danger' signs at either end. Moreover, the Pont-Neuf represented in the film is a reconstruction in the south of France: due to the extremely high profile of the film, it seems unlikely that it could have been understood at the time of its release as anything other than a reconstruction, unreal and artificial. The space in which the events take place is thus both physical and metaphorical.

Correspondingly, the problems which the text attempts to articulate and resolve are themselves symbolic. To this extent, it seems particularly important to underline the symbolic nature of the narrative space in *Les Amants du Pont-Neuf*, as any system of identification between bridge and protagonists will be inflected by this metaphorical identity, an identity crucial to the relationship between the central characters in the text; belonging neither to land nor water, the Pont-Neuf is the point of mediation between them. It is thus a stage upon which the (again metaphorical) identities attributed to the characters can be explored.

The film opens by charting the meeting of Michèle (Binoche) and Alex (Denis Lavant), both living rough, the former having abandoned her life in the wealthy suburbs because of an eye disease which is gradually turning her blind. Under the glare of the third main character, former caretaker Hans (Klaus-Michael Grüber), Alex and Michèle fall in love and live together on the bridge; however, despite Alex's attempts to keep the news from her, Michèle eventually learns that her eyesight can be saved. She spikes Alex's drink and leaves. Alex causes the death of a fly-poster and is imprisoned for manslaughter, having set fire to posters announcing the cure for Michèle's sight. On his release from prison three years later, Michèle and Alex meet on the restored bridge; Michèle's eyesight is also restored. Fearing a further betrayal, Alex pulls her into the river, where they are picked up by a barge heading for Le Havre.

The film's ending resolves the opposition between the couple throughout the narrative, which is articulated around elemental associations made between Alex and fire, and Michèle and water. Michèle longs for the sea, and when she washes, she washes naked; Alex watches, fascinated, as she cleanses her whole body with water. Later, insomniac, he intones her name as he throws stones into the river; when he washes he keeps the water literally at arm's length, immersing only his forearms and hands. Michèle sits framed against a fountain; when Alex passes, he passes to the side. When Michèle water-skis, he remains in the boat, surrounded and contained by electric light. At the seaside, Michèle looks at the horizon until her failing eyesight allows her to see it no longer; Alex's gaze is directed at the sand at his feet. Alex's alcove on the bridge resembles a lair, guarded by lamp-posts, whose light he controls; to earn money, he breathes fire.

Like *Subway* (Besson, 1985) before it, the narrative of Carax's film is structured around the interplay with previous texts, both cinematic and mythic; and specifically in this instance the myth of Beauty and the Beast. Whilst the camera returns to and lingers on Michèle's face, Alex is repeatedly shot from behind, often in close-up and out of focus, highlighting the back of his head, his neck, back, shoulders. When Michèle is seen bathing, the camera looks up at her, framing her within the columns of the bridge, casting her as a goddess.

Of the three characters on the Pont-Neuf cut off from the world around them, Alex alone is denied the 'bridge' of family relations linking him to surrounding society. Although Michèle and Hans carry tokens of their previous lives—portraits, memories, letters, keys—such links are denied to Alex; we are given no information about his past. Put simply, Alex does not exist before his residence on the bridge and nor can he exist independently of it: he is born of the Pont-Neuf. Shaven-headed and bare-chested, Alex operates halfway between nature and culture, fulfilling the same symbolic role as the bridge. He scrapes his head on the roadway at the beginning of the film, signalling both the closeness of his relationship to his physical environment and his alienation from it. Emerging from the earth, he cannot walk properly; he carries his physical handicap with him as a mark of his provenance, through his broken ankle and later loss of a shoe. He is inarticulate, given to incanted repetition ('Faut qu'j'retourne sur le pont', 'Michèle', 'où t'es?'); his writing, as with his note (declaring not so much his love for Michèle, as his own emotional fragility), is barely literate. Emotionally inarticulate also, he greets Michèle's successive betrayals with self-mutilation.

The narrative of *Les Amants du Pont-Neuf* is the transformation of Alex, the construction of his identity within societal relations. It is his pacification and socialization, his struggles against his inarticulacy to acquire language and find a voice which will enable him to enter the symbolic world of functional adult relations, his journey from beast to man, from nature to culture. There is thus a close—even extraordinary—correspondence between Alex's own narrative trajectory and the Lacanian narrative of the Oedipal trajectory, the formation of subjectivity and its construction in relations of sexual difference. Reworking Freudian psychoanalysis in the light of Saussure's model of structural linguistics, Lacan argued that the unconscious was structured like a language; correspondingly, subject construction should be understood in terms of the acquisition of language. The Oedipal trajectory was therefore a movement from the Imaginary to the Symbolic, a process he disaggregated into three stages.

The first stage is constituted by the mirror phase which, Lacan argued, needs to be understood '*as an identification* ... namely, the transformation that takes place in the subject when he assumes an image' (Lacan 1977: 2). Here, the infant (aged between six and eighteen months) begins to develop a sense of self as it encounters its self-image for the first time; in contrast to its experience of lack or *manque à être* since birth, the child 'responds jubilantly to this image whose completeness and unity contrast with its own experienced disunity and lack of motor control' (Lapsley and Westlake 1988: 68). However, this 'ideal of narcissistic omnipotence' (Stam et al. 1992: 129) or *ideal ego* is a misrecognition as it 'represents ... a degree of completeness and perfection never to be attained' and also produces alienation and division in the infant (Lapsley and Westlake 1988: 68). In Lacan's second stage (a reworking of the *fort/da* game developed by Freud), the infant acquires language, which prefigures the entry into the Symbolic. This can only be achieved, in the male child, by the resolution of the Oedipal complex, Lacan's third stage of subject construction. This stage is activated by the recognition of sexual difference and thus, in the male child, the threat of castration—but also of desire for the sexual other. Faced with sexual difference, the male child assumes masculine identity through identification with the father, an identification dependent on his compliance with the Name of the Father, conceived in linguistic terms by Lacan as the male child's acceptance of the prohibition of his incestuous desire for his mother and submission to the laws of society. The passage from Imaginary to Symbolic is thus articulated around three trajectories: from the pre-linguistic to the linguistic; from illusory sense of unity with the mother to patriarchal law; and, in the male child, from incestuous desire to acceptance of prohibition (Stam et al. 1992: 133).

One of the most fruitful ways in which Lacanian psychoanalytic theory has been applied to film has been in the analysis of spectatorship and the process of identification, in which the concept of the mirror phase has been particularly influential. Mulvey likens the process of spectatorship to one of identification with an ideal ego, arguing that, in mainstream cinema, film form reflects the unconscious of the patriarchal society which produced it. Cinema, Mulvey argued, is structured by three different looks; but in mainstream film those of the spectator and the camera are subsumed by the third, that of the central protagonist—and thus 'obsessively subordinated to the neurotic needs of the male ego' (Mulvey 1975: 18). Representation is accordingly structured around the opposition between active/male and passive/female, producing a determining, controlling male gaze. In this regime, 'the spectator identifies with the main male protagonist, he projects his look onto that of his like, his screen surrogate, so that the power of the male protagonist as he controls events coincides with the active power of the erotic look, both giving a satisfying sense of omnipotence' (Mulvey 1975: 12).

Applying this analysis to the central protagonists of Carax's three films is instructive. Writing on the representation of masculinity in mainstream film, Steve Neale stresses the narcissistic character of identification on the part of the spectator with such ideal egos as Jef Costello in Jean-Pierre Melville's Le Samouraï and the Clint Eastwood character in Sergio Leone's 'spaghetti Western' trilogy. This narcissism articulates 'phantasies of power, omnipotence, mastery and control' (Neale 1983: 5); omnipotence and inviolability are symbolized by silence, restraint, and emotional reticence (Neale 1983: 7; Green 1984: 41–2; Tasker 1993: 237). Silence signifies completeness, self-containment, self-sufficiency; not to voice is not to express desire, and therefore not to be in a state of lack; masculine identity is safe, fixed, whole. Alex, like the characters played by Eastwood and Delon, is remarkable for his economy with language; yet here this is not a sign of mastery and control but of a lack of facility, pushed in Les Amants du Pont-Neuf to prelinguistic inarticulacy; unformed, he must be constructed. Masculinity, socially constructed rather than timeless, universal, essential, is exposed as an effect of culture.

Psychoanalytic theory seeks to give an account of the construction of gender; my focus on Alex's Oedipal trajectory should be seen in the context of the construction not just of individual subjectivity, but specifically of masculine subjectivity. This is not just because Alex is, biologically, male; but rather because he is positioned by the text as masculine through his ownership and activation of the gaze (Kaplan 1983: 30). In Les Amants du Pont-Neuf, the crisis into which masculinity is placed does not open up a corresponding space for the assertion of female subjectivity: whilst Alex's Oedipal trajectory is the focus of the narrative, Michèle is objectified through voyeurism and fetishism (most obviously through the framing and excessive reproduction of her face on the posters). The degenerative eye disease from which she suffers means that she is unable to return the gaze: increasingly unable to contain Alex in her portraits, she cannot look at him during his fire-breathing performance; his essence, as delineated by the film, hurts her eyes too much. Further, we can see that this is also true of the camera: Alex is never held by the frame, masculinity is unrepresentable as spectacle; in Mulvey's (1975: 12) phrase, 'the male figure cannot bear the burden of sexual objectification'.

Implicit within my reading of Alex as the Lacanian pre-Oedipal subject is a corresponding identification of Michèle as mother and Hans as father. This identification is, of course, figurative, and is based on three observations. First, Alex's self-recognition in Michèle's paintings is analogous to the verification by the mother of the infant's sense of self; as Williamson points out, the illusory sense of unity experienced by the child in the mirror phase is usually considered to take place within the confines of the 'directing look' of the mother (Williamson 1987: 12). Secondly, as argued above, unlike Michèle and Hans, Alex has no prior history; to Alex, Michèle is his *premier amour*, analogous to Freud's designation of the mother as the first love-object of the male child (Freud 1977: 235, 371). Finally, Hans's desire for Michèle, consummated in the Louvre, is grounded in her supposed resemblance to his lost wife; his position as father-figure to Alex is reinforced by the position in each of Carax's previous feature films of an older man called Hans who, as here, dispenses drugs to Alex. The keys carried by Hans familiar as a metaphor of 'potential sexual awakening' (Hayward 1990: 129) from Jean Cocteau's 1946 version of *La Belle et la Bête*—are here a metaphor for patriarchal authority: they enable access to the spaces of knowledge and language closed off from Alex symbolized by the Louvre, but also to the space of non-transgressive adult sexuality.

Carax's films have been hailed as distinctive landmarks within a new youth cinema in France, commonly called the *cinéma du look*. Besides Carax, this is principally associated with Besson and Jean-Jacques Beineix, and is generally agreed to have been launched in 1981 by Beineix's *Diva* (Jameson 1990; Hayward 1993). Often likened to the 'look' of advertising and pop videos, the films of these directors tend to privilege spectacle over narrative, visual aesthetics over character and plot development; indeed, one familiar criticism levelled at *Les Amants du Pont-Neuf* was that it was 'vacuous', 'beautiful' but 'useless', as for Carax 'the packaging seems to be more important than the content, the gloss on the image more important than inner truth' (Pascaud 1991: 40–1).

In the *cinéma du look*, spectacle also displaces narrative through the structural use of intertextuality. Thus in *Subway*, Fred (Christophe Lambert) wields a fluorescent strip-light like a Jedi light-sword from *Star Wars* (Lucas, 1977); in *Diva*, a woman walks over an air-vent like Marilyn Monroe in *The Seven Year Itch* (Wilder, 1955); and in *Mauvais Sang*, Alex staggers like the wounded Maurice (Serge Reggiani) in *Le Doulos* (Melville, 1962). Moreover, these films are highly self-referential: thus Reggiani has a cameo part in *Mauvais Sang*; Besson's *Le Grand Bleu* (1988), *Nikita* (1990), *Léon* (1994), and *Le Cinquième élément* all begin with remarkably similar shots; and *Le Cinquième élément*, as well as quoting numerous other films, contains lengthy allusions to *Diva*. (Indeed, much could be made of the fact that the four element stones necessary to save the world are hidden inside the body of the diva, to which she 'gives birth' in her death.)

As references in Carax's films to other texts have already been extensively detailed (Revault d'Allonnes 1986; Thompson 1992; Reader 1993; Rosenbaum 1994; Powrie 1997), my emphasis here will be on the function of intertextuality as representational practice. Indeed, it is possible to isolate a relationship between Alex, Carax, and the intertextuality which structures his films; there is a sense that the most pertinent aspect of *Les Amants du Pont-Neuf*, like *Mauvais Sang* and *Boy Meets Girl* before it, is its self-reflexivity, the way it constantly refers to film and its processes of representation. Thus, as discussed above, Alex's Oedipal trajectory points to the construction of the narrative as a metaphor for the filmic process itself; further, it ends with the rejection of the symbolic order, of society and language. Much has been made elsewhere of Alex's position as Carax's alter ego (Thompson 1992; Rosenbaum 1994), but it is relevant to point out that the silence of Alex in all three films (in *Mauvais Sang*, he is ironically named *Langue-pendue*, 'Chatterbox') has been identified as the corollary of Carax's own past; as a youth he is reputed to have gone for long periods without speaking (Rosenbaum 1994: 15). In Carax's films, silent cinema provides some of the most fertile ground for intertextual plundering: it is fetishized, silence being privileged over sound. This is true of the film's denouement: in a strong analogy with the fantasy of *amour fou*, Alex's over-valuation of Michèle leads to his rejection of the Law of the Father and fusion with her in death (Krutnik 1991: 83–4). Narratives of *amour fou* were, of course, prominent in silent cinema, and are referred to throughout Carax's work (Rosenbaum 1994; Powrie 1997). Wherever the narrative leads, it seems, it always returns to the same place: to cinema.

As we have seen, in order for the relationship between Michèle and Alex to become whole, the opposition between their elemental identification—fire and water, Beauty and the Beast—must be resolved. This must be achieved through the pacification of the elements associated with Alex—the Beast within him—in order for him to enter the Symbolic order of functional adult relations. Alex's progression from nature to culture is echoed by the growing of his hair and his gradual acquisition of clothes; on his release from prison, his clothes finally become *his*. The socialization process begun by Michèle on the bridge—he learns to dry her hair, she attempts to teach him to articulate his emotions verbally—is partly achieved through the elements associated with Michèle; as visual metaphor for both true and finally requited love, the couple float underwater in the Seine, suspended as if in dream-time, invoking by citation Jean and Juliette in *L'Atalante* (Vigo, 1934).

L'Atalante is an important text for *Les Amants du Pont-Neuf*, which derives much of its narrative structure from Vigo's film. Like the bridge in Carax's film, the barge in *L'Atalante* exists within and outside Paris: the relationship between Jean and Juliette is charted by the excursions made by Juliette off the boat and into the capital itself. Similarly, the progress of the relationship between Michèle and Alex is charted by the excursions that they make together away from the bridge. Echoing Jean, Alex introduces Michèle to the instrument which, intended to keep her within the confines of his territory, becomes the agent of her departure from it: in *L'Atalante*, Jean turns on the radio in a bid to provide Juliette with all the entertainment she might need, removing any cause for her to leave the boat and seek it in the city; in *Les Amants du Pont-Neuf*, the radio that Alex brings onto the bridge allows Michèle to learn that her eyesight can be saved. (The Pont-Neuf is framed, rather ironically, by the Samaritaine building after Alex meets Michèle, and then again the building lights up as Michèle first takes hold of the radio. Each, it would seem, has his or her Good Samaritan.)

Taken as a whole, the textual citations in *Les Amants du Pont-Neuf* point to the reclamation of Alex's identity through the national and nationalizing myths of French cinema, which stands at the heart of modern France's cultural identity, and by extension at the heart of France's self-representation. In *Les Amants du Pont-Neuf*, a contrast is thus developed between the representation of national identity through France's re-enactment of the myth of its foundation (the Bicentennial), and its representation through cinematic production. The third element in Alex's recuperation is the state: Hans's disappearance creates a vacuum within the Oedipal triangle, allowing the replacement of the father by the state as representative of the patriarchal order. Nation and representation, exemplified by Jean-Paul Goude's *spectacle* on the one hand and by cinema on the other, are thus the second and third crises articulated in Carax's film.

Once pacified, Alex as social subject must still be constructed. To this effect, he must pass through the institutions of the French state in order to cut the umbilical cord with the Pont-Neuf and allow the possibility of his future integration into social relations; in order for the renovation work to be carried out on the bridge and for it to be reintegrated into Paris; in order that both of them may become *solide*. Until both processes are complete, Alex will be unable to leave Paris and the sanctuary of the bridge without incanting 'Faut qu'j'retourne sur le Pont' (Must go back to the bridge). Crucially, however, Carax presents the state as dysfunctional. Thus, whilst the Bicentennial provides a backdrop to the development of Alex and Michèle's relationship, the film shows us only the militarism of the celebrations; fighter planes are linked through editing to Alex's fire-breathing which hurts Michèle's sight; the images are constantly disrupted, cut up.

Alex's final mutilation, shooting his own finger off, is more than a symbol of his inarticulacy: it is a symbolic castration, the rejection of the patriarchal law, his refusal to negotiate his pre-Oedipal sexuality for entry into the Symbolic. My reading of the final sequence of the film, therefore, is based on the death of the two main characters. As the ending is ambiguous, I shall conclude by setting out my reasons for reading Alex and Michèle's 'rescue' as illusory.

We see, within the confines of the barge, three successive images: that of a tiny coal fire, representing Alex's potency, but contained and pacified within a wrought-iron frame; the picture of the barge-owners contained together within the narrow frame of the photograph; and then finally, juxtaposed, Michèle and Alex kitschly framed in a half-smile, the fully constituted couple. The framing produces containment in a way the camera previously has not; the vibrancy of the narrative is nullified. Restored, this is the only point where we see the Pont-Neuf whole, in its entirety; yet through the act of its reconstruction and sanitization, the bridge is now reduced to the clichéd image of picture postcard Paris, highlighting both the belated efficacy of the process and its status as illusion and image. Integrated into society through the grafting of a ready-made family, Alex and Michèle, also united, also functional, are similarly reduced to the clichéd image of the couple. Although Alex continues to bear the sign of his past identification—his mutilated hand is hidden in his pocket under a black glove—lest we are in any doubt as to the completeness of the success of Alex's pacification, the barge's cargo is sand, on hand to quench any prospective relapse. Moreover, the sand parodies the beach of Alex and Michèle's earlier escape from Paris, and conjures the Sandman, who finally brings the sleep which had proved so elusive to the pre-Oedipal Alex. As the film ends, the beast has finally been tamed and the process is complete.

Intertextual citation in Carax's films creates a complex web of references to other texts, but also—through its very excess—to the process of citation itself. Whilst bearing in mind the fact that excess does not necessarily denote either irony or self-awareness, it is perhaps here that, whilst ambivalent, Carax's use of intertextual quotation can be said to reflect on representation rather than simply be an indulgence in it. Carax's vision of the Parisian *clochard* is undoubtedly a Romantic, and romanticized, one; indeed, given the casting of Binoche in particular, it could perhaps hardly fail to be otherwise. Yet it is the juxtaposition of the Bicentennial celebration of state, nation, and culture with Alex's (and Michèle's) increasing iconic passage into French cinema which most serves to demonstrate the disparity between nation-constructing myth and the observed reality of urban deprivation. The possibility of narrative closure which 'reinforces patriarchal law by the effacement of the transgressive son and the normalization of the narrative structure' identified in *Mauvais Sang* (Powrie 1997: 137–8) is not available here. The closing sequence, whilst pointing initially to a celebration of spectacle through textual quotation, also brings eternal sleep and, by extension, Death. The patriarchal order is not affirmed; nation-constructing myths are shown to be sterile. Carax's use of intertextuality is therefore contradictory; whilst privileging spectacle, *Les Amants du Pont-Neuf* also seemingly points to such practice as a cul-de-sac. Indeed, on this level, we might argue that *Les Amants du Pont-Neuf* appears to foreground the impasse of the *cinéma du look* enterprise itself.

18

Cats in the 'Hood: The Unspeakable Truth about *Chacun cherche son chat* (Klapisch, 1996)

ELIZABETH EZRA

IN Cédric Klapisch's *Chacun cherche son chat*, Chloé, a painfully thin, Olive Oyle lookalike, is awkward and lonely. Treated with contempt at the modelling agency where she works as a make-up assistant, she has very few friends, and is alternately ignored and mistreated by men: she is looking for something, and not just her lost cat. Chloé's search for her beloved Gris-gris mobilizes most of the community; much of the film (which, like the cat, wandered out of its boundaries to become a feature-length work instead of the short subject initially planned) is spent following people as they scour the streets and alleyways of Paris's rapidly changing faubourg Saint-Antoine in search of the lost pet. However, for all the meandering the characters do, for all the distance they cover, the film is very narrowly confined geographically: it is fundamentally an anatomy of the local, a meditation not only on the concept of change but on changing conceptions of neighbourhood, neighbourliness, and community.

It is in this context that we can best understand the scene in which Chloé stands with Henriette Clavo, amateur cat psychologist and animal psychic, in front of the illuminated map of the eleventh *arrondissement*. 'He's here; he's not far; he's near us, I'm sure of it. He can't have gone anywhere else,' Mme Clavo says confidently. The cat, though it might wander far and wide, must surely understand and respect the arbitrary boundaries of the *arrondissement*— because anything else would be unimaginable. After all, there is no reason to suspect that the cat has lost its marbles, like the old woman from Chloé's building found wandering around the place de la République. When she is escorted home in a police van, a neighbour says to Chloé, 'since losing her husband, she gets lost in Paris'. With this, the film evokes a classic narrative theme: from Dante to the nineteenth-century *flâneur*, through surrealism and situationism, physical wandering has served as a metaphor for a psychological or spiritual quest. In the opening credits, a hodge-podge of letters gradually form the word 'Cherche'. 'Search', we are told—but, for what? When Chloé's cat disappears, she is provided with a physical search to match her emotional search for companionship. But, like the proverbial bluebird of happiness, both the cat and the man of Chloé's dreams are to be found in her own backyard: the cat is discovered hidden behind the stove of Mme Renée, the woman responsible for looking after it, and Mr Right turns out to be the next-door neighbour who offered the insight about the lost woman with the lost husband.

The film's lack of concern with anything beyond the borders of the *quartier* is breathtakingly explicit, and nowhere more apparent than in the depiction of Chloé's vacation, which, after countless preparations, lasts no more than three seconds: Chloé is shown walking, equipped with backpack, across a busy Paris intersection; the scene cuts to her bobbing alone in the sea, exhaling; a moment later, we are back at the intersection, where she crosses in the oppo-site direction, returning from her trip. The shot of Chloé in the water, like many others in the film, emphasizes her isolation: she appears to be alone in the ocean as she will later be shown alone against the sky in the dream sequence on top of the Bastille monu-ment. In opposition to many Eric Rohmer films, whose *raison d'être* would be the holiday, here, the vacation, although it sets the plot in motion (motivating Chloé's search first for someone to look after her cat, and then for the cat itself), is incidental.

This is because the film's setting is also its main subject. The opening shot, an establishing shot in a thematic as well as a narra-tive sense, shows Parisian rooftops dominated by a tall crane in the centre. The views of the skyline that punctuate the film alternate between shots of cranes and shots of the Bastille monument, suggesting that the tall crane has become a kind of modern-day Bastille—in short, a prison. Characters in the film frequently pause to lament the endless construction in and concomitant destruction of their neighbourhood: the film is littered with wrecking balls, building sites, temporary passageways, and the sound of drills, all of which converge on a demolition site whose name could not possibly be more ironic: Notre-Dame d'Espérance (Our Lady of Hope). As the geographical search is coextensive with an emotional search, so the breaking up of cement and stone is paralleled by the disintegration of the community.

From the very first moments of the film, we are shown images of people experiencing difficulty in forming or maintaining attachments. Chloé implores a friend on the phone to catsit for her while she goes on vacation, and is frustrated when the friend will not reciprocate for an earlier favour. Chloé's gay flatmate Michel then announces that he has broken up with his boyfriend. Later, when Mme Renée opens her door to Chloé for the first time, she is wary of the young newcomer, refusing to reveal her identity until she is certain that Chloé has come on important business (namely, the search for a catsitter). Loneliness afflicts most of the characters in the film, which is rife with scenes of people thrown together who cannot make each other happy. When an obnoxious man tries to pick up Chloé in a bar, she is accused by his girlfriend of having tried to seduce him; Chloé in turn rejects the sexual advances of the female bartender who intervenes on her behalf, and who is shown walking away alone, dejected and sad. Then, Chloé herself is rejected by Michel, whom she tries to seduce in a moment of desperation; we see the two of them lying together in bed, turned away from each other, embarrassed and irritated. When Chloé finally sleeps with the boy she has been flirting with throughout the film, she appears to feel as lonely as ever, while lying right next to him. It is thus not for lack of opportunities that these people feel isolated. The film repeatedly emphasizes the fact that mere proximity is not enough to bring them together—as the walls around them come crashing down, new, invisible ones appear to spring up between people.

This repeated failure to connect is literally echoed in the constant presence of noise that interferes with people's efforts to communicate. Throughout much of the film, Chloé and Mme Renée are shown shutting their windows to drown out the raucous sound of a drum kit, which makes it almost impossible to hear anything else. The drums can be heard in the background when Chloé is talking frustratedly on the phone in the opening scene; the noise, which Chloé manages to drown out a little by closing the window, also accompanies her tiff with Michel, as he tells her, 'I'm not your husband, okay? We're not married,' and it accompanies Chloé's unpleasant exchange with the concierge, who refuses to watch her cat. The next time we hear the drum music is when Chloé stops by Mme Renée's apartment to pick up her cat, and discovers it has gone. This time, the music is connected to a voice, but a voice making its own brand of noise: 'Ta gueule, la vioque' (Put a lid on it, you old bag), the voice yells after Mme Renée shouts at him to stop the racket. The drum noise turns out to have been made by the boy with whom Chloé has a series of flirtatious encounters, culminating in a brief sexual liaison that leaves her feeling even more isolated.

To the drum music, the film opposes other, more communal kinds of music. While walking through an outdoor market, Chloé comes upon a local brass band playing a cheerful tune; and on her way to a bar, she passes a couple dancing vigorously to fast-paced salsa music. On both occasions, Chloé stops to watch, and smiles, showing an expression of genuine happiness that we do not otherwise see until the final moments of the film. In both instances, she is admiring forms of music that are socially inclusive, instead of alienating, as the drum music is represented in the film.

The film begins, in fact, with a communicative obstacle course: the opening credits roll to the accompaniment of brash, percussive funk music, sung in English, a foreign tongue, and thus tantamount to gibberish for the average French viewer. The impression of nonsense is heightened visually by the hodgepodge of letters that crowd onto the screen, only gradually decipherable as the film's opening credits. When Chloé is on the phone with Henriette Clavo, cat psychologist, Michel makes it difficult for her to speak (for laughter) by making silly noises in the background, which prompts Mme Clavo to say, 'I can't hear you. Is there music on there?' Finally, Djamel, the intellectually backward man who latches on to Chloé, also has trouble speaking; he prefaces everything he says with 'Comment . . .' (what), and is taunted for being unable to find the right words.

Auditory dissonance functions as both a sign and an index of alienation, as is demonstrated in the nightmare that Chloé has when she is in the depths of despair. In the dream, Chloé tentatively peeks out of a darkened doorway into dazzlingly bright sunlight; the filmstock is slightly overexposed to make her look washed out, and to set this sequence off from the rest of the film. Soft, delicate flute music plays on the soundtrack, in sharp contrast to the pulsating electronic percussion that played in the two previous scenes. A voice on the soundtrack begins singing, in English: 'I hear a scream,' and there is a cut to a shot of Chloé screaming above the rooftops, which we see but do not hear: at first, we hear only the next lyric of the song: 'I see me scream; is it from memory?' Then, we do hear Chloé's screams (she is calling, 'Gris-gris!' repeatedly), but in what is obviously post-synchronous sound. Her cries are drowned out by the sound of a brass band playing a vaguely mariachi tune. The soundtrack—from the screams to the music—is perfectly suited to this sequence precisely because, like Chloé's dress, it does not fit.

The very first words of the film—'Ah, mais écoute...' (Hey, now listen...)—are thus at once rhetorical and very literal. These words, as it happens, are spoken on the telephone, like a large proportion of the film's dialogue; in fact, we hear Chloé before we see her. Our first glimpse of the place she works, too, is of a man on a mobile phone, walking directly in front of the camera, speaking in heavily accented English: 'Allo? No, he can't talk to you now. Not available.' Communication is here impeded by a double obstacle: first, the language barrier, and then, the 'unavailability' of the person being asked for. (Similarly, many of the songs on the soundtrack, in addition to the one that accompanies the opening credits, are sung in English, which adds an extra layer of impenetrability for French characters and audiences.) This scene is echoed later in the film, when the stylist says that she cannot speak but takes a call anyway: 'No, I don't have time to talk to him; let me talk to him,' telling the caller in struggling English that she is 'really beezy beezy'. These pseudo-conversations are analogous to the noise of the drums: the sounds being made are preventing communication from occurring. Similarly, the stylist seems unwilling, or unable, to speak to Chloé directly. Although she is standing right in front of her, she gives her instructions via her assistant, and is repeatedly unable to remember her name. In this environment, people talk constantly, but communication is replaced by noise—the noise of the drums, of the drills, of people barking orders through a third party or jabbering on the phone in order to say that they are not available.

This refusal of contact contrasts with the old women's insistence on contact. These women have a communication network whose speed and efficiency surprises Chloé: women she has never met come up to her in the street to talk about her cat, and call her at home when she herself has only just learned of its disappearance.

This network is represented in one scene of the film as an amalgamation of disembodied telephone conversations that rise above the rooftops. Unlike the people Chloé works with, who use the telephone to avoid saying anything, these women call each other even (and, perhaps, especially) when they have nothing substantial to say, for the purpose of reinforcing the community of gossip. Chloé refuses to be drawn into this network at first, abruptly cutting Mme Verligodin's telephone call off, just as she refuses to engage in conversation with the chatty young bakery cashier in the next scene. The *boulangère* belongs to the old-style neighbourhood; her marked southern French accent indicates that she comes from a part of France that still clings to some of the traditional ways. At this point in the film, though, Chloé is not interested in traditional community structures. Yet, she is just as alienated from the culture that the film opposes to that of the traditional community: the world of fashion.

The world of fashion comes complete with its own language. This is made abundantly clear in an amusing scene in which Chloé, making up a model for a fashion shoot at work, is made to fiddle endlessly with a hairclip, or barrette, while the stylist decides what look she wants. As all concerned agonize over that aspect of the vestimentary code that Barthes has called the 'variant of assertion of existence' (Barthes 1983: 115) (with/without barrette), and then, on top of that, the variant of species (if with, blue or red?), it becomes clear that the function of detail, according to Barthes, is that '*nothing* can signify *everything*' (Barthes 1983: 243; Barthes's emphasis). The investment of so much in so little is the source of the scene's humour. When the stylist's assistant suggests the addition of a leather bracelet, the whole system is thrown off; the stylist looks at her as though she has said something heretical and replies, horrified, 'oh no, absolutely not!' To those who speak this language, these seemingly insignificant details are everything. Lacan was almost right: it is actually a barrette that separates signifier from signified.

Chloé, however, does not speak this language very fluently, as an exchange with her flatmate Michel demonstrates. As Chloé, attempting to change her image at the urging of her co-workers, tries on outfit after outfit, Michel rejects most of them; he tells her what each outfit says about her, literally reading her wardrobe to her. On two occasions, when she does not understand him, he must translate or gloss his own words for her: the English word 'glitter', and 'coincé de chochotte' ('candy-assed', as the subtitles have it). Perhaps, the film is implying, Michel can speak the gendered language of fashion better than Chloé because he has come to terms with the 'feminine' side of his nature in a way that Chloé has not. Michel advises Chloé to wear something more 'bouffeuse de mecs' (man-eating), more 'jeteuse' (bewitching), in order to emphasize her femininity. When she does this, puts on make-up, which she does not appear to wear normally, and ventures out in the hope of attracting a man, she gets more than she bargained for. She is repeatedly hassled and even physically accosted by several aggressive men, who respond to her new look by objectifying her. Even in her dreams, Chloé's encounters with men have been less than fulfilling. It is for this reason that she is so touched by Bel Canto's painting of her, whose bare outlines and broad strokes show the simplest clothing (and are too basic to register make-up). The implication is that he sees the 'essential' Chloé, and his opinion of her does not change according to what she is wearing—for although the painting may be analogous to a fashion photo, it is much more permanent. As long as she follows the vagaries of fashion, however, she only attracts men who are always on the lookout for *new* women.

For fashion privileges the ever-new: it is about jettisoning one thing and replacing it with another, constantly. Barthes writes that the rhetoric of fashion serves to 'blur the memory of past Fashions' (Barthes 1983: 300). Fashion is founded on a lack of continuity, which is precisely what Mme Renée bemoans when she observes the gentrification of the old neighbourhood; 'once it's transformed, you forget what was there before', she says, adding later, 'I liked my music store better.' The music store has been replaced by a clothing boutique run by the stylist for whom Chloé works. The stylist, in the little shop she has purchased, gushes, 'it's like a little village, don't you think?'—perfectly oblivious to the fact that, in contributing to the gentrification of the neighbourhood, she is destroying the very community she finds so charming. Chloé replies, 'yes, but not for long, because the old women are being evicted; everything's being torn down'. People are being evicted from their homes as if they were outmoded fashions being thrown out to make way for new purchases. This ethic is mocked at the beginning of the film, when we are told that the new look is 'un peu trash' (a little trashy)—a word that hits the nail on the head, because fashion is by definition destined to end up as trash, as old items are discarded to make way for the new season. When Chloé is walking with the old women after leaving the stylist's boutique, they ask if she likes to wear the kind of clothes displayed in the shop window. 'Moitié moitié' (Half and half), she says; and indeed, she is half in and half out of the fashion community, not fitting in completely to either world—despite the fact that her severe thinness, in addition to making her appear all the more fragile, makes of her literally a fashion victim.

Chloé's isolation does not last forever. There is a moment in the film when she begins to appreciate the company of the old women, and stops shunning their attempts to befriend her. This transformation is made explicit when Chloé snaps at the stylist, who has made fun of the older women, that 'those are my friends', and walks off with them. This alliance is not one that Chloé would have forged earlier in the film; it comes only after the film's turning point, which is marked by the discovery of a dead cat.

When Chloé receives a second call from Mme Verligodin, she rolls her eyes, expecting a repetition of the woman's previous newsless update. But this time, it is serious: Mme Verligodin thinks she has found Chloé's cat. Chloé, Mme Verligodin, and Mme Renée meet at the building site where a black cat has been seen, and, holding on to each other for physical and moral support, slowly make their way across the rubble of broken concrete to identify the body. When they discover that the cat in question is not Gris-gris after all, they heave a collective sigh of relief and stroll off merrily, as Chloé suggests that they go somewhere for a cup of coffee. The feline corpse is a sacrificial victim, a necessary prerequisite for the formation of the bond between the women. René Girard has noted that the role of the sacrificial victim is to ensure the survival of the community—and so it does in this film, after a fashion (see Girard 1972). As the three women walk hesitantly towards the cat before learning it is not Gris-gris, Renée says, 'I hope we've made a mistake. There's misery among animals just as there is with people, you know.' Her touching analogy between animals and people evokes the larger issue of cultural exclusion. The idealized image of community, problematic throughout French history, is shown to be especially fragile in this film. Even the film's buoyantly cheerful ending, which reunites most of the cast members in the local café for a rousing sing-along, does not extend to everyone: most notably, Djamel is left out. At one point, he bursts into tears, finally cracking under the strain of the relentless humiliation he is made to endure. At the end of the film, sensing the growing attraction between Chloé and Bel Canto, he mutters, 'Moi je trouve que la vie est mal faite!' (If you ask me, life is unfair!). The African carpenters in the shop next to Chloé's building, too, remain segregated from the rest of the community: there appear to be only Africans employed in the workshop, and we are shown no sub-Saharan Africans anywhere else in the film. The fact of segregation is underwritten by attitudes such as the one espoused by the neighbour who introduces Chloé to Djamel: 'They didn't invent hot water, did they? They come from warm countries and they didn't invent warm water.' She then adds, 'but they're not the worst, the Africans are. Yeah, you have to watch out for the blacks.' Chloé is of course duly disgusted by these sentiments, but they are none the less shown to be lurking in the shadow of the Bastille monument, symbol of the new form of community that sprang up in the wake of the Revolution, whose name was the République—which is where the woman who lost her husband wanders every chance she gets, until she is picked up and returned to the Bastille neighbourhood by the police. The film is set during the presidential elections of 1995: campaign posters for Lionel Jospin are juxtaposed with flyers describing the missing cat. When Chloé wakes up in Michel's bed after her wretched evening at the bar and subsequent rejection at home, Chirac's victory is being announced on the radio. Even the pretence of the socialist dream of a community of equals has come to an end.

In this postcolonial republic, the structures of exclusion that are often thought to threaten the cohesion of the community actually ensure its survival. As the sacrificial kitten cemented the bonds between Chloé and the old women, so another sacrificial creature cements relations in the community at large: Djamel. Resembling the 'village idiot' from the Middle Ages, both scorned and fiercely protected by the community, he is, like the sacrificial victim that Girard describes, 'simultaneously outside of and enclosed' (Girard 1972: 405) within the community. Djamel longs to go away (with Chloé, to the seaside), but he will never leave, whereas Bel Canto would like to stay in Paris, but is forced to move when he is evicted.

The revelation of Djamel's sacrificial status unfolds in two stages. First, an analogy is established between Djamel and Chloé's cat when we are told that Djamel, like Gris-gris, fell off a roof when he was young, resulting in his stunted cerebral development. The association between Djamel and the lost cat is then extended metonymically to the dead kitten found on the building site and reinforced visually in the scene in which Chloé, Renée, and Mme Verligodin are walking down the street after stopping at the stylist's clothing boutique. We see an overhead long shot of the three women in front of a large shop with two signs that read: '400 TAPIS D'ORIENT SACRIFIÉS' (400 oriental carpets must go) in the shape of arrows pointing downward; below one of these signs, the words 'Le Sud' (the South) are visible, while below the other sign, we see the words 'Retour foire de Paris' (Return Paris fair) with 'retour' and 'Paris' set off in red letters from the other words, which are blue. As they walk past these signs, another woman runs up to them and points upward toward the camera. There is then a cut to Djamel tiptoeing precariously across the rooftop in search of Chloé's cat. The word 'sacrifiés', repeated twice and occurring shortly after the discovery of the dead cat and immediately prior to the discovery of Djamel on the roof, provides a symbolic linkage between the two scenes. Moreover, the arrow pointing to the words 'Le Sud', followed by the woman pointing to Djamel, indicates that his ethnic origin from somewhere south of France—namely, North Africa—might have something to do with his sacrificial status (an idea that is reinforced by the words 'd'Orient'). At the same time, the words 'Retour/Paris' suggest that such a 'sacrifice' might bring about a return of the old Paris, a mythical community whose harmony was unbroken by cultural difference. The exclusion of the postcolonial subject is a prerequisite for the cohesion of this traditional community. Paris, so the song goes, 'est une blonde' (is a blonde).

This cohesion of the community is signified and accompanied, as we have seen, by the sound of music. In interviews, Klapisch has invoked a musical metaphor to describe the group dynamic depicted in this and his previous films, *Riens du tout* (1992) and *Le Péril jeune* (1994), as well as in *Un air de famille* (1996), which had been shot but not yet released when *Chacun cherche son chat* premièred: 'It's true that my films speak of nothing else: relations between the individual and the group. How to unite, how to form a group, a chorus. How to sing together. How to be happy both on one's own and with others' (Klapisch 1996). In *Chacun cherche son chat*, when Chloé chooses communal music over the drummer's self-absorbed noise, she is choosing music that many can sing at the same time. At the end of the film, Chloé awakens to the mutual attraction that she shares with Bel Canto, whose name suggests a beautiful song and a traditional musical form; their liaison is accompanied by the sound of a hearty French *chanson populaire* being sung by the people in the café, most of the film's cast members piled in, like the big finale of an opera. The song, titled 'Ça c'est Paris' (That's Paris), compares Paris to a (blonde) woman; Mme Renée and the café's *patronne* alter the words slightly, substituting themselves for the city: 'Tous ceux qui nous connaissent, grisés par nos caresses, s'en vont, mais reviennent toujours. Paris, à nos amours. Ça c'est Paris!' (All those who know us, giddy from our caresses, although they may leave, always come back. Paris, here's to our love. That's Paris!) The song's crescendo, marked by the words 'mais reviennent toujours' (always come back), can be heard as Bel Canto walks toward his moving van: we know that, although he is moving to the suburbs, he and Chloé will maintain their relationship. But the happy ending is marked by an ambivalence: when the painter says goodbye to Mme Renée, she says, 'Et adieu Paris' (Good bye Paris), meaning both that Bel Canto is leaving Paris, and that Paris is disappearing.

All of which bestows a retrospective significance on the song that is playing as we are first shown the modelling agency where Chloé works. It asks, in American-accented English, 'Is this really the end? Or is it a new beginning?' The film seems undecided; on the one hand, it appears to come down on the side of the new beginning, leaving a space for the creation of new forms of community on the rubble of the old structures. But on the other hand, it is acknowledging that this 'new beginning' is rooted in nostalgia, and reproduces the same structures of exclusion that characterized the (retrospectively) idealized community of the past.

The singing café patrons succeed in drowning out the noise of change all around them, but theirs is the voice of nostalgia, the only voice that can make itself heard amidst the hammering and the drilling—that is, apart from any voice speaking (or singing) English, sign and symbol of the new cultural imperialism: the *chanson populaire* is ultimately replaced by Portishead's 'Glory Box',

1990s anthem to budding womanhood. But in this era located between France's imposition of one form of imperialism and its subjection to another, the French language echoes with the refrains of nostalgia. Without this nostalgia, the destruction of the traditional community would be impossible to articulate, because it challenges received notions of Paris as the city of love, or the city of beautiful monuments, presenting it instead as the city of loneliness, the city of wrecker balls and construction sites. So, although there is noise everywhere, as jackhammers drill holes in the ground and buildings and institutions come crashing down, beneath the cobblestone streets—beneath even the utopian *plage* (beach) of May 1968—there is an unspeakable silence.

Which brings us to the most important question of all. What, finally, is the significance of the film's title, *Chacun cherche son chat?*

It's hard to say.

19

Remaking Paternity: *Mon Père ce héros* (Lauzier, 1991) and *My Father the Hero* (Miner, 1994)

LUCY MAZDON

THE 1980s and the early 1990s proved to be a fruitful period for the cinematic remake (the term is used here to refer specifically to Hollywood remakes of French cinematic works). Between 1980 and 1990 fifteen French films were remade by Hollywood, and another sixteen between 1990 and 1997. Thus the 1980s and 1990s have been the most productive period in terms of the remake in the history of cinema. French critics typically describe the process as a straightforward vertical trajectory from the 'art' of French cinema to the 'popular' commercialism of Hollywood; American studios, in need of new ideas, are said to use their economic power to purchase the rights to successful French films and thus undermine their career in the American market. They describe the process in terms of a debased commercialism which unavoidably reduces the French original to a popular copy.

Such critique is located in wider discourses about American cultural imperialism, particularly via the mass media, and a concomitant threat to French culture. Interestingly, earlier remakes are rarely mentioned by those who condemn the films of the 1980s, despite their high numbers during the 1930s and 1940s. By ignoring the prehistory of the practice in this manner, French critics seem to suggest that it is a new phenomenon, a fresh onslaught upon French culture on the part of Hollywood. Thus it is inscribed in a general history of 'American cultural invasion' whilst abstracted from its particular past in order to lend it increased significance.

Clearly material and commercial practices are not negligible. Indeed they can be seen to play a significant role in both the prevalence of the remake during particular periods of time and the commercial trajectories of source film and remake. However, the remake process cannot be reduced to commercial issues alone, nor indeed to a straightforward opposition between French 'art' and American 'popularism'. The critical discourse outlined above frequently condemns the Hollywood remake as an undisguised attack upon the French cinematic industry, conveniently failing to acknowledge the not insignificant profits garnered by French producers through the sale of rights. Moreover, it should be noted that an increasing number of remakes involve French co-producers, for example Canal Plus for *Sommersby* (Amiel, 1993) and Film par film, DD Productions, and Cité films for *My Father the Hero* (1994). As a result the remake can actually be seen to create profit for the French industry rather than simply preventing its commercial success.

The problematic nature of definitions of French and American cinema is echoed by a similar instability in the oppositions established between French 'art' and Hollywood 'mass entertainment'. A brief survey of the remakes of the 1980s and the 1990s reveals that of the twenty-eight films remade since 1980, eighteen are connected in some way with popular comic genres. It is somewhat paradoxical that whilst many French critics decry the commercial nature of the remake process, claiming that it is purely a matter of financial gain, the films selected for transposition are often commercial successes within their country of production. Thus the tendency to remake French comedies can perhaps be partly attributed to the enduring success of domestic comedy in France and the fact that it is the only indigenous genre able to resist Hollywood competition at the box office. Indeed, it is evident that, despite the critical tendency to construct French cinema in terms of 'art' or 'auteurism', French production is in fact marked by a flourishing popular cinema. It is these popular films which are most frequently selected for remaking, thus rendering somewhat equivocal calls for the protection of French 'art' in the face of Hollywood. It would seem that it is not French 'art' which is under threat from the remake, but rather those popular domestic genres which are themselves dismissed by many French critics.

Even if the popular nature of much French remake material is accepted, it is nevertheless a critical commonplace to suggest that these popular films are remade because they are intrinsically unexportable. It is claimed that popular genres, especially comedy, are highly culturally specific; that which proves amusing to an audience in Paris will invariably fail to raise a laugh amongst spectators in New York. Clearly there is some truth in this claim; films do indeed invoke 'national' discourses. However, this definition of the popular needs to be relocated within broader notions of the intertextuality and hybridity of popular genres. Indeed, the very diversity of the films chosen for remaking suggests the impossibility of constructing limits and boundaries for any description of a 'national-popular' cinema. Moreover, many of these films can be seen to play upon and rework the traditions or conventions of Hollywood cinema and this intertextuality, both cinematic and cultural, is carried through to the remakes themselves.

If we now turn our attention to Gérard Lauzier's *Mon Père ce héros* (1991) and Steve Miner's remake of 1994, *My Father the Hero*, we can perceive this hybridity. As previously stated, any attempt to define the remake as unproblematically 'American' is complicated by the involvement of French co-producers. Moreover, the screenplay was co-written by Francis Veber, a highly successful French comic scriptwriter and director, many of whose works have themselves been the source of subsequent remakes (*Le Jouet*, 1976, *Les Fugitifs*, 1986, *La Chèvre*, 1981, *Les Compères*, 1983). Above all, this cultural interconnection and exchange is located in the double presence of Gérard Depardieu, star of both films. Clearly Depardieu's role in the remake plays upon his work in Lauzier's film. However, both films extend these allusions to the actor's previous work, to the particular connotations of his star persona and, in the case of the Hollywood production, to specific cinematic constructions of French identity embodied in the screen presence of Depardieu. His moonlight tryst beneath the balcony with his love-struck daughter recalls his role in *Cyrano de Bergerac* whilst the remake also alludes to the actor's other major success in the American market, Weir's *Green Card*.

Both films thus establish intertextuality via the screen presence of Depardieu; however, it should be noted that in each case the connotations provided by his star persona are rather different. In France the actor's career has straddled both popular genres and art or auteur cinema and this has developed a star image incorporating both comedy and tragedy (Vincendeau 1993c: 343–61). In *Mon Père ce héros* Depardieu plays upon both of these aspects; he is both a comic figure caught up in the confusion that follows his daughter's claims that he is her lover and at the same time a source of melancholy, of paternity in crisis, as he struggles to come to terms with their changing relationship and his concomitant jealousy. In the remake Depardieu is reduced to pure comedy. He is not able to connote the duality and ambiguity inscribed in his French star image; rather his success in the United States is based upon a particular notion of Frenchness constructed through cliché and stereotype. This was exemplified in *Green Card* by his Gauloise-smoking, steak-eating, entirely non-politically-correct character, and the process is furthered in Miner's film as André's 'relationship' with Nicole is repeatedly ascribed to his 'Frenchness'. This construction also articulates previous American cinematic representations of a French identity; early in the film some of his fellow residents at the Caribbean hotel compare him to Louis Jourdan and Catherine Deneuve and, perhaps most blatantly of all, at the hotel's talent night Depardieu bursts into a spirited, heavily accented rendition of 'Thank Heaven for Little Girls', echoing that seminal Hollywood depiction of France, Vincente Minnelli's *Gigi* (1954) and its star, Maurice Chevalier.

The evident intertextuality of both of these films, and indeed of their star, suggests the problematic nature of attempts to describe popular cinematic works or genres in terms of a straightforward national identity. Indeed the very popularity of Hollywood productions in France suggests that they too should be perceived as part of a French or European popular cinema; definitions of the popular should after all be constructed as much through processes of consumption as through production. The hybridity of popular genres breaks down the hegemonic critical account of the remake as a transposition from French 'art' to American 'mass culture'. It reveals the tension between claims as to the unexportability of popular cinematic works (often attributed to American insularity) and descriptions of remakes as mere 'copies' of a superior 'original'. The popular films remade are part of a cinema (or cinemas) which may be described as French or European but which clearly incorporates and alludes to cinemas extending well beyond national boundaries. Moreover, the remake is not a simple copy; rather, within the hybridity of popular genres it reworks narratives, film and acting styles, and ideological content according to the conventions of a new cinematic context. The remake is neither entirely different nor entirely the same and it is in the process of transformation that the actual work of transposition can be perceived.

Mon Père ce héros and *My Father the Hero* are clearly quite different films despite their apparent narrative similarities. Both recount the exploits of a single father (Depardieu) as he takes his adolescent daughter on an exotic holiday only to discover that she pretends to be his lover in order to impress a boy she meets at the beach. However, the Hollywood film is significantly shorter than its French source and the narrative is simplified through the absence or reduction of certain digressions and twists. Thus the film, like many other remakes, can be seen to conform to the conventions of classical Hollywood cinema in its streamlining or literalizing of narrative; ambiguities are eschewed in favour of a goal-oriented narrative structure.

As previously stated, both films are essentially popular comedies; however, here again differences can be perceived. The French film is perhaps best described as a *comédie de mœurs* which incorporates the tropes of both comedy and melodrama. It is significant that the video release of the film in Britain attempted to incorporate the film into a tradition of auteurist comedy of manners, describing it as a 'charming and warmly diverting comedy . . . in the tradition of Eric Rohmer's *Comédies et proverbes*'. The film's comic/melodramatic focus on the father–daughter relationship is replaced in the remake by physical comedy and broad farce. This difference is made immediately apparent by the publicity for the two films; whereas that for the French production represents a close-up of a serious-looking André and Véronique, the poster for the remake shows a smiling Depardieu whilst in the background he struggles on a pair of water-skis. This contrast between the French film's emphasis on a low-key verbal comedy and the remake's exploitation of physical farce should be situated within broader comic traditions. Although neither 'national' cinema can be said to focus exclusively on either physical or cerebral comedy (witness the work of Jacques Tati and Woody Allen), French cinema does have a strong tradition of verbal humour whilst physical comedy has proved enduringly successful in the United States.

Despite their contrasting use of comic conventions, both films negotiate the theme of paternity via the relationship between a father and his teenage daughter. However, once again the films' specific treatment of this theme shows how the remake is a process of transformation. *Mon Père ce héros* represents this father–daughter dyad in terms of incipient sexuality and Oedipal conflict. In contrast the remake suggests this incestuous threat, and then hastens to disavow it, reinscribing the narrative within the tribulations of single parenthood and confusion and conflict through absence and distance.

The sexual ambiguity of the relationship between father and daughter is repeatedly stressed in the French film. As Véronique and André sit close to one another in the restaurant in an early scene, Chrystelle, a fellow guest, refers to them as 'les amoureux'. Towards the end of the film, André accompanies Véro to a midnight tryst with Benjamin. However, as they wait for Ben's arrival, the local police appear and André is taken for his daughter's lover. In the remake this ambiguity is both suggested and almost hysterically repudiated. Nicky is shown to be a sexual being; she is constantly revealed as the object of both the non-diegetic and the diegetic masculine gaze. In an early scene we see her lying in bed, her legs bare and uncovered by the sheets. The camera pans slowly up her body in an explicit reification and sexualization of her adolescent physique. However this process and the concomitant suggestion of sexual ambiguity in her relationship with her father is vociferously negated; the boundaries of propriety are clearly defined. As Nicky and André wait at the airport towards the beginning of the film, André goes to the bar and is complimented by the female bar attendant on his 'beautiful daughter'. Whereas in the French source André and Véro share a room and undress in front of one another, here Nicky refuses to sleep with her father, claiming that she cannot sleep with a strange man and instructing him not to walk around in his underwear. Thus the possibility of incestuous confusion is made visible and then rapidly defused; it is covered up just as André covers up his daughter's backside as she walks by the pool in a highly revealing swimsuit. The remake seems to suggest that any confusion as to the relationship between André and Nicky stems only from her lies; in the French film this confusion is revealed as an integral part of the father–daughter relationship.

The role of André's lover is significant in this process of representation and denial. In both films he is shown to make numerous attempts to phone Isabelle in Paris, anxious to rectify the problems in their relationship; however, these calls are far more frequent in the remake and we both see and hear Isabelle as he delivers his messages to her answer-phone. This reinforcement of the relationship between André and Isabelle clearly works to underline the disavowal of incest. Furthermore, the early focus on Nicky's attraction to Ben (she sees him as soon as she arrives at the hotel in contrast to Véro who meets him on the beach about ten minutes into the action) constructs a linear romance narrative between the pair which also serves to present a 'suitable' relationship capable of negating the threatening possibilities of the father–daughter dyad.

In the tropes of psychoanalysis the relationship between father and daughter is shown to be fraught with difficulty. As the object of the daughter's love after the transference of her initial attachment to her mother, the father must be capable of both providing an ideal heterosexual object choice and defusing the dangerous ambiguities of this attraction, ensuring successful transition of the Oedipal phase. It is this problematic relationship which is explored in *Mon Père*. Both André and Véronique are shown to be unable to accept the other's love-object; Véro leaves the restaurant in tears after André admits he would like to marry Isabelle, and André repeatedly shows his jealousy, for example forbidding her to see Pablo, the resident musician. Particularly striking is his reaction to her conversation with a much older man at the poolside bar. He drags her away, calling the man 'Papy' and thus stressing his age, and asks her why she cannot find 'somebody of her own age'. He then does just this, introducing her to a highly serious adolescent boy. Thus André is shown not only to be unable to accept his daughter's choice of potential love object, but also to be particularly jealous of an older man, another father-figure, capable of usurping his role as patriarch.

The ambiguities and tensions of this Oedipal scenario are defused in *My Father*. Rather than representing the father–daughter relationship through this conflict with its attendant suggestions of incestuous sexuality, the remake inscribes paternity in terms of single parenting. Unlike the French film in which it is suggested that father and daughter, although not living together, see one another frequently, here the film opens as André arrives in New York from Paris. Nicky's mother, his ex-wife, reminds him that their daughter is now 14 years old and that she has changed a great deal, thus immediately stressing the father's absence, his distance from his daughter. Subsequently André buys Nicky a drink at the airport bar; he buys her a Shirley Temple which she refuses to drink. Clearly she is beginning to grow and his absence has made him unaware of this change and unable to cope with its consequences. Like Véro, Nicky becomes jealous at the prospect of her father's remarriage. However, the Oedipal subtext of the French film is denied as Nicky tearfully explains that André's relationship with Isabelle caused him to miss her thirteenth birthday; here the daughter's jealousy is explicitly ascribed to the father's absence through divorce and any suggestion of sexual jealousy is negated.

The remake's treatment of paternity can then be seen to be centred in confusion rather than crisis. Much of the film's humour stems from André's failure to understand that his daughter is no longer a child; as she tells Ben that her mother was a prostitute and her father a drug pusher, André assures Diana that 'Nicky knows nothing about love . . . she thinks it is a fairy tale'. Thus the film can be seen to deal with a father's attempts to accept that his child is growing up, a process rendered more difficult by his status as absent single parent. This focus is underlined in a scene towards the end of the film in which André sits reading a copy of *Time* magazine whose cover title is 'Kids, Sex and Values'. It would seem that the film is able to negotiate adolescent sexuality whilst vigorously denying the sexual ambiguities of the father–daughter relationship. These ambiguities simmer below the surface yet are constantly suppressed; as the hotel guests become 'aware' that André's daughter is in fact his 'lover', the relationship is ascribed to his French identity: his transgression is made acceptable only by being 'othered'. It should be noted that in both films the daughters choose to call their father by his first name. In *Mon Père* Véro constantly switches between Papa and André, so underlining the ambivalence of their relationship, his immanent status as both father and lover. In the remake Nicky also uses both names but here the issue becomes one of translation. Nicky will neither be Nicole nor call André *Papa* until after the windsurfing incident when, by attempting to rescue her, he has once again proved his love for her, has become a true father and hence her *Papa*.

As previously stated the American production can be seen to be about paternity in confusion, how to come to terms with a daughter's growing up and her incipient sexuality. In contrast, the French film's exploration of the ambiguities of the father–daughter couple reveals a crisis in paternity, the inability to negotiate successfully the dangers of the Oedipal complex. This contrast is made explicit by the endings of the two films. In the French film Véro leaves André to go on a cruise with Benjamin. Her absence throughout the night provokes his explicit jealousy (he slaps her) which is only soothed by her physical gestures (she puts her hands on his shoulder, turns him around and then embraces him). As they depart the scene cuts between André watching her from a window and a lingering point-of-view shot of her waving up at him. André is then shown lying on his bed, tears in his eyes. The phone rings, it is Isabelle, and he asks her to marry him and to have another daughter with him. Thus his apparent acceptance of his daughter's new love-object and his rejection of incestuous desires through marriage to Isabelle is undermined as he asks for another daughter to fill the place of the one he has lost. This ambivalence is reinforced as the film ends with a long close-up on André's point-of-view shot of Véro whilst in the background we hear the refrain of a melancholy tune which has been played throughout the film each time André sees his daughter with Ben, this time with the words sung by Depardieu, 'Les filles et leurs papas, c'est des drôles de fiançailles. Le temps de s'aimer un peu et puis elles s'en aillent' (It's a funny kind of engagement between girls and their Dads. Just the time to love each other a little and then they go away). Clearly this explicit reference to *fiançailles*, a form of marriage between father and daughter, can only serve to underline the film's focus upon the sexuality integral to the father–daughter relationship and André's inability to accept fully the necessary rejection of this desire. That this dyad is the film's main concern is also restated as the work ends with a dedication to the daughters of the director, producers, and star.

The ending of the remake is far less ambiguous. The melancholy exchange of looks described above takes place as Nicky leaves the hotel with Ben; however, it is much more brief than that of the French film. The film ends with André watching the young couple embrace on the beach. Nicky's skirt blows up in the wind revealing her underwear and underlining the film's dual exploitation and denial of the sexuality between father and daughter. He then rings Isabelle and also asks her to marry him and to have his daughter. This time, however, closure is achieved as we see André laughingly make this request whilst Nicky and Ben kiss in the background; thus he can be seen to have accepted that his daughter is growing up, he has got to know her again and can now become a true father once more within a stable (read married) family group.

These variations in the films' representations of paternity clearly reveal the remake as a process of transformation rather than a mere copy. Ultimately these differences must be located within the specific cinematic and cultural context of each production. *Mon Père*'s negotiation of the incestuous possibilities of the father–daughter relationship cannot be abstracted from a wider examination of these concerns in French culture. Indeed, such representations of paternal seduction can be discerned across a broad range of French cultural artefacts; consider Françoise Sagan's *Bonjour Tristesse* (1954) and Serge Gainsbourg's celebrations of his daughter in his film *Charlotte Forever* (1986) and a subsequent song, 'Lemon Incest'. Within this particular tradition, the title song of *Mon Père ce héros* is not insignificant; it is performed by Marie Gillain (Véro) in a breathy, childlike voice which reinforces the similarly infantile yet suggestive lyrics. The popularity of this particular 'Lolitaesque' performance style, exemplified by the likes of Jane Birkin and Vanessa Paradis, suggests a fascination with the young girl, still childlike yet resonant with sexual promise. Ginette Vincendeau describes the relationship between an older man and a younger woman, often cast in terms of paternity, as a 'master-narrative' of French cinema (Vincendeau 1992: 14). Tracing this tradition back to the films of the 1930s, Vincendeau argues that it has been constantly reworked in both popular and art-house genres, becoming increasingly frequent during the 1980s and early 1990s in films such as *La Puritaine* (Doillon, 1986), *A nos amours* (Pialat, 1983), *La Belle Noiseuse*, and *Nikita*. Whilst stressing the long history of the father–daughter theme in French culture, Vincendeau relates its preponderance in the 1980s and 1990s to both aesthetic conventions (the association of feminine beauty with youth and the concomitant lack of starring roles for mature women actors) and social developments (anxieties about the role of masculinity in the light of feminism).

Clearly then *Mon Père ce héros* can be inserted into a broad French tradition of cultural production which both explores and exploits the ambiguities of the father–daughter relationship. It is surely not insignificant that an iconic image of Frenchness in contemporary Britain is the Nicole/Papa couple of the Renault Clio publicity campaign. In contrast the remake both presents and puritanically disavows these ambiguities, reworking them in terms of single parenthood and the difficulties of adolescence. Both films deny maternity; André is shown to fulfil both roles and in each case the mother is shown to be near-hysterical and unsuccessful in her parenting. Thus I would suggest that both the French production and its remake can be inserted into a renegotiation of paternity and an ensuing denial of maternity in the light of the social changes brought about by feminism described above.

However, whereas the French production can also be inserted into a tradition of previous explorations of the sexual nature of the father–daughter dyad, the remake negates such possibilities. Such denial is surely bound up with the fact that within the hegemony of political correctness, incest and paedophilia have become the great taboos of American society (witness the media controversy of 1996 over Larry Clark's *Kids*). Moreover, the physical comedy of the American film and its focus on the adolescent romance suggests that as a Disney production it was aimed at a young audience, in contrast to the rather more serious French film; clearly this would make the negation of a problematic sexuality even more imperative.

My Father can be seen to form part of a broader renegotiation of masculinity within Hollywood through the tropes of fatherhood and family. As Susan Jeffords remarks, recent Hollywood productions have tended to replace the muscular action hero with a more nurturing family man, thus creating a new space for masculinity within the context of post-feminist society (Jeffords 1993: 196–208). It is not insignificant that many of the remakes of the 1980s and 1990s can be seen to deal with this theme: *Three Men and a Baby* (1987), *Three Fugitives* (1989), *Paradise* (1991), *True Lies* (1994), and *Father's Day* (1997). Thus the representations of paternity in the two films under discussion can be seen both to demonstrate the process of transformation of the remake, as a French film is reworked within a different cultural and cinematic context, and at the same time to underline the intertextuality of popular film as each draws upon a recurrent motif of French and Hollywood contemporary production. In condemning the remake as a 'copy' of a clearly defined 'original' text we deny both this difference and the shared identities of these thoroughly hybrid and intertextual works.

20

Nationality, Authenticity, Reflexivity: Kieslowski's *Trois couleurs*: *Bleu* (1993), *Blanc* (1993), and *Rouge* (1994)

JULIA DOBSON

KIESLOWSKI'S *Three Colours* trilogy comprising *Bleu* (1993), *Blanc* (1993), *Rouge* (1994), three films of enormous emotional impact and complex ethical engagement, occupies an important place in the study of contemporary French cinema as locus of engagement with constructions of both French cinema and film itself. The pan-European success of the trilogy and the attendant high-profile media coverage of the films (see, for example, the special number of *Télérama* with its glossy film stills, interviews with large numbers of the crew and cast, and obsessive relation of on-set anecdotes) have represented it as the apogee of 1990s European art-house cinema. Kieslowski's announcement of his retirement from film-making during the making of the trilogy and his sudden death after its completion have engendered a critical reception of the films dominated by the desire to read them as a defining culmination of his film-making career. Deemed an appropriate closure, *Rouge* has been lauded as consoling evidence of an ultimately less pessimistic world view to counter his earlier work (Peck 1994: 147; Kehr 1994: 12). Whilst acknowledging the considerable body of interpretative work on Kieslowski's œuvre,[1] I do not have room here to address his earlier works in the light of my arguments. This chapter originated in a double sense of unease with both the secondary critical discourse (primarily the reviews in *Cahiers du cinéma*) around *Bleu* and *Rouge*, and the textual complexity of the final frames of *Rouge*. A closer examination of both reveals their engagement with different mobilizations of the notion of authenticity; it is implicated in both the reviews' construction of national cinemas, and the trilogy's deconstruction of film, represented in its increasingly reflexive mode.

In its conception, funding, and casting, the *Three Colours* trilogy serves as a notable example of the current trend (whether a consequence of desire or financial necessity) towards international co-productions. The three films' embrace of different national locations, languages, and stars positions them as an interesting challenge to notions of national cinemas in the 1990s.

The concept of a national cinema clearly serves complex ideological purposes in both its reflection of, and contribution to, shifting constructs of national (cultural) identity (Bhabha 1990: 2). I will not discuss the representation of national culture within the filmic text or 'national typologies' (Hayward 1993: 8), but rather the role of secondary, critical discourse in maintaining such constructs. Postcolonial theory has reminded us of the crucial role of the Other in the dialectic of identity formation, and the construction of the concept of a national cinema equally requires the positing of an Other (which may shift in different political and socio-historical contexts) from which to distinguish itself. Hollywood continues to occupy the position of the dominant Other of French cinema,[2] yet critical responses to Kieslowski's trilogy suggest the attempt to define French cinema through an assertion of the difference between French and Eastern European cinemas.[3] This is clearly not a reaction to a threat of cultural imperialism from the East, but may be read as a confused anxiety over the transgression of boundaries of national cinemas, enacted by the phenomenon of international co-productions which the trilogy represents.

Critical discourse around Kieslowski's cinema has overwhelmingly insisted upon drawing a distinction between his 'Polish' films and his later 'French' films, a reductive opposition which has greatly hindered critical engagement with the development of his aesthetics and his constant self-reflexive interrogation of different modes of film-making. This distinction has been widely made, but the response of prominent French critics to the trilogy constitutes a simplistic discourse around notions of nationality and authenticity which deserves closer examination.

The almost hysterical desire to reinforce traditional boundaries is centred upon the linking of national identity and authenticity and is reflected in the reviews of *Bleu* and *Blanc*.[4] On *Bleu*: 'Not only does Kieslowski present us with a French reality devoid of all documentary truth, but he constructs characters, a story, at the limits of kitsch and pomposity . . . the settings, like that of the rue Mouffetard, filmed with the eye of the conventional tourist in a search for the most unadulterated picturesque' (Ostria 1993: 65). This reductive discourse privileges a director's nationality as definitive factor influencing the authentic representation of particular narratives and locations. Kieslowski's representation of Paris in *Bleu* is deemed inauthentic due to his status as emigrant outsider, and his presumed lack of perception of the specific nature of different parts of Paris (an awareness Kieslowski demonstrates in his discussion of this very location; see Stok 1993: 223). Ostria's dismissal of Kieslowski's representation of Paris implies an unconstructed authenticity accessible only to the French (or perhaps only to certain Parisians) and denies its role as a constantly reinterpreted cultural site. Such remappings of Paris are prevalent within contemporary French cinema, notably in films such as *La Haine* (Kassovitz, 1995) and *Sélect Hôtel* (Bouhnik, 1996).

Whilst western critics' construction of East European cinema includes several major tropes which are equally restrictive (Baecque 1990: 32), the main criterion underlying these constructions of Polish cinema is the projection of a moral duty to foreground the country's economical and political crises (Ostria 1993: 67). Thus *Bleu* is considered to be an abjuration of this responsibility and a problematic divergence from the 'cinema of moral anxiety'. Polish critics made similar criticism of *La Double Vie de Véronique* (1991) and *Bleu*, evoking the Romantic tradition of the artist in Polish culture as an individual who defends both the population and the perceived national culture under the rule of imposed oppressive regimes. Clearly definitions of Polish national cinema are equally constructed (Skwara 1993: 230). If other reviewers of *Bleu* are less explicit in their criticism than Ostria, they none the less imply a displacement of Kieslowski's true nature in the film through their reception of *Blanc* as a welcome return to form and proof of his aesthetic affinity with 'Polish reality' (Jousse 1994: 72) and even with a Polish crew (Amiel 1994: 16). As *Blanc* is interpreted exclusively as a fable of Polish society, defined wholly by its setting (Jousse 1994: 71; Kehr 1994: 16), so Kieslowski as Polish director is seen to return reassuringly to his proper mode, adhering to the projected codes of his national cinema. The *Cahiers* critics do not however imply that Kieslowski's status as émigré, resident in France, precludes him from authentic representation of contemporary Poland.

The reviews discussed appeared primarily in *Cahiers du cinéma*, for whom such controversial judgements play a central role in the construction of the institution's status as arbiter of cultural value and bestower of the mantle of auteur. These assumptions allow Jousse to label Kieslowski as a 'grand petit maître' (Jousse 1994: 73). The glossier coverage of the trilogy (notably the special number of *Télérama*) evoked a reflected glory for French cinema as a consequence of Kieslowski's adoption of France as location and of such icons of contemporary French cinema as Binoche and Trintignant.

The secondary discourse around the *Three Colours* trilogy forms a striking contrast to the narrative content of the films as they reflect Kieslowski's interest in the complex interface between the ethics of the individual and the moral, legal, and financial codes of contemporary society. Such issues, as demonstrated through the different settings of the three films, explicitly transcend all notions of national specificity, notions which Kieslowski consistently attacked in interviews at the time (Stok 1993: 193; Kieslowski 1993: 30; Trémois and Remy 1994: 96). The films maintain the same oblique connections with the constitutional tenets of the French tricolour, which might have suggested a national specificity, that the films of the *Decalogue* have with the Ten Commandments, employing them solely as a springboard for their existentialist explorations of the human condition in a concrete contemporary setting.

The films themselves contest the simplistic discourse of authenticity articulated in the reviews and turn to address the authenticity of cinema. Whilst the films can be read as an 'examination of revolutionary concepts in a post-ideological world' (Hoberman 1994: 50), they remain preoccupied by a reflexive interrogation of the medium of film. Kieslowski's work represents a consistent engagement with the function and role of the cinematic image. His documentaries explore and blur the boundaries between the objective and the subjective image, documentary and fiction, and demonstrate his fascination with the power or impotency of the cinematic image to convey emotion. Kieslowski stated his reasons for moving from documentary to fiction film as a combination of his awareness of the blurring of these distinctions and his anxiety over the unintended role of the documentary camera (Pangon 1988). The trilogy's questioning of the authenticity of the image resides in its reflexive study of the nature of cinema, one which both informs and constitutes a complex representation of Kieslowski's apparent weariness of the cinematic medium (Amiel and Ciment 1994: 32). This reflexivity pervades the trilogy; its presence in *Bleu*, *Blanc*, and *Rouge* serves simultaneously to affirm and question the potential of film.

Bleu, arguably the most intimate and moving of the three films, centres on the grief, self-willed isolation, and ultimate reintegration into society of the central protagonist, Julie. Julie is in almost every frame as the film searches for a means of representing her emotional state. Kieslowski's use of significant objects in characterization is consistent throughout his work (see Pangon 1989), and is evident here in Julie's association with a sensual blue glass mobile. This, however, plays a minor role in comparison to Kieslowski's interrogation of the limits of conventional film language in evoking the invisible core of human subjectivity. The conventional use of close-up in the portrayal of a character's state of mind is taken to extreme lengths in *Bleu*. The first clear shot we have of Julie in hospital after the accident does not encourage the spectator's identification via a conventional close-up but, through the use of a 200 mm lens, fills the screen with the image of her eye. Yet technological advances are of no assistance in representing subjectivity; the eye does not prove to be a window of the soul and functions ironically as another lens whose surface reflects her surroundings and permits us no privileged access to her emotions. The point is emphasized as the shot is repeated at the end of *Bleu*. Other lengthy close-ups of the luminously lit Binoche are equally ambivalent; as Julie sits passively in the sun we can appreciate the quality of the light playing on her face, but cannot determine her state of mind. The ability of film to approach the character in such shots is undermined by the persistent emphasis on reflection and light which presents Julie as icon and ultimately represses her subjectivity.

Kieslowski also investigates the portrayal of subjective time and sound. He subverts the conventional use of the fade to denote the passage of time by inserting fades to black after which we return to the same moment (Stok 1993: 215–16). These fades articulate neither temporal progression nor flashback (Estève 1994: 124), but the privileging of subjective time as narrative time is suspended. Kieslowski's work often contains structures or devices which are seemingly built into a pattern only to be abandoned or subverted. Thus we find a parody of this only recently adopted use of the fade in *Blanc* as Karol's recovery from sexual impotency is signalled by the representation of Dominique's orgasm by a fade to white. The exploration of subjective sound communicates moments of emotional intensity through the asynchronistic echoes of earlier traumatic events. As Julie closes the cupboard door in distress after unleashing her neighbour's cat on the new-born mice, the sound we hear is that of the car crash in which she lost her husband and child. Similarly, the sound of pigeons taking flight recurs throughout *Blanc*, reminding Karol and the audience both of the hallucinatory flashback of his wedding day and his humiliation at the Palais de Justice, thus evoking both his obsession with Dominique and his desire for revenge.

The use of extradiegetic music to suggest or emphasize emotional mood is a frequently abused cinematic convention, yet Preisner's music for *Bleu*, which was composed before filming began (Ciment and Niogret 1993: 22), clearly occupies a central thematic and structural role; indeed the gradual revelation of the concerto provides a sense of progression which offsets the predominantly static camera. (The music in *Blanc* and *Rouge* is employed to conventional effect. The melodies in *Blanc* recall both the Polish mazurka and accompaniments to silent films. The use of the bolero in *Rouge*, its two separate themes which ultimately combine, serves as musical *mise en abyme* of the narrative.) Sudden changes in volume and the accompaniment of bright blue light heighten the multiple roles and impact of the music, whilst the extreme close-ups of the score foreground both its construction and the ambiguity over its authentic authorship. The music seems to be straining to represent what the visual image cannot capture. We may recall the final image of the film as an aural experience in the impact of the chorus. Kieslowski's questioning of the capacity of this wide range of film language to represent subjectivity reflects his frustration with cinema: 'The goal is to capture what lies within us, but there's no way of filming it . . . Literature can achieve this, cinema can't. It can't because it doesn't have the means. It's not intelligent enough' (Stok 1993: 194–5).

Through its lingering shots of photographs, posters, and screens, *Bleu*'s final overwhelming sequence, a montage of the characters who have informed Julie's final self-affirmation, provides multiple references to the attempts of visual images to capture subjectivity. These references all dissimulate emotive images, from lost memories to future lives, yet the manner in which some of them are filmed undermines their authenticity. Julie and Olivier's lovemaking is shot through a fish tank (a device which complements the blue wash of the sequence), but Julie's face is pressed against the glass which functions as a visible surface, a reminder of the screen. The final close-up of her crying encourages catharsis, yet, as the shot progresses, reflections of trees on the glass that separates us from her become increasingly intrusive.[5] The ending of *Bleu* thus foregrounds the limitations of the cinematic image as Kieslowski insists upon the two-dimensional nature of the screen and the ambiguous transparent but tangible barrier that it represents.

The black humour of *Blanc* relies greatly upon our awareness of the potential alienation of the protagonists in the workings of powerful social, financial, and legal institutions, the transgression of subject/object boundaries. In the first part of the film a series of denials (sexual, linguistic, and financial) of the central protagonist Karol's subjectivity culminates in his return to Poland as freight rather than passenger. It is implied that the failure of his marriage is due in part to his objectification of Dominique, shown by his adoption of the bust (also reminiscent of Marianne, symbol of France) and his frequent occupation of the position of voyeur in relation to her.

This thematic concern is paralleled in the reflection upon cinema invited by the film's emphasis on the representation of Karol looking (Peck 1994: 158), through which *Blanc* reminds us constantly of our position as spectators and voyeurs outside the cinematic text. The structures of voyeurism are frequently addressed in Kieslowski's films and central to *Decalogue* 6 and 9 (1988). In *Bleu*, a site of extreme voyeurism, the live sex show, serves as the setting for an ultimately more voyeuristic documentary on Julie's dead husband. The alternation of the camera between the adoption of Karol's voyeuristic position and close-ups of him watching punctuates the pivotal scenes of the narrative. He watches Dominique's silhouette through her bedroom window, spies upon her at his own funeral, and finally watches her when she becomes a literal prisoner of his obsession, objectified in the frame of the prison window. When Karol invites his new friend Mikolaj to share his voyeurism by watching Dominique through her bedroom window, Mikolaj misunderstands and comments on a two-dimensional image, the poster of Bardot that is adjacent to the window. The conventional image of Bardot as fetishized object is, however, subverted by the clear indication that this is a poster for *Le Mépris* (Godard, 1963), a narrative which reflects ironically on Karol's situation.

The act of looking is emphasized both at the funeral and in the last scene by Karol's use of opera glasses, an instrument which introduces the notion of spectacle central to the final sequence's evocation of the structure of cinema itself. Karol stands in the dark, looks up at the illuminated prison window, and is mesmerized by Dominique's gestural performance of their future remarriage which constitutes a mute, unthreatening projection of his desires. The scene complements the references to silent cinema present in the music and Kieslowski's visual characterization of Karol as Chaplin (Trémois 1993: 36). However, the rectilinear composition and artificial reframing of Dominique (the prison bars are removed by a change in focal depth) work reflexively to remind us of the two-dimensional nature of film. This *mise en abyme* of cinema serves to ensure that questions of spectatorship and voyeurism remain foregrounded at the closure of the film. The final close-up of Karol's tear-streaked face remains ambiguous as it encourages our compassion for him whilst reminding us once again of the artificial construction of the text and of our spectatorship.

Rouge is the most explicitly reflexive film of the trilogy and constitutes a multifaceted enquiry into the authenticity of cinema in the context of its contemporary status as consumer product. *Rouge* remains the most intriguing of the three films both in the complexity of its central protagonists (Joseph/Trintignant as the judge arguably provokes a stronger engagement than Valentine/Jacob) and the structure of its narrative. However, the apparent victory of Valentine's compassion over the judge's world-weary cynicism, and the ludic mappings of fate and chance which maintain themes recurrent in Kieslowski's *œuvre*, are articulated within a highly reflexive filmic text.

Whilst this reflexivity is apparent throughout the film, there is only space here to explore brief examples. The smooth, dramatic sweep of the puzzling, autonomous camera movement which punctuates an important conversation between Valentine and Joseph serves little narrative purpose (indeed it contrasts with the careful use of the house interior to represent the moral labyrinths presented by the judge), but reminds us that we are watching a film. Similarly, Kieslowski's use of the Technocrane to create seamless and highly self-conscious camera movements between Valentine's and Auguste's flats, and the dramatic evocation of the judge's book falling from the theatre stalls into the orchestra pit, serve to draw our attention to the intermediary of the camera and the construction of the filmic text.

The judge's role as cynical questioner of the Law (his name, Joseph Kern, identifies him with the central protagonist of Kafka's *The Trial*) is ultimately secondary to his influence over the lives of those around him. Associations of the character of the judge with Kieslowski are unjustified in their biographical specificity (Masson 1994: 21; Hoberman 1994: 53), yet the judge's apparent proclivity for the temporal and spatial manipulation of the other characters and his sensitivity to the quality of the light create a figure analogous to a film-maker.

Commenting on Godard's film language and his creation of a reflexive cinematic discourse, Stam describes the main characteristics of presentation:

Actors are posed against blank walls or schematic backgrounds which block perspectival lines. Rectilinear compositions and abstract framing force us to contemplate rather than 'enter' the image, while the inclusion of two-dimensional materials—paintings, photographs, posters, newspapers, book covers—call attention to the screen as a two-dimensional surface. (Stam 1985: 255)

Whilst Kieslowski's interrogation of cinema in *Rouge* does not amount to an 'attack on illusionistic representation' (Stam 1985: 266), it does create a complex, multilayered text that affirms the pleasures of cinema whilst undermining its authenticity. *Rouge* is full of two-dimensional images, including the newspaper pictures of Valentine's brother, the multiple results of the photo-shoot, and the excessively sized advertising posters. The authenticity of all these images is called into question: Valentine rebukes the enquiries of her gloating neighbour by pretending that the newspaper picture of the drug user is someone who merely resembles her brother, the photographer insists that she adopt a sad pose for the photographs so undermining the authenticity of her expression, and the function of the poster image, replicated in the television news footage of the ferry disaster, is rendered ambiguous precisely as a consequence of this dual function within the narrative.

Valentine works as a model in a fashion industry which is founded upon the financially driven manipulation of aesthetics, and her profession plays an important role in the reflexivity of the film, functioning as allegory of the film industry. This analogy is made explicit through the inspired subversion of product placement in the revelation of the product marketed by the advertising campaign; the aptly named Hollywood gum. As the judge watches the news footage, the clicking of the press cameras provides an aural reminder of the photo-shoot before the significance of the image is emphasized by the repositioning, within the cinematic frame, of the picture on the judge's television screen. The picture is first frozen and then moves through a slow zoom to deliver an exact replication of the poster. The revelation of the artificial construction of the image, and our recognition of its previous role, call into question the authenticity of both Valentine's sad expression and the function of the cinematic image before us. Our subsequent reflection on both the manipulation of the image and the parallel manipulation of our position as spectator-consumer obliges us to question whether the discourses of financial and emotional investment can be mutually accommodated. The use of the shot to market *Rouge* adds another layer to this relationship.

The critique of the commodification of culture, introduced in the work of Adorno and developed in the work of Baudrillard and others (including its articulation in Godard's cinematic discourse), is a familiar trope of contemporary cultural theory. Kieslowski's *Rouge* constitutes a complex interrogation and illustration of such debates. The 'rescue' of the main protagonists from the three films and their subsequent inscription as survivors of the shipwreck is moving, yet the impact of this happy ending (which glosses over the thousand passengers who have drowned) is also diminished in the light of the judge's assertion that Valentine's rescue of his dog did not represent a purely altruistic gesture, but rather a self-interested assuagement of her own guilt at having run it over.

The final frozen frame of *Rouge* leaves the spectator not with an easily assimilated closure to the trilogy, but with an immensely complex and multilayered image whose disquieting nature lies precisely in the juxtaposition of the tangible compassion of a director 'saving' his characters and the emphatic undermining of the authenticity of the image with which he communicates this compassion.

The problematic assumptions which underwrite the critical reception afforded the films in *Cahiers* and the reflexivity of the filmic texts have been shown to rely upon very different engagements with concepts of authenticity. Indeed, the limited parameters of the reviews, based on a reductive defence of simplistic constructions of national cinemas, sets Kieslowski's exploration of the authenticity of film into favourable relief. Kieslowski's reflexive engagement with the filmic medium increases in amplitude as the trilogy progresses, however the three endings all foreground evocations of cinema. *Bleu* ends with a virtuoso demonstration of both the potential and the limits of cinema's capacity to represent human subjectivity. *Blanc*'s ending invites our compassion for Karol whilst also implicating his voyeuristic desires in Dominique's imprisonment, an implication which implicitly reflects upon our own spectatorship. *Rouge* employs an image whose double function as commercial advertisement and narrative climax disturbs our identification both with the character of Valentine and with the narrative closure.

Ultimately the final frames of *Bleu*, *Blanc*, and *Rouge* include a lengthy close-up of Julie, Karol, and the judge in their positions as implicit spectators. The closures of the three films coincide with the emotional openings of the protagonists who are seen to be moved to tears by their respective metaphors of cinema. Kieslowski, in the trilogy, invites us to consider the authenticity of both image and cinema whilst (not at all paradoxically) delivering a forceful reminder of the power and pleasures of cinema; that manipulated play of time, space, and image which should be capable of engaging both our emotions and our thought.

Notes

1. I would also like to acknowledge the work of the Film Studies seminar groups at Madingley Hall, July 1997.

2. The divide between French and Hollywood production has been blurred by films such as Besson's *Léon* (1994) and more recently *Le Cinquième élément* (1997). However, the constructions remain intact as audience response to *Léon* revealed that it was thought too 'French' by American audiences and too 'American' by French cinema-goers (Austin 1996: 132).

3. Orientalist discourse asserts the western viewpoint as the self-reflexive origin of knowledge and views other cultures as eternal and unchangeable, fetishizing what it posits as their essential characteristics, which consequently denies and represses representations of independent subjectivities (Said 1991; Bhabha 1990; Spivak 1989).

4. See also Kehr 1994: 16. *Rouge* did not receive such 'coloured' reviews. This is perhaps due to the 'neutral' location of Geneva or the knowledge that this was to be Kieslowski's last film.

5. The metaphorical use of windows and distorting glass prisms to denote freedom and subjectivity is important throughout Kieslowski's *œuvre*; see Dobson 1996.

21

Besson's 'Mission Elastoplast': *Le Cinquième élément* (1997)

SUSAN HAYWARD

LE *Cinquième élément* continues the tradition begun with *Le Grand Bleu* of 'serious' critics trashing Besson's work, but popular audiences acclaiming it in their millions. The film is Besson's most audacious coup to date: a French-financed blockbuster, a special-effects film that beats Hollywood at its own game. Completely financed by the French producers Gaumont for 500 million francs ($90 million), it had already made its money back in pre-production sales before Besson had shot his first image, a phenomenon unheard of in the French film industry. Criticized for not being 'French', because the dialogue is in English and the setting a futuristic New York of the twenty-third century, it was none the less—like *Le Grand Bleu* before it (1988, also in English)—selected to open the 1997 Cannes Film Festival. Eyebrows were raised: 'how could an English-speaking French film be opening the 50th Cannes Film Festival?' The French film industry needs Besson's work to be deemed French, however, if only because of the huge revenues his films bring into the CNC and Gaumont coffers, which subsidize other, less popular projects, such as Godard's *Histoires du cinéma* and Kassovitz's *Déjà vu*.

Le Cinquième élément is a visually resplendent film. And it is certainly more than a French film masquerading as a Hollywood product (or as 'less-than' a Hollywood product). First, it is a film which, through its spectacularization of costume design, is dedicated to a new generation of French haute-couturiers, most particularly the branch of couture that is interested in the intellectual transgressive potential of fashion and cross-dressing, namely the couture of Jean-Paul Gaultier (see Bruzzi 1997). The opening of the film at Cannes was itself preceded by a Gaultier catwalk fashion parade. As a further challenge, cyborg and aliens in this film are just as important as fashion-carrying bodies as are the humans. But the fashion itself carries its own signification, forming a discourse that runs independently throughout the film, and acting as one of the strongly motivating signs of the narrative.

Besson's film also spectacularizes technology—as have all his previous films. But it is a conscious spectacularization. In *Le Cinquième élément*, Besson brings together cinemascope (his favourite format) and digital technology for the computer-generated images of twenty-third-century New York. Besson consciously experiments with photographic imagery and digital (post-photographic) imagery. He has been criticized for making a special-effects cinema, but special effects has always been an ethical preoccupation of Besson's since his first film (*Le Dernier Combat*, 1983). His question has always been 'how not to cheat with special effects'. It is not accidental, therefore, that he chose to work with Digital Domain in California rather than any of the other digital effects companies in the USA.[1] James Cameron, one of the co-founders of Digital Domain, was the special-effects man for *Aliens* (Cameron, 1986) and *Terminator 2* (Cameron, 1991). Cameron's guiding principle, which he took with him to Digital Domain, was to make special effects an integrated and integral part of the movie and not to fetishize special effects by flagging them up, priming the spectator for them, as occurs in *Jurassic Park*, say, with its computer-generated dinosaurs. In other words, Besson turned to Cameron because the challenge for him in his film was to make the photographic image and the post-photographic image make sense together, rather than aiming to obtain the maximum extraordinary effects (as so often occurs when new technology comes onto the scene/screen). In this respect, Besson is following the tradition first set by George Lucas in 1977 with his *Star Wars* where the 'natural' of his hyper-space contrasted markedly with what had preceded in sci-fi cinema (particularly that of the 1950s; see Cantaloube 1997).

The New York of *Le Cinquième élément* was created from images shot of a scaled model of the city (Manhattan) that were subsequently digitally manipulated. The special effects, then, are not entirely numerical, but a combination of old film practices (scale models) and new technology (digital). The whole thing could have been numerically pulled out of a bank of prefabricated images in a computer, a hyper-realization of special effects that Besson opted against, clearly for aesthetic purposes. His choice is for a degree of naturalism compounded by the camerawork:

The film's extraordinary cityscapes and flying vehicles were created by cutting edge SFX company Digital Domain. Besson himself provided more than 8000 drawings, created by a nine-strong team in the 12 months before shooting. The director and special visual effects supervisor Mark Stetson then worked on the detailed miniatures and computer-generated effects, blending them with the director's photo-realistic cinematic style. 'I tried to stay totally anonymous with my camera; as if I were shooting in the street,' says Besson. 'I think it gives the film a sense of reality; the camera doesn't suddenly shift speed or change style to suit a special effect. A shot of the New York skyline with 400 flying cars is enough.' (Floyd 1997: 17)

This aesthetic sensibility is described by one of Digital Domain's representatives as a European approach to special effects which refuses to privilege the technical over the artistic (the representative is Delahaye, quoted in Cantaloube 1997: 84). Thus, the effects themselves tell part of the story. In *Le Cinquième élément* they are a force driving the narrative, and therefore constitute, as with the fashion designs, a strongly motivating sign of the narrative. This again detaches Besson's film from accusations that it is poor Hollywood pastiche. He is trying out other ideas with the technology available—making an actualizable world of the future-present which it is unlikely Hollywood would attempt. The point with Hollywood sci-fi films is not just the scarcely hidden political agendas, but the happy ending which tells us that we need not fear we will end up in such an imaginary world because the hero will disable the technology that makes such a world possible. In Besson's film, the opposite occurs and the hero prevents twenty-third-century New York, the futuristic new world, from being destroyed. In fact, Besson's world has today's technology (radio, cellphones) living alongside that of the future (Zorg's magnificent multi-purpose weapon of destruction, space stations, flying taxis). The past floats in as well, quite comfortably, in the form of reference to other sci-fi films (most obviously *Blade Runner*, Scott, 1982); food is parodied in a past-present tension with the Chinese junk carrying exotic memories of Los Angeles (*Blade Runner* again) and McDonald's gratuitously going up in smoke (a counter-cocacolanization the French audiences must surely have enjoyed). Besson's future-present world is not necessarily a world we might want to live in, but it is not one in which the city itself is a menacing presence. It is fast, potentially dangerous, under heavy surveillance, and the lower regions of the city are dirty and smog-ridden. We already live in cities such as this one. We cannot therefore reject it from our consciousness as easily as we might other imagined cities in the sci-fi genre.

There are ways in which Besson's film can be read as a postmodern nightmare, however. *Le Cinquième élément* is in many regards a film that takes on board the effects of cyberspace and technology on human consciousness. The world it presents is one where the modernist world is crumbling in the face of a virtual world that is post-narrative, post-photography, and post-biological. The paradox of Besson's movie is that Leeloo, the supreme being, embodies or—better put—is the site where these two worlds collide. The love story, which is one of the core narratives, is bound up with the race against time (indeed even back in time). This traditional narrative is under constant threat from a techno-erotics (technology as a projection/displacement of the erotic body) in which the technology to delete the body threatens to outsmart more conventional ways of resolving the crisis (through love and intelligence). The classical narrative, of man making his break from the tribe, proving his manhood, overthrowing the malevolent forces, and killing the chief to finally reap his rewards of security and marriage, almost does not happen. Leeloo, the virtual embodiment of woman, only relents at the eleventh hour to Korben's entreaties to love him, that is, to assert his subjectivity and help him fulfil his Oedipal trajectory. The classical narrative is under numerous threats, not just from the aliens and Zorg (different aspects of techno-erotics), but also from the pure (but apparently forgettable) embodiment of techno-erotics itself, Leeloo. In other words, the narrative is saved only if we forget that Leeloo is not human. We know for a fact that she is a cyborg (at best); however, the Oedipal narrative works very hard to make us forget this. The outcome, man having intercourse with a cyborg, is a far from classical one. Thus the narrative ends up in a postmodern capsule; we are, literally, on the verge of the post-narrative.

As for the other issues of the postmodern nightmare (post photography and post-biological), here too we are almost already there. We are already in an age of post-photography, where images—including images of the human form—can be numerically invoked onto the computer screen. The material body need no longer figure since it can be seen and experienced virtually. The recreation of Leeloo in the film makes this clear, as does the scientist's blissful reaction ('perfect') to her digitalized reconstruction. Indeed, the ethics of reconstructing Leeloo come down to a degree zero; the question becomes whether it is safe to do so, not whether it is morally a good idea. Leeloo is also post-biological in that she may well be a DNA sample, but she is not meat—effectively she is reconstructed as the body without meat (muscles and 'covering' are bio-technically imaged onto her frame that itself has been bio-technically rebuilt). A positive reading of this could lead us to say that whilst man seeks to delete the body (through his pursuit of techno-erotics—investing his subjectivity in technics), he cannot actually allow himself to let it happen. To the question 'can thought go on without a body?' the answer is, at present, 'no'.[2] A less positive reading brings us to an analysis of the characterization of Leeloo herself, who, to all intents and purposes, is the font of all knowledge, and yet we see very little manifestation of this. If anything, she is merely the key to the puzzle, and men have to find out where she fits. As we see, it is the men who resolve the enigma. She, meantime, spends a great deal of her intellectual energy absorbing man's past (off digitally created images on the computer!). 'Can thought go on without male body' might be a better way of rephrasing the question.

A crucial problem is posed by the embodied presence of Leeloo. The question is not who, but what is she? Is she a cyborg? an alien? an android even? Perhaps we can assume she is not an android, since androids are robots masquerading as humans (like the replicants in *Blade Runner*). Nor indeed is she an alien, although she comes close, since these are extra-terrestrial beings, and, whilst Leeloo seems to come to us from outer space, she is in fact very clearly a re-creation—genetically engineered—from a mummified body which we presume had a terrestrial past since it appeared to originate from Egypt from where it was taken to a place of safety. So we must perhaps think of her as a cybernetic organism, a techno-body maybe? What she is not is massively (en masse, as matter) her original self. That got burned up, only the charred remains of one hand/claw remain, a transparent intertextual reference to *Terminator 2* (Cameron, 1991). Two writers offer some useful definitions and distinctions between different types of cyborgs which can help our analysis here (Balsamo 1997: 11; Springer 1996: 19–20). The two most common types as represented in popular culture are, first, the cyborg which 'combines the human organic body, which either preexisted as a person or was genetically engineered, with non-organic mechanical or electronic implants or protheses' (Springer 1996: 19). The second type 'has no organic form but consists of the human mind preserved on computer software' (Springer 1996: 19–20). In respect of this second type, one thinks immediately of Hal in Kubrick's *2001: A Space Odyssey* (1968). Humans who download software directly into their electronically wired brains are also cyborgs (Kathryn Bigelow's *Strange Days*, 1995, comes to mind). In a sense, Leeloo crosses both types. She is the result of a human–machine coupling, and, thanks to her massively over-endowed DNA structure, she can download at the rate of cyber-knots the entire history of man into her memory.

Balsamo's definitions concur with Springer's. She adds, however, that the human body itself already has the ability to be compared to a cyborg since nowadays so many of its parts (she counts twenty-seven in all) are replaceable either through prosthesis or implant (Balsamo 1997: 7–9). She goes on to say, and this is interesting in the context of Leeloo's identity, that

Cyborgs are hybrid entities that are neither wholly technological nor completely organic, which means that the cyborg has the potential not only to disrupt persistent dualisms that set the natural body in opposition to the technologically recrafted body, but also to fashion our thinking about the theoretical construction of the body as both a material entity and a discursive process . . . Cyborg bodies are definitionally transgressive of a dominant culture order, not so much because of their 'constructed' nature, but rather because of the indeterminancy of their hybrid design. The cyborg provides a framework for studying gender identity as it is technologically crafted simultaneously from the matter of material bodies and cultural fictions. (Balsamo 1997: 11)

In other words, because cyborgs are like us and yet not like us, and because their identity is 'predicated on transgressed boundaries' (Balsamo 1997: 32), they foreground 'the constructedness of otherness' (Balsamo 1997: 33). Cyborgs show that gender identity is socially ideologically predicated, because the cyborg body is not a 'natural' body, and yet it appears in popular culture (film and fiction for example) as gendered (for example, *RoboCop*

(Verhoeven, 1987) is definitely male). But how can this be, since definitions of gender rely upon 'appeals to the natural body' (Balsamo 1997: 25)? This is the point of exposure: the actuality of the cyborg (as human/machine) means it is 'other' than natural; and yet it passes as natural, as human, and becomes engrained/enchained in the ideology of the gender divide. Through its transgressiveness (as a technologically recrafted body), it exposes the ideological constructedness of otherness that is based in the (psychoanalytical) principle of difference. Freud and Lacan explain that male subjectivity (sexual identity) is dependent on and affirmed by the female other (she who is sexually marked as different from the male). Since we cannot in truth impute a sexual identity to a cyborg, how can it be possible to inscribe it within the concept of gender?

Because we do, however, impute gender identity to cyborgs, it becomes clear, then, that gender is an ideological concept that emanates not from the 'natural' body itself, but from the exchange between the physical body and the social body (alternatively known as the social order of things, patriarchal law, the Symbolic). In other words, gender is not something your body intrinsically is. Gender is not your sex, but how you socially act or perform your sex. The social body requires, for example, that heterosexuality prevail in order for the social order of things to be perpetuated through procreation. Clearly, a transgressive body will cause problems for the social body; indeed, it will expose the anxieties felt by ideology (patriarchy) about the social body and its securedness (see Balsamo 1997: 17–28). If we just pause for a moment and consider the still very real hostility towards an everyday transgressive body, that of the homosexual or lesbian, we can see how the reaction says more about fear for the securedness and legitimacy of the social body than it does about the transgressive body itself, about which so little can be known. How does one control a body that is not entirely knowable? If we impute a gender to cyborgs, it is because the cyborg body, the techno-body, is in fact an unruly body; one that disrupts because it is not of the centre, is obscene in its uncentredness, potentially exposing the fragility of the social body.

If we accept this reading of transgressiveness, why then does man spend so much of his scientific energies trying to reproduce the human in robotic or cyborg form, the very essence of the transgressive body? Why does the military invest massively in Artificial

Intelligence (AI)? Why does man make transgressive, unknowable forms of simulated life? Why does he seek his own obsolescence? There are two obvious answers: to avoid investment in the improvement of social relations (which would eventually dispense with power relations); and to overcome, through displacement, man's deep-rooted fear of his own sexuality.[3] If we are at the dawn of a new revolutionary age (of life 'in silico', which, according to Springer, is a dream of articifical-life computer scientists and biologists; Springer 1996: 21), then we are at the dusk of the sexed body, possibly man's greatest ambition. And the way to get to it is by dissolving the distinction between technology and humanity. Genetic engineering, cloning (begun a century ago with frogs), templating the human brain onto computers (AI) are but the latest manifestations of man's desire to 'not be' (a film example of which is Bigelow's *Strange Days*, co-authored by James Cameron). They are also part of man's ongoing desire to remove that which, to his own mind, most threatens his subjectivity/sexuality (because her presence reminds him of it all the time): woman. Equally, they represent the desire to replace, through bio-technological repro duction, the female's function of reproduction. The paradox, as always, is that man seeks to perfect the very thing that will expose what he most wants to hide. Cyborgs and robots are the projections of what man fears most: fear of his own sexuality (including its precarious security dependent on the female other), progress in the system of human relations (an end to hierarchies of power), and, of course, fear of his own death. These techno-bodies, then, are simultaneously a containment and a displacement of those fears, and so they are always already transgressive in that they stand for what the social body (patriarchal law) most desperately wants not to be or not to happen.

Leeloo, as a cyborg body, is an extremely complex set of hybridizations. And yet we never really get to read her body as transgressive. In fact, she reads as a throwback to earlier, nine-teenth-century science-fiction writing where woman is constructed as the one who retains moral purity (there is much insistence on her virginity); she is the one who will redeem the capitalist (now post-capitalist) world and save it from its worst excesses (such as total annihilation). Leeloo seems to fit all of these descriptions, and yet she is a cyborg. The question becomes why, after all, in Besson's film, is the fifth element a woman? We recall that the explorer in

Egypt explained that it is the fifth element alone that can save the world in the twenty-third century. The assumption made is that this supreme being will be a male. Yet it is female. In the film narrative, rather than transgress the social body, Leeloo helps to restore it, to make it secure, much like the nineteenth-century science-fiction characterization of woman before her. She is the (male) scientist's dream cyborg: truly contained and not threatening to man. In fact, she becomes very much a cipher (to complement her waif-like body), and it is mostly Korben Dallas who does the figuring out. It is true that she almost refuses at the end of the film to 'save humanity', but finally she succumbs, as well as succumbing to that other exigency of the social body: the heterosexual imperative. She has sex with Korben in the very capsule that made her! In other words, Leeloo is the very last 'person' to foreground the constructedness of otherness. Her body only transgresses as an idea, not as a fact. We are led to believe that she is amazingly strong (her hand-to-gun combat on the paradise planet/space-hotel Fhloston), but she has none of the muscularity and vigorous health we associate with techno-bodies. Cyborg bodies are supposedly hyper-built, not just DNA structures in excess. Leeloo is never the opposite of what she appears to be. She is never allowed to look or be transgressive (unlike her fore-sister Nikita). To have had the muscularity of the techno-body would have meant that she would herself have recrafted the body that emerges from the capsule (through body-building). We note that she has an enormous appetite, but it does not get transformed into any change of matter. But we do know that techno-bodies, like those of female body-builders, are, as Balsamo points out, 'delegitimated as cultural markers of proper femininity' (Balsamo 1997: 47). There can, it would appear, be no improper female masculinity for Leeloo (any more, ultimately, than for Nikita in Besson's earlier film). In fact, her cyborgness is suppressed, which is perhaps why we get none of the male rage and aggression we normally see directed against the female (cyborg) in American sci-fi movies (e.g. *Alien*, Scott, 1979; *Aliens*, Cameron, 1986; *Alien 3*, Fincher, 1992). In the final analysis, Leeloo challenges nothing. She is the mere (sartorial) mirror to Korben Dallas. As Jean-Paul Gaultier made clear, 'her braces are orange, the same colour as Bruce Willis's T-shirt, to suggest they are made for each other' (Gaultier 1997: 9). And in case we had missed that point, her hair is orange too.

If the inherent paradoxes of the social body or the realities of 'forbidden' fantasies are repressed, then, they reappear elsewhere, often in the form of pathologies or as displaced excess. In Besson's film, interestingly, the challenge to the social body does not occur through the presence of the cyborg body at all (Leeloo), but rather through the transgressive male body. Both Zorg and Ruby Rhod are transgressive male bodies; both, in different ways, embody improper masculine femininity. They ultimately become—visually at least—more interesting (to look at) than Leeloo, and almost than Korben Dallas who, thanks to his sexy latex trousers and T-shirt (rubber was used to make Willis sweat for his vanity, Gaultier naughtily tells us; Slater 1997: 27), saves the day for proper masculine masculinity. Clothes design becomes the play arena for questions of male sexuality in this film. We should not forget that, back in the 1980s, Gaultier designed the male skirt. Zorg's skirted coats with their nipped-in waistlines recall the earlier design. Gaultier explains that he pulls from past designs—not just his own—to create his effect (Gaultier 1997: 9). Zorg is of course a re-imagined Hitler of the twenty-third century (that is how Besson spoke to Gaultier about the character). But, more significantly, he is a putative cyborg because of his plexiglas skull. He wears his transgression (doubly so, skull and clothes) on his body, and is surrounded by robotic domestic knick-knacks that serve only to undermine his 'hard' image, particularly when they are thrown out of control as he nearly chokes to death on a cherry stone. Indeed, in the final analysis, none of his fancy technics work for him; they end by blowing him up. He falls victim to his own desire to delete humanity, to obsolesce the body. Zorg, the techno-body, mechanical man, arms dealer, confirms his impotence. He can no more hide behind the multi-functional arms he sells than he can behind the skirt of his coat.

If Zorg is the 'bad' side of the coin of transgression, the same is not true of Ruby Rhod. S/he crosses every line possible and helps to save the day. Ruby performs all the sexes, in dress and implicitly in action; and s/he camps up all the generic roles s/he can muster. One critic describes Ruby as swathed in leopard-skin with Cruella de Vil collars (Slater 1997: 27). S/he also drips with ostentatious (costume?) jewellery. Ruby's dress code is a pot-pourri of the blaxploitation-look movies of the 1970s and the black hip-hop style of the 1980s, both of which in their own right derive their style from parodies of other earlier styles. The former 1970s clothes-chic of flares and tight polyester tops and platform shoes is derived from the dress codes of black pimps and prostitutes and the latter 1980s city-slicker cool suits (often with high necks) and masses of thick gold chains, chokers, and rings come from Coco Chanel's use of ostentatious fake jewellery to adorn her classic cut suits.

Rhod becomes a hero despite herself. It is s/he who complements the masculine Korben Dallas: s/he is the ultra-feminine black body to his ultra-masculine white body. Both are in excess, but Rhod is more visibly transgressive; her/his body manifests an ability to play with sexuality in a way that the very white Korben cannot. The challenges around sexuality and gender performativity that *Le Cinquième élément* puts on display (or at the very least the *mise en scène* of these excessive and transgressive bodies) mark the film as a contestation of dominant ideology to a degree. It parodies genre and stereotypes, raises issues around race and male sexuality, but it stops short of a resistance to the social order of things through its misogynistic representation of Leeloo. Her name is a diminutive (reduced from her very long one). A diminutive name is hardly the appropriate one for a 'supreme and perfect being' because it brings her purported power down to size (as 'less than'). Although she is clearly very smart and redolent of bio-energy, she becomes weak in knowledge and power by the end of the film, and is saved only by Korben's declaration of love for her. Throughout, she acts as a child, not as a sexualized woman. She is in the end reduced to the symbol of salvation (as the fifth element and as the reproduction machine). Ultimately, she is controlled by man who can make her (through bio-technology and words of love), and just as easily unmake her. As such she is a very conventional female characterization, fitting into (amongst others) the classic film noir genre with its tropes of 'woman as enigma' and 'man as unravelling the enigma of woman'.

In this oversized humanated scope cartoon, good triumphs over evil; and France triumphs over Hollywood. As Besson himself makes clear, no American major would have touched his script, which in Hollywood would have cost $140 million to produce (Frodon 1997*b*: 18). Nor would they have touched it because of Hollywood's golden rules for blockbusters: nothing foreign and nothing queer. Its play with male sexuality, though not a specificity of French cinema, certainly demarcates Besson's films as non-mainstream Hollywood. But as to its Frenchness, there are many levels of production of meaning that do align it with its nation of origin. All the creative staff were French; of the 450 technicians working on the film, one third were French. And, of course, the film is a French artefact in that it relies for its overall look on two major French designers: Gaultier for the clothes, and Jean Giraud, the cartoonist, for the sets and decors. On the other hand, it is truly a massively intertextual film, starting with the bodily intertext of the star persona Bruce Willis, and it is also heavily cross-fertilized technologically speaking (French, British, and American). However, it is ineluctably a deeply personal film as well. First, because the genesis of the film is Besson himself who wrote a rough sketch for it when he was 15. And, second, because he made this film, as he himself states, to please his audience, and to give some momentary relief from that which he cannot do, which is to reduce unemployment and diminish social injustice (Frodon 1997*b*: 18). As he says, his work is 'Mission Elastoplast' (Frodon 1997*b*: 18). Perhaps we must let it go as that.

Notes

1. For example, he chose not to work with Pixar (linked with Disney) and PDI (with Dreamworks), precisely because they are attached to the majors in the industry and have formulaic ways of making their special effects felt. Interestingly, Besson did not choose Industrial Light and Magic (ILM) either. This company was founded by George Lucas and is the only other independent company in California. However, ILM did make the special effects for *Jurassic Park* and *Lost World* (1997), reflecting Spielberg's own choices. It could be that Besson, in his concern not to flag up the special-effects imagery in the ostentatious way they are signalled in *Jurassic Park*, decided to opt for Digital Domain.

2. See Springer 1996 and Balsamo 1997 for further discussion of techno-erotics.

3. For a more developed discussion of this idea of obsolescence and robotics, see Baudrillard 1996: 109–33, and for a more detailed analysis of Besson's films and technology, see Hayward 1998: 94–118.

Filmography

THE following list contains those Francophone films distributed in the UK from 1990 to December 1998. Full technical details including a plot summary and a critical review can be found in the issue of the British Film Institute periodicals *Monthly Film Bulletin* (*MFB*) and *Sight and Sound* (*SS*) referred to in column 4; references here give the year followed by volume and issue numbers. The list also contains films which were released in the 1990s and which are referred to in this volume, but which were not distributed in the UK; such films do not have *Monthly Film Bulletin* or *Sight and Sound* references. Details for these films, and those distributed in the UK, should normally be found electronically in the BFI CD-ROM catalogue *Film Index International*, or on the *Internet Movie Database*. Column 5 gives the number of spectators in France until December 1998, where available. These statistics were obtained from the Centre National de la Cinématographie. The final column lists the references for the videocassette version of the film (subtitled) when available; original French SECAM versions are not given.

Title of Film	Year	Director	BFI Ref.	Spectators > = less than	Video
Accompagnatrice, L'	1992	Miller	*SS* (1993), 3: 11	724,423	TVT1140
A la campagne	1995	Poirier		121,694	
Amant, L'	1992	Annaud	*SS* (1992), 2: 3	3,156,124	
Amants du Pont-Neuf, Les	1991	Carax	*SS* (1992), 2: 5	867,197	ART047
Anges gardiens, Les	1995	Poiré		5,735,244	
Annabelle partagée	1990	Comencini	*SS* (1993), 3: 3	>5000	TVT1084
Appartement, L'	1996	Mimouni	*SS* (1997), 7: 10	156,857	ART147
Appât, L'	1995	Tavernier	*SS* (1995), 5: 9	721,715	ART117
Apprentis, Les	1995	Salvadori	*SS* (1996), 6: 8	538,684	TVT1257
Après l'amour	1992	Kurys	*SS* (1993), 3: 9	542,174	G0034
Artémisia	1997	Ferlet	*SS* (1999), 9: 5	105,060	
Assassin(s)	1997	Kassovitz		441,157	
A toute vitesse	1996	Morel	*SS* (1998), 8: 2	80,633	DTK020

Table (*continued*)

Title of Film	Year	Director	BFI Ref.	Spectators > = less than	Video
Autre Côté de la mer, L'	1997	Cabrera		169,130	
Aux yeux du monde	1991	Rochant	SS (1992), 2: 3	149,198	ART042
Baule-les-Pins, La	1990	Kurys	MFB (1990), 58: 686	724,141	
Beaumarchais, l'insolent	1996	Molinaro	SS (1996), 6: 9	1,927,397	ART129
Belle Noiseuse, La	1991	Rivette	SS (1992), 1: 12	277,696	ART038
Belle verte, La	1996	Serreau		747,952	
Bonheur est dans le pré, Le	1995	Chatiliez	SS (1996), 6: 12	4,930,127	G8904S
Bossu, Le	1997	de Broca	SS (1998), 8: 9	2,318,338	P8957W
Bye Bye	1995	Dridi		129,581	
Caprices d'un fleuve, Les	1996	Giraudeau		835,182	
Captive du désert, La	1990	Depardon	SS (1991), 1: 2	154,795	
Cérémonie, La	1995	Chabrol	SS (1996), 6: 3	1,000,271	TVT1258
C'est arrivé près de chez vous	1992	Belvaux, Bonzel, Poelvoorde	SS (1993), 3: 1	536,490	TVT1074
Chacun cherche son chat	1996	Klapisch	SS (1996), 6: 11	678,950	ART137
Château de ma mère, Le	1990	Robert	SS (1991), 1: 4	4,269,126	ART097
Cible émouvante	1993	Salvadori	SS (1994), 4: 8	63,856	TVT1181
Cinquième élément, Le	1997	Besson	SS (1997), 7: 7	7,681,803	G8920W
Cité des enfants perdus, La	1995	Jeunet, Caro	SS (1995), 5: 9	1,304,794	EVS1213
Classe de neige, La	1997	Miller	SS (1999), 9:1	87,170	
Clubbed to Death	1997	Zauberman	SS (1998), 8: 2	12,684	ART153
Colonel Chabert, Le	1994	Angelo	SS (1995), 5: 5	1,693,840	G8810
Comment je me suis disputé... ('ma vie sexuelle')	1996	Desplechin	SS (1997), 7: 8	253,850	G8937S
Confessional, Le	1995	Lepage	SS (1996), 6: 6	11,503	ART136
Contes des quatre saisons: conte d'automne	1998	Rohmer	SS (1999), 9:4	362 775	
Contes des quatre saisons: conte d'été	1996	Rohmer	SS (1996), 6: 10	316 463	ART134
Contes des quatre saisons: conte d'hiver	1992	Rohmer		210,087	ART052
Couloirs du temps, Les: Les Visiteurs 2	1998	Poiré		7,880,446	

Table (*continued*)

Title of Film	Year	Director	BFI Ref.	Spectators > = less than	Video
Crise, La	1992	Serreau	*SS* (1994), 4: 3	2,350,189	EP0062
Cyrano de Bergerac	1990	Rappeneau	*MFB* (1991), 58: 684	4,731,625	ART015, TVT1307
Daddy Nostalgie	1990	Tavernier	*SS* (1991), 1: 2	141,747	
Décroche les étoiles	1996	Cassavetes Kassovitz	*SS* (1997) 7: 7	95,723	
Déjà vu					
Delicatessen	1990	Jeunet, Caro	*SS* (1992), 1: 9	407,784	EP636470
Diên Biên Phu	1992	Schoendoerffer		915,807	
Dobermann	1997	Kounen	*SS* (1999), 9:1	789 944	TVTTBA7
Docteur Petiot	1990	de Chalonge	*SS* (1991), 1: 6	529,730	EP0014
Double Vie de Véronique, La	1991	Kieslowski	*SS* (1992), 1: 11	592,070	TVT60
Douce France	1995	Chibane		28,882	
Élisa	1994	Becker	*SS* (1995), 5: 12	2,473,193	TVT1256
Elles ne pensent qu'à ça	1993	Dubreuil		42,706	
Elles n'oublient pas	1994	Frank	*SS* (1994), 4: 11	128,682	TVT
En compagnie d'Antonin Artaud	1993	Mordillat	*SS* (1996), 6: 6	10,215	
Enfer, L'	1993	Chabrol	*SS* (1995), 4: 11	916,460	G0052
État des lieux	1995	Richet		201,695	
Fabuleuses Aventures de Madame Petlet, Les	1995	Casabianca		32,303	
Farinelli	1995	Corbiau		1,320,574	G8862s
Fausto	1992	Duchemin		64,072	CV0048
Fille de d'Artagnan, La	1994	Tavernier	*SS* (1995), 5: 7	1,490,496	ART115
Fille de l'air, La	1992	Bagdadi	*SS* (1993), 3: 11	45,645	TVT1137
Fracture du myocarde, La	1990	Fansten	*SS* (1992), 1: 12	441,901	
Gadjo dilo	1997	Gatlif	*SS* (1998), 8: 8	360,247	
Gazon maudit	1995	Balasko	*SS* (1996), 6: 3	3,990,094	G8840s
Gens de la rizière, Les	1994	Panh	*SS* (1995), 5: 6	97,401	
Gens normaux n'ont rien d'exceptionnel, Les	1995	Ferreira-Barbosa		154,565	
Germinal	1993	Berri	*SS* (1995), 4: 5	6,158,401	G8774
Gloire de mon père, La	1990	Robert	*SS* (1991), 1: 2	6,286,481	ART097
Haine, La	1995	Kassovitz	*SS* (1995), 5: 11	2,041,960	TVT1239
Hasards ou coïncidences	1998	Lelouch	*SS* (1999), 9:6		
Hexagone	1994	Chibane		47,304	
Homme de ma vie, L'	1993	Tachella	*SS* (1995), 5: 10	21,947	TVT1096

Table (continued)

Title of Film	Year	Director	BFI Ref.	Spectators > = less than	Video
Hommes femmes: mode d'emploi	1996	Lelouch	SS (1997), 7: 6	1,253,895	TVT1277
Hors la vie	1991	Bagdadi	SS (1992), 1: 10	204,274	NP0011
Huitième jour, Le	1996	Van Dormael	SS (1996), 6: 113,589,501		EP0453883
Hussard sur le toit, Le	1995	Rappeneau	SS (1996), 6: 1	2,434,883	ART128
Île au trésor, L'	1991	Ruiz	SS (1992), 2: 3	>5000	
Indochine	1992	Wargnier	SS (1993), 3: 4	3,198,663	EP0033
IP5	1992	Beineix	SS (1993), 3: 12	855,136	ART088
Irma Vep	1996	Assayas	SS (1997), 7: 3	31,035	ICAV1029
Jacquot de Nantes	1991	Varda	SS (1992), 1: 10	239,701	TVT1090
J'ai horreur de l'amour	1997	Ferreira-Barbosa		199,633	
J'ai pas sommeil	1993	Denis		52,453	
Jeanne la pucelle	1994	Rivette	SS (1995), 5: 9	143,445	
J'embrasse pas	1991	Téchiné	SS (1992), 1: 12	472,187	TVT1094
Jeune Werther, Le	1992	Doillon	SS (1995), 4: 9	158,043	TVT1168
Jour des rois, Le	1990	Treilhou		83,293	
Journal de Lady M, Le	1992	Tanner	SS (1995), 4: 5	11,763	
Krim	1995	Bouchaala		>5000	
Leolo	1992	Lauzon		51,617	TVT1101
Léon	1994	Besson	SS (1995), 5: 2	3,545,019	D4000022 D474322
Love etc.	1996	Vernoux	SS (1998), 8: 4	135,539	P89445
L.627	1992	Tavernier	SS (1993), 3: 1	715,206	ART055
Lucie Aubrac	1997	Berri	SS (1998), 8: 2	1,690,460	P8945W
Madame Bovary	1991	Chabrol	SS (1993), 3: 7	1,292,075	AV019
Mari de la coiffeuse, Le	1990	Leconte	SS (1991), 1: 2	356,980	VDM1004
Marion	1996	Poirier		132,668	
Marius et Jeannette	1997	Guédiguian	SS (1997), 7: 12	2,627,827	TVT1309
Marquise	1997	Belmont		471,337	
Ma Saison préférée	1993	Téchiné	SS (1994), 4: 8	1,000,667	AV017
Ma 6T va crack-er	1997	Richet		67,631	
Ma Vie en rose	1997	Berliner	SS (1997), 7: 11	267,549	BL09
Ma Vie est un enfer	1991	Balasko		1,170,523	
Mensonge	1992	Margolin	SS (1993), 3: 11	155,329	TVT1125
Merci la vie	1991	Blier	SS (1992), 1: 9	1,088,777	ART027
Métisse	1993	Kassovitz		89,036	
Microcosmos	1996	Nuridsany, Pérennou	SS (1997), 7: 6	3,371,883	G89225
Mina Tannenbaum	1993	Dugowson	SS (1994), 4: 10	381,913	G0053
Misérables du ving-tième siècle, Les	1995	Lelouch	SS (1996), 6: 2	986,078	5014141
Mon homme	1996	Blier	SS (1997), 7: 6	468,019	ART144
Mon Père ce héros	1991	Lauzier	SS (1992), 2: 7	1,428,871	TVT1069

Table (*continued*)

Title of Film	Year	Director	BFI Ref.	Spectators > = less than	Video
Nelly et M. Arnaud	1995	Sautet	*SS* (1996), 6: 4	1,521,041	G8869
Nés quelque part	1997	Chibane			
Nikita	1990	Besson	*MFB* (1990), 57: 682	3,786,613	ART063
Noce blanche	1989	Brisseau	*SS* (1991), 1: 4	1,819,289	TVT062
No smoking	1994	Resnais		352,716	
N'oublie pas que tu vas mourir	1995	Beauvois	*SS* (1996), 6: 10	119,889	
Nuit et jour	1991	Akerman	*SS* (1992), 2: 5	40,407	
Nuits fauves, Les	1992	Collard	*SS* (1993), 3: 6	2,811,073	ART064
Odeur de la papaye verte, L'	1993	Hung	*SS* (1994), 4: 4	383,750	ART093
Olivier Olivier	1992	Holland		49,109	TVT1088
Ombre du doute, L'	1992	Issermann	*SS* (1995), 4: 9	75,295	EP0074
On connaît la chanson	1997	Resnais	*SS* (1998), 8:12	2,632,850	FXP8955W
Parfum d'Yvonne, Le	1994	Leconte	*SS* (1995), 4: 9	156,968	ART102
Pas très catholique	1994	Marshall		266,502	
Péril jeune, Le	1994	Klapisch		644,893	
Personne ne m'aime	1994	Vernoux		113,213	
Pétain	1992	Marbœuf	*SS* (1994), 4: 4	244,802	TVT1164
Petit Prince a dit, Le	1992	Pascal	*SS* (1994), 4: 5	566,404	
Pigalle	1994	Dridi		49,568	
Ponette	1996	Doillon	*SS* (1998), 8: 7	271,192	TVT1302
Portraits chinois	1996	Dugowson	*SS* (1997), 7: 8	107,400	VC3624
Quadrille	1997	Lemercier		133,739	
Raï	1995	Gilou		127,601	
Rayon vert, Le	1994	Rohmer		459,401	ART032
Regarde les hommes tomber	1993	Audiard	*SS* (1997), 7: 6	218,831	
Reine Margot, La	1994	Chéreau	*SS* (1995), 5: 1	1,978,776	G8803s
Rendezvous de Paris, Les	1995	Rohmer	*SS* (1996), 6: 2	81,040	ART118
Ridicule	1996	Leconte	*SS* (1997), 7: 2	2,060,139	PG 0453303
Rien à foutre d'aimer	1997	Giacobbi			
Rien ne va plus	1997	Chabrol	*SS* (1998), 8:11	401,380	ART165
Riens du tout	1992	Klapisch		469,425	
Romaine	1997	Obadia		30,117	
Roseaux sauvages, Les	1994	Téchiné	*SS* (1995), 5: 3	573,840	TVT1228
Salut cousin!	1996	Allouache	*SS* (1998), 8: 5	73,598	
Secret défense	1997	Rivette	*SS* (1998), 8: 10	34,399	ART163
Sélect Hôtel	1996	Bouhnik	*SS* (1997), 7: 7	21,368	
S'en fout la mort	1990	Denis		51,507	
Séparation, La	1994	Vincent	*SS* (1995), 5: 10	486,751	G8815s
Seul avec Claude	1996	Beaudin		6,321	
Seul contre tous	1998	Noé	*SS* (1999), 9:4		

Table (continued)

Title of Film	Year	Director	BFI Ref.	Spectators > = less than	Video
Silences du palais, Les	1994	Tlati	SS (1995), 5: 3	195,610	ICAV 10818
Sitcom	1997	Ozon	SS (1999), 9:1	159,384	
Smoking	1994	Resnais		402,914	
Soif de l'or, La	1993	Oury		1,517,880	
Souviens-toi de moi	1996	Volta			
Tango	1993	Leconte	SS (1993), 3: 8	632,223	ART065
Tatie Danielle	1990	Chatiliez	SS (1991), 1: 1	2,151,463	EP6327383
Thune, La	1991	Galland		39,582	
Total Eclipse	1995	Holland	SS (1997), 7: 4	27,199	
Toto le héros	1991	Van Dormael	SS (1992), 1: 9	539,344	EP0006
Tous les matins du monde	1992	Corneau	SS (1993), 3: 1	2,152,934	EP0026
Toxic Affair	1993	Esposito		197,654	
Trois couleurs: Blanc	1993	Kieslowski	SS (1994), 4: 6	472,895	ART100
Trois couleurs: Bleu	1993	Kieslowski	SS (1993), 3: 11	1,237,269	ART085
Trois couleurs: Rouge	1994	Kieslowski	SS (1995), 4: 11	820,935	ART105
Trois frères, Les	1995	Bourdon and Campan		6,667,207	
Trop de bonheur	1994	Kahn		47,083	
Un air de famille	1996	Klapisch	SS (1998), 8: 3	2,406,195	TVT1284
Un cœur en hiver	1991	Sautet	SS (1993), 3: 5	1,349,483	ART060
Un cœur qui bat	1991	Dupeyron	SS (1997), 7: 2	77,989	
Un, deux, trois soleil	1993	Blier		419,406	
Une femme française	1994	Wargnier	SS (1996), 6: 6	860,368	G8883S
Une histoire inventée	1990	Forcier	SS (1992), 2: 1	9,478	
Un grand cri d'amour	1998	Balasko		442,340	
Un héros très discret	1996	Audiard	SS (1997), 7: 4	582,508	ART143
Un Indien dans la ville	1994	Palud		7,879,943	
Uranus	1990	Berri	SS (1991), 1: 6	2,545,412	
Van Gogh	1991	Pialat	SS (1992), 2: 1	1,307,000	ART040
Vérité si je mens, La	1997	Gilou		4,872,506	
Vie de Jésus, La	1996	Dumont	SS (1998), 8: 9	114,045	
Vieille qui marchait dans la mer, La	1992	Heynemann		526,018	
Vie rêvée des anges, La	1998	Zonca	SS (1998), 8:11	1,265,418	TVT1311
Vie sexuelle des Belges 1950–1978, La	1994	Bucquoy	SS (1995), 5: 6	28,860	TVT1215
Visiteurs, Les	1993	Poiré	SS (1994), 4: 2	13,782,698	AV013
Voleurs, Les	1996	Téchiné	SS (1998), 8: 4	919,015	TVT1283
Western	1997	Poirier		1,083,254	ART155
Y aura-t-il de la neige à Noël?	1996	Veysset	SS (1997), 7: 11	829,336	ART150
Zone franche	1996	Vecchiali		>5000	

Bibliography

ABEL, R. (1984), *French Cinema: The First Wave, 1915–1929*. Princeton: Princeton University Press.

AMIEL, V. (1994), 'Trois couleurs: Blanc: le milieu, les origines', *Positif*, 396: 16–17.

—— and CIMENT, M. (1994), 'Entretien avec Kieslowski', *Positif*, 403: 26–32.

ASSOULINE, P. (1993), *Germinal: l'aventure d'un film*. Paris: Fayard.

AUDÉ, F. (1979), *Ciné-modèles, cinéma d'elles*. Lausanne: L'Âge d'homme.

AUSTIN, G. (1994), 'History and Spectacle in Blier's *Merci la vie*', *French Cultural Studies*, 4: 73–84.

—— (1996), *Contemporary French Cinema*. Manchester: Manchester University Press.

BACHELARD, G. (1957), *La Poétique de l'espace*. Paris: Gallimard.

BAECQUE, A. DE (1990), 'Faut-il entrer dans l'église de Kieslowski?', *Cahiers du cinéma*, 429: 32–3.

—— (1997), '*Histoire(s) du cinéma* de Jean-Luc Godard', *Cahiers du cinéma*, 513: 36–55.

BAKHTIN, M. (1968), *Rabelais and his World*, trans. H. Iswolsky. Baltimore: MIT Press.

BALDIZZONE, J. (1992), 'Discours officiel et contre-discours', *Les Cahiers de la cinémathèque*, 57: 40–6.

BALIBAR, E. (1990), 'La Forme nation: histoire et idéologie', in E. Balibar and I. Wallerstein (eds.), *Race, nation, classe: les identités ambiguës*. Paris: La Découverte: 117–43.

BALIBAR, R. (1985), *L'Institution du français: essai sur le colinguisme des Carolingiens à la République*. Paris: Presses Universitaires de France.

BALSAMO, A. (1997), *Technologies of the Gendered Body: Reading Cyborg Women*. Durham, NC: Duke University Press.

BALSAN, H. (1997), 'Y aura-t-il des films indépendants cet automne? Entretien avec Humbert Balsan', *Cahiers du cinéma*, 511: 4–5.

BARTHES, R. (1957), *Mythologies*. Paris: Seuil.

—— (1975), 'En sortant du cinéma', *Communications*, 23: 104–7.

—— (1977), *Fragments d'un discours amoureux*. Paris: Seuil.

—— (1983), *The Fashion System*, trans. M. Ward and R. Howard. New York: Hill & Wang.

—— (1988), *Camera Lucida*, trans. R. Howard (2nd edn.). London: Fontana.

—— (1990), *A Lover's Discourse: Fragments*, trans. R. Howard. London: Penguin.

BAUDRILLARD, J. (1996), *The System of Objects*, trans. J. Benedict. London: Verso.

BECKER, C. (1986), *Émile Zola: la fabrique de Germinal*. Paris: Sedes.

BENJAMIN, W. (1969), *Illuminations*, trans. H. Zohn. New York: Shocken Books.

BERGSON, H. (1940), *Le Rire*. Paris: Presses Universitaires de France.

BERRI, C. (1993), '. . . signé Zola-Berri', *Le Quotidien de Paris*, 4314 (28 Sept.), 18–19.

BHABHA, H. (ed.) (1990), *Nation and Narration*. London: Routledge.

—— (1993), 'Foreword: Remembering Fanon', in F. Fanon, *Black Skin, White Marks*, trans. C. Farrington. London: Pluto.

BOSSÉNO, C. (1992), 'Immigrant Cinema: National Cinema—the Case of *Beur* Film', in R. Dyer and G. Vincendeau (eds.), *Popular European Cinema*. London: Routledge: 47–57.

BOULANGER, G. (1997), 'Le Sens de l'affaire Papon', *Le Figaro magazine*, 884 (4 Oct.), 55.

BOULANGER, P. (1975), *Le Cinéma colonial de l'Atlandide à Lawrence d'Arabie*. Paris: Cinéma 2000 Seghers.

BOURDIEU, P. (1996), *Sur la télévision: suivi de L'Emprise du journalisme*. Paris: Liber.

BRAHIMI, D. (1997), *Cinémas d'Afrique francophone et du Maghreb*. Paris: Nathan.

BRECHT, B. (1970), *Sur le cinéma*. Paris: L'Arche.

—— (1972), *Écrits sur le théâtre*, vol. i. Paris: L'Arche.

BRUZZI, S. (1997), *Undressing Cinema: Clothing and Identity in the Movies*. London: Routledge.

BURGIN, V. (1986), 'Diderot, Barthes, Vertigo', in V. Burgin, J. Donald, and C. Kaplan (eds.), *Formations of Fantasy*. London: Methuen: 85–108.

BUTLER, J. (1990), *Gender Trouble*. New York: Routledge.

—— (1997), *Excitable Speech*. London: Routledge.

CAHEN, J. (1997), 'Douze cinéastes témoignent de leur engagement citoyen', *Le Monde* (19 Mar.), 25.

CALLAHAN, V. (1996), 'Zones of Anxiety: Movement, Musidora and the Crime Serials of Louis Feuillade', *Velvet Light Trap*, 37: 37–50.

CANELLAS, C. (1997), 'Deux historiens s'opposent sur Vichy au procès Papon', Reuters, 31 Oct.

CANTALOUBE, T. (1997), 'La Magie digitale', *Cahiers du cinéma*, 513: 81–4.

CERTEAU, M. DE (1988), *The Writing of History*, trans. T. Conley. New York: Columbia University Press.

CHAMBERS, R. (1991), *Room for Maneuver*. Chicago: University of Chicago Press.

CIMENT, M., and NIOGRET, H. (1993), 'Interview with Kieslowski', *Positif*, 391: 20–5.

CinémAction (1997), 82, 'Le Comique à l'écran'.

CNC (1995), *Bilan 1994*, special issue of *CNC Info 256*.

—— (1996), *Bilan 1995*, special issue of *CNC Info 261*.

—— (1997), *Bilan 1996*, special issue of *CNC Info 265*.

COLLARD, C. (1992), 'Me concentrer sur le désordre qui consiste à faire un film: recueilli par Gérard Lefort', *Libération* (21 Oct.), 38–9.

—— (1993), *Les Nuits fauves*. Paris: J'ai lu. Originally pub. Paris: Flammarion, 1989.

COOK, P. (1982), 'Masculinity in Crisis?', *Screen*, 23/3–4: 39–46.

COPJEC, J. (1995), *Read my Desire: Lacan against the Historicists* (2nd edn.). Cambridge Mass.: Massachusetts Institute of Technology.

CREED, B. (1994), *The Monstrous-Feminine: Film, Feminism, Psychoanalysis* (2nd edn.). London: Routledge.

CUTHBERT, P. (1997), 'Going to Court' (interview with Patrice Leconte), *Eye Weekly* (12 Dec.), 20.

DA COSTA, B. (1978), *Historie du café-théâtre*. Paris: Buchet-Castel.

DANAN, M. (1998), 'Trois comédies et une nation: la communauté du rire au cinéma', *French Review*, 273–84 (in press).

DARKE, C. (1993), 'Rupture, Continuity and Diversification: *Cahiers du cinéma* in the 1980s', *Screen*, 34/4: 362–79.

—— (1996), 'When the Cat's Away . . . /Chacun cherche son chat', *Sight and Sound*, 6/11: 62.

—— (1997), 'Irma Vep', *Sight and Sound*, 7/3: 51–2.

—— (1998), 'Lucie Aubrac', *Sight and Sound*, 8/2: 46–7.

DEBRAY, R. (1993), *L'État séducteur: les révolutions médiologiques du pouvoir*. Paris: Gallimard.

DELEMEUILLE, F. (1992), 'Fictions cinématographiques et guerre d'Indochine', *Les Cahiers de la cinémathèque*, 57: 63–72.

DENIS, C. and FARGEAU, J.-P. (1997), *I Can't Sleep*, trans I. Burley, *Scenario*, 3/2: 53–83.

DESPLECHIN, A. (1997), 'Douze cinéastes témoignent de leur engagement citoyen', *Le Monde* (19 Mar.), 24.

DIASTÈME, K. and DIASTÈME, K. (1995), 'Le Bonheur a encore frappé', *Première*, 224: 64–9.

DIAWARA, M. (1992), *African Cinema: Politics and Culture*. Bloomington: Indiana University Press.

DOANE, M. A. (1982), 'Film and Masquerade: Theorizing the Female Spectator', *Screen*, 23/3–4: 34–88.

—— (1991), *Femmes Fatales: Feminism, Film Theory, Psychoanalysis*. London: Routledge.

—— (1993), 'Technology's Body: Cinematic Vision in Modernity', *Differences*, 5/2: 1–23.

DOBSON, J. (1996), 'The Double Framing of Véronique', unpublished paper given at 'film/culture/history', University of Aberdeen.

DONAHOE, J. I. (ed.) (1991), *Essays on Quebec Cinema*. East Lansing, Mich.: Michigan State University Press.

DOWNING, J. D. H. (1996), 'Post-Triclor African Cinema: Toward a Richer Vision', in D. Sherzer (ed.), *Cinema, Colonialism, Postcolonialism: Perspectives from the French and Francophone Worlds*. Austin: University of Texas Press: 188–228.

DRIDI, K. (1997), 'Douze cinéastes témoignent de leur engagement citoyen', *Le Monde* (19 Mar.), 24.

ELSAESSER, T. (1992), 'Rivette and the End of Cinema', *Sight and Sound*, 1/12: 20–3.

ERICKSON, S. (1997), 'Making a Connection between the Cinema, Politics and Real Life: An Interview with Olivier Assayas', *Cineaste*, 22/4: 6–9.

ESTÈVE, M. (1994), 'Trois couleurs bleu ou l'apprentissage de la liberté', *Études cinématographiques*, 203–10: 121–7.

—— (1995), '*La Haine*: jusqu'ici tout va bien...', *Le Français dans le monde*, 275: 6–7.

EVERETT, W. (1995), 'The Autobiographical Eye in European Film', *Europa: An International Journal of Language, Art and Culture*, 2/1: 3–10.

—— (ed.) (1996), *European Identity in Cinema*. Exeter: Intellect.

EVIN, K. (1993), 'Mine d'or', *La Tribune Desfossés* (29 Sept.), 35.

FANON, F. (1971), *The Wretched of the Earth*, trans. C. Farrington. London: Penguin.

FAVIER, G., and KASSOVITZ, M. (1995), *Jusqu'ici tout va bien*. Paris: Actes Sud.

FELMAN, S., and LAUB, D. (1992), *Testimony: Crises of Witnessing in Literature, Psychoanalysis, and History*. New York: Routledge.

FERRAN, P., and DESPLECHIN, A. (1997), 'Lettre ouverte aux députés français', *Le Monde* (18 Feb.), 13.

FEUILLADE, L., and MEIRS, G. (1916), *Les Vampires: les yeux qui fascinent*. Paris: Librairie contemporaine.

FINNEY, A. (1996), *The State of European Cinema: A New Dose of Reality*. London: Cassell.

FISHER, L. (1996), *Cinematernity: Film, Motherhood, Genre*. Princeton: Princeton University Press.

FISKE, J. (1991), *Television Culture*. London: Routledge.

FLOYD, N. (1997), '*The Fifth Element*', *Time Out* (11 June 1997), 17.

FONTENAY, E. DE (1976), 'Pour Émile et par Émile, Sophie ou l'invention du ménage', *Les Temps modernes*, 378: 1775–95.

FOUCAULT, M. (1971), *L'Ordre du discours: leçon inaugurale au Collège de France prononcé le 2 décembre 1970*. Paris: Gallimard.

FREUD, S. (1977), *On Sexuality*. London: Pelican.

FRODON, J.-M. (1994), 'L'Année des Visiteurs', Le Monde (4 Jan.), 22.

—— (1995a), L'Âge moderne du cinéma français: de la Nouvelle Vague à nos jours, Paris: Flammarion.

—— (1995b), 'Le Jeune Cinéma français connaît un renouveau prometteur', Le Monde (29 June), 32.

—— (1997a), 'Une initiative exceptionnelle venant du monde du cinéma', Le Monde, 16189 (12 Feb.), 9.

—— (1997b), 'Je connais bien ce monde du XXIIIe siècle, j'y ai longtemps habité', Le Monde (9 May 1997), 18.

GARBAZ, F. (1997), 'Le Renouveau social du cinéma français', Positif, 442: 74–5.

GARBER, M. (1993), Vested Interests: Cross-dressing and Cultural Anxiety. London: Penguin.

—— (1996), 'Custody Battles', in M. Garber, R. L. Walkowitz, and P. Franklin (eds.), Field Work: Sites in Literary and Cultural Studies. New York Routledge: 27–33.

GARCIN, J. (1993), 'Les Français ont voté... pour Les Visiteurs', L'Événement du jeudi (1–7 Apr.), 92–4.

GARDEL, L. (1980), Fort Saganne. Paris: Seuil.

GASPÉRI, A. DE (1992), 'Les Nuits fauves, ou le romantisme hard', Le Quotidien de Paris (21 Oct.).

GASTON-MATHÉ, C. (1996), La Société française au miroir de son cinéma. Paris: Panoramiques-Corlet.

GAULTIER, J.-P. (1997), 'Jean-Paul Gaultier on his Designs for The Fifth Element', Evening Standard (5 June 1997), 9.

GAUTHIER, G. (1992), 'Indochine, rêve d'Empire', Revue du cinéma, 483: 52.

GEORGE, K. (1993), 'Alternative French', in C. Sanders (ed.), French Today: Language in its Social Context. Cambridge: Cambridge University Press: 155–70.

GILLESPIE, M. (1995), Television, Ethnicity and Cultural Change. London: Routledge.

GIRARD, R. (1972), La Violence et le sacré. Paris: Grasset.

GOUPIL, R. (1997), 'Douze cinéastes témoignent de leur engagement citoyen', Le Monde (19 Mar.), 25.

GRAMSCI, A. (1971), Selections from the Prison Notebooks, ed. Q. Hoare and G. Nowell Smith. New York: International Publishers.

—— (1985), Selections from Cultural Writings, ed. D. Forgacs and G. Nowell Smith. Cambridge, Mass.: Harvard University Press.

GREEN, I. (1984), 'Malefunction', Screen, 25/4–5: 36–48.

GREENE, N. (1996), 'Empire as Myth and Memory', in D. Sherzer (ed.), Cinema, Colonialism, Postcolonialism: Perspectives from the French and Francophone Worlds. Austin: University of Texas Press: 103–19.

GUÉDIGUIAN, R. (1997), 'Douze cinéastes témoignent de leur engagement citoyen', *Le Monde* (19 Mar.), 25.

—— (1998), 'Le Goût de l'Estaque: entretien avec Robert Guédiguian', *Cahiers du cinéma*, 518: 58–61.

GUNNING, T. (1989), 'An Aesthetic of Astonishment: Early Film and the (In)credulous Spectator', *Art and Text*, 34: 31–45.

HARGREAVES, A. (1991), *Voices from the North African Community in France*. New York: Berg.

—— (1995), *Immigration, 'Race' and Ethnicity in Contemporary France*. London: Routledge.

HAUSTRATE, G. (1988), *Bertrand Blier*. Paris: Edilig.

HAYWARD, S. (1990), 'Gender Politics: Cocteau's Belle is not that Bête', in S. Hayward and G. Vincendeau (eds.), *French Film: Texts and Contexts*. London: Routledge: 127–36.

—— (1993), *French National Cinema*. London: Routledge.

—— (1998), *Luc Besson*. Manchester: Manchester University Press.

HERPE, N. (1996), '*Irma Vep*: on dirait qu'on jouerait aux vampires', *Positif*, 429: 35–6.

—— (1998), 'Y aura-t-il un jeune cinéma français?', *Positif*, 443: 53–5.

HEWITT, N. (1998), *Modern French Politics*. London: Polity Press.

HILLAIRET, P., LE BRAT, C., and ROLLET, P. (eds.) (1985), *Paris vu par le cinéma d'avant-garde: 1923–1983*. Paris: Paris Expérimental.

HOBERMAN, J. (1994), '*Red, White* and *Blue*', *Première*, 8: 50–3.

HORTON, A. (ed.) (1991), *Comedy, Cinema, Theory*. Berkeley and Los Angeles: University of California Press.

JÄCKEL, A., and DUVERGER, X. M. (1993), 'Far from Vietnam', *Sight and Sound*, 3/4: 23.

JAMESON, F. (1990), *Signatures of the Visible*. London: Routledge.

JEANCOLAS, J.-P. (1997), 'Une bobine d'avance: du cinéma et de la politique en février 1997', *Positif*, 434: 56–8.

JEFFORDS, S. (1993), 'The Big Switch: Hollywood Masculinity in the Nineties', in J. Collins, A. P. Collins, and H. Radner (eds.), *Film Theory Goes to the Movies*. London: Routledge: 196–208.

JONES, K. (1997), 'Night Exterior', *Filmmaker*, 5/3: 37, 76.

JOUSSE, T. (1994), 'Marché noir', *Cahiers du cinéma*, 476: 71–3.

—— (1995), 'Le Banlieue-film existe-t-il?', *Cahiers du cinéma*, 492: 37–9.

—— and STRAUSS, F. (1994), 'Entretien avec Claire Denis', *Cahiers du cinéma*, 479/80: 25–30.

KAPLAN, E. A. (1983), *Women and Film: Both Sides of the Camera*. London: Routledge.

—— (ed.) (1994), *Women in Film Noir* (8th edn.). London: BFI.

KATSAHNIAS, I. (1989a), 'Noir sur blanc', *Cahiers du cinéma*, 418: 50–1.

KATSAHNIAS, I. (1989*b*), 'Le Scénario introuvable du cinéma français', *Cahiers du cinéma*, 419: 15–18.

KEHR, D. (1994), 'To Save the World: Kieslowski's *Three Colours Trilogy*', *Film Comment*, 30: 10–20.

KIESLOWSKI, K. (1993), 'Interview', *Screen International*, 894: 28–30.

Kiosque en vue (1997), 'Le Contrat publicitaire d'Emmanuelle Béart avec Dior ne sera pas renouvelé', *Le Monde* (3 Apr.), 31.

KLAPISCH, C. (1996), Interview with M.-N. Tranchant, *Le Figaro* (4 Apr. 1996).

—— (1997), 'Douze cinéastes témoignent de leur engagement citoyen', *Le Monde* (19 Mar.), 25.

KRUTNIK, F. (1991), *In a Lonely Street: Film Noir, Genre, Masculinity*. London: Routledge.

KUHN, A. (1990), *The Women's Companion to International Film*. London: Virago.

LACAN, J. (1977), *Écrits: A Selection*, trans. Alan Sheridan. London: Tavistock.

LANG, J. (1993), 'Il faut se battre!', *Le Nouvel Observateur*, 1507 (23 Sept.), 63.

LAPLANCHE, J. (1976), *Life and Death in Psychoanalysis*, trans. J. Mehlman. Baltimore: Johns Hopkins University Press.

—— (1989), *New Foundations for Psychoanalysis*, trans. D. Macey. Oxford: Blackwell.

LAPSLEY, R. and WESTLAKE, M. (1988), *Film Theory: An Introduction*. Manchester: Manchester University Press.

LAVOIGNAT, J.-P. (1992), 'Cyril Collard, le jeu avec le feu', *Studio Magazine*, 67: 118–19.

—— and D'YVOIRE, C. (1995), 'Étienne Chatiliez: les clefs du bonheur', *Studio Magazine*, 105: 109–12.

LE CLÉZIO, J.-M. (1980), *Désert*. Paris: Gallimard.

LEFORT, G. (1993), 'Le Dernier Berri', *Libération* (29 Sept.).

LEJEUNE, P. (1987), *Le Cinéma des femmes*. Paris: Lherminier.

LIPPY, T. (1997), 'Writing and Directing *I Can't Sleep*: A Talk with Claire Denis', *Scenario*, 3/2: 84–7, 185–7.

LURY, C. (1998), *Prosthetic Culture: Photography, Memory and Identity*. London: Routledge.

MACDOUGALL, D. (1994), 'Films of Memory', in L. Taylor, *Visualizing Theory*. New York: Routledge: 260–70.

MAFFESOLI, M. (1996), 'Socialité et polythétisme sociétal', *Échos*, 78–9: 12–17.

MAHONEY, E. (1997), ' "The People in Parentheses": Space under Pressure in the Post-modern City', in D. B. Clarke (ed.), *The Cinematic City*. London: Routledge: 168–85.

MALCOLM, D. (1996), 'The greatest story ever told?' *The Guardian* (13 Apr.), 30.

Manifesto (1997), 'Cinquante-neuf réalisateurs appellent à "désobéir" ', *Le Monde*, 16189 (12 Feb.), 9.

MARKER, C. (1996), 'Defying the Censor: Resistance to the Algerian War in French Literature and Cinema', Ph.D. dissertation (Ann Arbor).

MARSHALL, T. (1997), ' "Les Intermittents de la politique" ', *Positif*, 436: 44–7.

MARS-JONES, A. (1995), *Independent* (16 Nov.), 10–11.

MASPÉRO, F. (1990), *Les Passagers du Roissy-Express*. Paris: Seuil.

MASSON, A. (1994), '*Trois couleurs: rouge*: la naïveté du manipulateur', *Positif*, 403: 21–3.

MAZDON, L. (1996), 'Rewriting and Remakes: Questions of Originality and Authenticity', in G. T. Harris (ed.), *On Translating French Literature and Film*. Amsterdam: Rodopi; 47–63.

MÉDIAMÉTRIE (1997), survey in *Le Film français*, 2662: 14–15.

MEMMI, A. (1965), *The Colonizer and the Colonized*, trans. H. Greenfeld. London: Orion P . ˙s.

MÉRIGEAU, P. (199 ˙ ˙ ˙ ˙ice Leconte: la joie d'être "Reine d'un jour" ', *Le Monde* (su ˙ ˙ ˙ t Cannes 1996, 10 May), iv.

MESNIL, M. (19 ˙ ˙ ˙ *rci la vie* ou l' "imaginaire à la française" ', *Esprit*, 5: 126–35.

MEYER, A. ˙ ˙ ˙ 'City Centre and Suburban Periphery: Literary Represe˙ ˙ ˙ of Paris, 1926–1928', in *Mythologies of Paris*. Stirling: Stirling ˙ ˙ ˙ Publications: 1–24.

MONGIN ˙ ˙ ˙ 7), *La Violence des images ou comment s'en débarrasser?* Pari ˙ ˙ ˙

MOOR˙ ˙ ˙ 995), 'Note on *La Haine*', *Screen International*, 1010/31 (2 June), 2.

MORICE, J. (1996), '*Irma Vep*', *Télérama*, 2414: 34–5.

MORRISON, S. (1997), '*Irma Vep*', *Cineaction*, 42: 63–5.

MOULET, L. (1994), 'Le Néo-irréalisme français', *Cahiers du cinéma*, 475: 48–9.

Moving Pictures (1994), 'Prime Couleurs', *Moving Pictures International*, 189: 13.

MULVEY, L. (1975), 'Visual Pleasure and Narrative Cinema', *Screen*, 16/3: 6–18.

NAU, J.-Y. (1996), 'La Gestion de l'ARC est gravement mise en cause par la Cour des comptes', *Le Monde* (6 Jan.), 7.

N'DIAYE, M. (1990), *En famille*. Paris: Minuit.

NEALE, S. (1983), 'Masculinity as Spectacle', *Screen*, 24/6: 2–16.

NESSELSON, L. (1994), 'Arabz N the Hood', *Variety* (21–7 Feb.), 46.

NICHOLS, B. (1994), *Blurred Boundaries*. Bloomington: Indiana University Press.

NIMIER, R. (1950), *Le Hussard bleu*. Paris: Gallimard.

NOIRIEL, G. (1996), *The French Melting Pot*, trans. G. de Laforcade. Minneapolis: University of Minnesota Press.

NORA, P. (1984–92), *Les Lieux de mémoire*. Paris: Gallimard.

NORINDR, P. (1996), 'Filmic Memorial and Colonial Blues: Indochina in Contemporary French Cinema', in D. Sherzer (ed.), *Cinema, Colonialism, Postcolonialism: Perspectives from the French and Francophone Worlds*. Austin: University of Texas Press: 120–46.

NOWELL-SMITH, G. (ed.) (1997), *The Oxford History of Cinema*. Oxford: Oxford University Press.

NWACHUKWU, F. U. (1994), *Black African Cinema*. Berkeley and Los Angeles: University of California Press.

ORSENNA, E. (1988), *L'Exposition coloniale*. Paris: Seuil.

ORY, P. (1985), *L'Anarchisme de droite*. Paris: Grasset.

O'SHEA, S. (1995), 'Raï', *Variety* (7–13 Aug.), 37.

OSTRIA, V. (1993), 'Le Hasard et l'indifférence', *Cahiers du cinéma*, 471: 65–7.

PALLISTER, J. L. (1995), *The Cinema of Quebec: Masters in their Own House*. Cranbury, NJ: Fairleigh Dickinson University Press.

PANGON, G. (1988), interview with Kieslowski, *Télérama* (26 Oct. 1988).

—— (1989), interview with Kieslowski, *Télérama* (11 Oct. 1989).

PASCAL, M. (1994), 'Camille le Maudit', *Le Point*, 1131: 100–1.

PASCAUD, F. (1991), 'Vision infantile', *Télérama*, 2179: 40–1.

PAXTON, R. (1972), *Vichy France*. New York: Alfred A. Knopf.

PECK, A. (1994), '*Trois couleurs Bleu/Blanc/Rouge*: une trilogie européenne', *Études cinématographiques*, 203–10: 147–62.

PENNAC, D. (1987), *La Fée Carabine*. Paris: Gallimard.

—— (1990), *La Petite Marchande de prose*. Paris: Gallimard.

PERRIN, L. (1994), *André Téchiné, après la nouvelle vague*. Video Collection *Cinéma de notre temps*. France: AMIP La Sept Arte, INA.

PETRIE, D. (ed.) (1992), *Screening Europe: Image and Identity in Contemporary European Cinema*. London: BFI.

PHILLIPS, A. (1994), *On Flirtation*. London: Faber.

PIAZZO, P. (1998), review of *Un grand cri d'amour*, *Aden* (7–13 Jan.), 13.

PILLET, E. (1995), 'Thérésa et Yvette: à propos du comique féminin au café concert', in G.-V. Martin (ed.), *Féminin/masculin: humour et différence sexuelle*, *Cahiers de recherche de CORHUM-CRIH*, 3: 29–47.

PITHON, R. (1987), 'Retour à Feuillade', *Positif*, 312: 49–51.

POWRIE, P. (1997), *French Cinema in the 1980s: Nostalgia and the Crisis of Masculinity*. Oxford: Clarendon Press.

PRATT, M. L. (1991), 'Arts of the Contact Zone', *Profession* 91 (MLA), 33–40.

PRÉDAL, R. (1991), *Le Cinéma français depuis 1945*. Paris: Nathan.
—— (1996), *50 ans de cinéma français*. Paris: Nathan.
READER, K. (1992), 'How to Avoid Becoming a Middle-Aged Fogey, with Reference to Three Recent French Films', *Paragraph*, 15: 97–104.
—— (1993), 'Cinematic Representations of Paris: Vigo/Truffaut/Carax', *Modern and Contemporary France*, NS 1/4: 409–15.
—— (1995), 'After the Riot', *Sight and Sound*, 5/11:12–14.
—— (1996), 'Review of French Cinema in 1995', *Modern and Contemporary France*, 3: 348–51.
—— (1999), 'Belgian Film Comedy and National Identity', in J. Andrew, M. Crook, and D. Holmes (eds.), *Why Europe? Problems of Culture and Identity*, ii: *Media, Culture and Representation*. London: Macmillan, forthcoming.
REVAULT D'ALLONNES, F. (1986), '*Mauvais Sang* ne saurait mentir', *Cinéma*, 378: 4–7.
REY, H. (1996), *La Peur des banlieues*. Paris: Presses de la Fondation Nationale de Sciences Politiques.
REYNAUD, B. (1997), 'I can't sell my acting like that', *Sight and Sound*, 7/3: 24–6.
RICH, R. (1985), 'In the Name of Feminist Film Criticism', in B. Nichols (ed.), *Movies and Methods*. Berkeley and Los Angeles: University of California Press: 340–58.
RIEDMATTEN, L. A. DE (1996), *L'Affaire du sang contaminé*. Paris: Du Rocher.
ROLLET, B. (1994), 'Le Sida dans *Les Nuits fauves* et *Mensonge*: représentation et "misrepresentation" ', unpublished paper given at the French Cinema Conference, Nottingham University.
—— (1997), 'Two women speak out: Serreau and Balasko and the Inheritance of May 68', in M. Cross and S. Perry (eds.), *Voices of France*. London: Pinter: 100–13.
—— (1998), *Coline Serreau*. Manchester: Manchester University Press.
ROMNEY, J. (1994), '*Germinal*', *New Statesman* (6 May), 33.
ROSELLO, M. (1996a), *Infiltrating Culture: Power and Identity in Contemporary Women's Writing*. Manchester: Manchester University Press.
—— (1996b), 'Third Cinema or Third Degree: The "Rachid System" in Serge Meynard's L'Œil au beurre noir', in D. Sherzer (ed.), *Cinema, Colonialism, Postcolonialism: Perspectives from the French and Francophone Worlds*. Austin: University of Texas Press: 147–72.
—— (1998), *Declining the Stereotype: Ethnicity and Representation in French Cultures*. Hanover, NH: University Press of New England.
ROSENBAUM, J. (1994), 'The Problem with Poetry: Leos Carax', *Film Comment*, 30: 12–23.

274 Bibliography

ROUCHY, M. E. (1993), 'Sida: Si d'amour les films...', *Télérama*, 2244: 20–3.

ROUSSEAU, J.-J. (1979), *Émile or on Education*, introd., trans. and notes A. Bloom. New York: Basic Books.

ROUSSO, H. (1991), *The Vichy Syndrome: History and Memory in France since 1944*. Boston: Harvard University Press.

—— (1997), 'Pour les jeunes, un passé très présent', *L'Express* (2–8 Oct.), 14–16.

ROWE, K. (1995), *The Unruly Woman: Gender and the Genres of Laughter*. Austin: University of Texas Press.

ROZE, A. (1995), *La France arc-en-ciel: les Français venus d'ailleurs*. Paris: Julliard.

ROZEN, L. (1996), review of *Ridicule*, *People* (9 Dec.).

SAID, E. (1991), *Orientalism*. Harmondsworth: Penguin.

SANDERS, C. (1993), 'Sociosituational Variation', in C. Sanders (ed.), *French Today: Language in its Social Context*. Cambridge: Cambridge University Press: 27–53.

SANITAS, J. (1995), *Le Sang et le sida: une enquête critique sur l'affaire du sang contaminé*. Paris: L'Harmattan.

SCHWARTZBAUM, L. (1996), 'Snide Goeth before a Fall: French Phonies Get their Comeuppance in "Ridicule" ', *Entertainment Weekly*, 356 (pagination unknown).

SEBBAR, L. (1982), *Shérazade*. Paris: Stock.

—— (1984), *Le Chinois vert d'Afrique*. Paris: Stock.

SEGURET, O. (1992), 'Cyril Collard: fauve qui peut', *Libération* (21 Oct.), 38.

SHAVIRO, S. (1993), *The Cinematic Body*. Minneapolis: University of Minnesota Press.

SHERZER, D. (ed.) (1996), *Cinema, Colonialism, Postcolonialism: Perspectives from the French and Francophone Worlds*. Austin: University of Texas Press.

—— (1998), 'Colonial and Postcolonial Hybridity: Condition métisse', *Journal of European Studies*, 28: parts 1 and 2: 103–20.

SHOHAT, E. (1991–2), 'Gender and the Culture of Empire', *Quarterly Review of Film and Video*, 13: 45–84.

SHOWALTER, E. (1991), *Sexual Anarchy: Gender and Culture at the Fin de Siècle*. London: Bloomsbury.

SICLIER, J. (1993), '*Germinal*', *Le Monde* (30 Sept.), 26.

SILVERMAN, K. (1996), *The Threshold of the Visible World*. London: Routledge.

SKWARA, A. (1993), 'Film Stars do not Shine in the Sky over Poland', in R. Dyer and G. Vincendeau (eds.), *Popular European Cinema*. London: Routledge, 220–31.

SLATER, L. (1997), 'Fashion is about enjoying yourself', *Daily Telegraph* (6 June 1997), 27.

SONTAG, S. (1996), '100 Years of Cinema', *Guardian* (2 Mar.), 27.

SORLIN, P. (1977), *Sociologie du cinéma: ouverture pour l'histoire de demain*. Paris: Aubier Montaigne.

—— (1980), *The Film in History: Restaging the Past*. Totowa, NJ: Barnes & Noble.

SPIVAK, G. (1989), 'Questions of Multiculturalism', in M. Broe and A. Ingram (eds.), *Women's Writing in Exile*. Chapel Hill, NC: University of North Carolina Press: 412–20.

—— (1996), 'Diasporas Old and New: Women in the Transnational World', *Textual Practice*, 10: 245–69.

SPRINGER, C. (1996), *Electronic Eros: Bodies and Desire in the Post-industrial Age*. London: Athlone Press.

STAM, R. (1985), *Reflexivity in Film and Literature: From Don Quixote to Jean-Luc Godard*. Ann Arbor: UMI Research Press.

—— (1989), *Subversive Pleasure: Bakhtin, Cultural Criticism and Film*. Baltimore: Johns Hopkins University Press.

—— BURGOYNE, R., and FLITTERMAN-LEWIS, S. (1992), *New Vocabularies in Film Semiotics*. London: Routledge.

STERN, J., and BOUJNAH, M. P. (1992), 'Collard: le cinéma est régi par la peur', *Sept à Paris* (21 Oct.), 15–16.

STOK, D. (ed.) (1993), *Kieslowski on Kieslowski*. Boston: Faber.

STORA, B. (1997), *Images de guerre*. Paris: La Découverte.

STRAUSS, F. (1994), 'Tu ne jouiras point', *Cahiers du cinéma*, 483: 62–3.

TABOULAY, C. (1991), 'Le Pari neuf de Carax', *Cahiers du cinéma*, 448: 14–17.

TAGUIEFF, P.-A. (1996), 'Identité nationale: un débat français', *Échos*, 78–9: 82–92.

TARR, C. (1993), 'Questions of Identity in Beur Cinema: From *Tea in the Harem* to *Cheb*', *Screen*, 34/4: 321–42.

—— (1995), '*Beurz* N the Hood? The Articulation of French and *Beur* Identities in *Le Thé au harem d'Archimède* and *Hexagone*', *Modern and Contemporary France*, 3: 415–25.

—— (1997a), 'Ethnicity and Identity in *Métisse* and *La Haine* by Mathieu Kassovitz', in T. Chafer (ed.), *Multicultural France: Working Papers on Contemporary France*. Portsmouth: University of Portsmouth: i. 40–7.

—— (1997b), 'French Cinema and Post-colonial Minorities', in A. G. Hargreaves and M. McKinney (eds.), *Postcolonial Cultures in France*. London: Routledge: 59–83.

—— (1997c), 'Gender, Ethnicity and Identity in Contemporary French Cinema: The Case of the Young Maghrebi-French woman', *Iris*, 24: 123–33 (to be reprinted in *Interface*, Bradford University Press, 1999).

TASKER, Y. (1993), 'Dumb Movies for Dumb People: Masculinity, the Body and the Voice in Contemporary Action Cinema', in S. Cohan and I. R. Hark (eds.), *Screening the Male: Exploring Masculinities in Hollywood Cinema*. London: Routledge: 230–44.

TAVERNIER, B. (1997), 'Douze cinéastes témoignent de leur engagement citoyen', *Le Monde* (19 Mar.), 24.

Télérama (1993), special no. 'La Passion Kieslowski'.

TEMPLE, M. (1998), 'It will be worth it', *Sight and Sound*, 8/1: 20–3.

THOMPSON, D. (1992), 'Once upon a Time in Paris', *Sight and Sound*, 1/5: 6–11.

THORNS, D. C. (1972), *Suburbia*. London: MacGibbon & Kee.

TIGNÈRES, S. (1992), 'Vietnam et l'opinion publique en 1984', *Les Cahiers de la cinémathèque*, 57: 57–9.

TOBIN, Y. (1995), 'État des (ban)lieues', *Positif*, 415: 28–30.

TODD, E. (1994), *Le Destin des immigrés*. Paris: Seuil.

TODOROV, T. (1993), *On Human Diversity: Nationalism, Racism, and Exoticism in French Thought*. Cambridge, Mass.: Harvard University Press.

TOUBIANA, S. (1991), 'Entretien avec Bertrand Blier', *Cahiers du cinéma*, 441: 22–7.

—— (1992), 'Carpe diem and Night', *Cahiers du cinéma*, 460: 22–5.

—— (1997), 'Retour du politique (suite)', *Cahiers du cinéma*, 511: 28–9.

TOURNIER, M. (1986), *La Goutte d'or*. Paris: Gallimard.

TRÉMOIS, C. M. (1992), 'Cyril Collard: la vie sur le vif', *Télérama*, 2232: 40–1.

—— (1993), 'Zamachowsky, le "possédé" du cinéma', *Télérama* (Sept.), 36–9.

—— (1997), *Les Enfants de la liberté: le jeune cinéma français des années 90*. Paris: Seuil.

—— and REMY, V. (1993), 'Je doute, je doute toujours: entretien avec Kieslowski', *Télérama*, special no. (Sept.), 90–6.

TURIM, M. (1989), *Flashbacks in Films: Memory and History*. New York: Routledge.

VACHEZ, L. (1993), '*Les Visiteurs* ont le sourire Émail Diamant', *Libération* (23 Apr.).

VASSÉ, C. (1995), 'Un regard métisse', *Positif*, 415: 6–7.

VINCENDEAU, G. (1992), 'Family Plots: The Father and Daughters of French Cinema', *Sight and Sound*, 1/1: 14–17.

—— (1993a), 'Fire and Ice', *Sight and Sound*, 3/4: 20–2.

—— (1993b), 'Hijacked', *Sight and Sound*, 3/7: 23–5.

—— (1993c), 'Gérard Depardieu: The Axiom of Contemporary French Cinema', *Screen*, 34/4: 343–61.

—— (1995), 'Unsettling memories', *Sight and Sound*, 5/7: 30–2.

—— (1997), review of *Ridicule*, *Sight and Sound*, 7/2: 56.

WACQUANT, L. J. D. (1992), '*Banlieue*s françaises et ghetto noir américain: de l'amalgame à la comparaison', *French Politics and Society*, 10/4: 81–103.

WARGNIER, R. (1992), 'Pour revenir sur *Indochine*: entretien avec Régis Wargnier', *Revue du cinéma*, 482: 37.

WATNEY, S. (1993), 'The French Connection', *Sight and Sound*, 3/6: 24–5.

WHITE, A., and SUTTON, P. (1997), 'Framing the Text: *In the Company of Wolves*', *Manuscript*, 2/1: 27 38.

WIEVIORKA, M. (1993), *La Démocratie à l'épreuve: nationalisme, populisme, ethnicité*. Paris: La Découverte.

WILLIAMSON, D. (1987), 'Language and Sexual Difference', *Screen*, 28/1: 10–25.

YOUNG, J. (1993), *The Texture of Memory: Holocaust Memorials and Meaning*. New Haven, Conn.: Yale University Press.

ZACHAREK, S. (1997), '*Irma Vep* captures the larcenous, breaking allure of cinema itself', Salon, May 1997: 1–3 [at http://www.salonmagazine.com/may97/vep970509.html].

ZIZEK, S. (1994), *The Metastases of Enjoyment: Six Essays on Woman and Causality*. London: Verso.

ZOLA, E. (1964), *Germinal*, in *Les Rougon-Macquart*, vol. iii. Paris: Gallimard. Translations by R. Cousins.

Index of Films and Proper Names